IMPARTIALITY IN
MORAL AND POLITICAL PHILOSOPHY

Impartiality in Moral and Political Philosophy

by
Susan Mendus

OXFORD
UNIVERSITY PRESS

OXFORD
UNIVERSITY PRESS

Great Clarendon Street, Oxford OX2 6DP

Oxford University Press is a department of the University of Oxford.
It furthers the University's objective of excellence in research, scholarship,
and education by publishing worldwide in

Oxford New York

Auckland Bangkok Buenos Aires Cape Town Chennai
Dar es Salaam Delhi Hong Kong Istanbul Karachi Kolkata
Kuala Lumpur Madrid Melbourne Mexico City Mumbai Nairobi
São Paulo Shanghai Singapore Taipei Tokyo Toronto
with an associated company in Berlin

Oxford is a registered trade mark of Oxford University Press
in the UK and in certain other countries

Published in the United States
By Oxford University Press Inc., New York

British Library Cataloguing in Publication Data
Data available

Library of Congress Cataloging in Publication Data
Mendus, Susan.
Impartiality in moral and political philosophy / by Susan Mendus.
p. cm.
Includes bibliographical references and index.
1. Justice. 2. Fairness. 3. Political science–Philosophy. 3. Ethics. I. Title.
JC578 .M437 2002   320'.01'1–dc21   2001059139
ISBN 0–19–829781–5 (alk. paper)

1 3 5 7 9 10 8 6 4 2

Typeset by Kolam Information Services pvt. Ltd.,
Printed in Great Brtain by T.J. International Ltd., Padstow, Cornwall

For Matt
who helped me Light out for the Territory

Acknowledgements

The bulk of this book was written during the academic year 1999–2000. That year was a uniquely fortunate one for me: first, I was awarded a British Academy/Leverhulme Trust Senior Research Fellowship which enabled me to take leave of absence from my teaching and administrative duties at the University of York; second, the Research School for Social Science at the Australian National University granted me the status of Visiting Fellow for the first four months of the new millennium; third, my colleagues in the Politics Department at the University of York covered for me during my absence by taking on onerous administrative responsibilities which should, in justice, have been mine. I have been the recipient of immense personal and institutional generosity, for which I express my sincere thanks.

David Miller, Onora O'Neill, and Albert Weale were supportive of my initial application to the British Academy, and I am grateful to them for their help in this, as in so many things over the years. At the ANU, I was privileged to attend the weekly 'Wednesday Reading Group' organized by Michael Smith and attended by Claire Finkelstein, Karen Jones, Barbara Nunn, Philip Pettit, Josh Parsons, Mike Ridge, and Jay Wallace—to name but a few. Those occasions were all that academic discussions should be: highly critical, deeply irreverent, and immense fun. I learned an enormous amount from all the participants, but especially from Michael Smith, whose command of moral philosophy leaves me awe struck. I am deeply indebted to him.

Closer to home, I would like, once again, to express my thanks to the C. and J. B. Morrell Trust which has funded research in political philosophy at the University of York for over twenty years. It is through the generosity of the Trust, and the personal support of the Trustees (Geoffrey Heselton, Nicholas Morrell, Margaret Morrell, and Martin Wainwright) that York remains one of the best places in which to study political philosophy. It is also one of the most stimulating and collegial places in which to study political philosophy. This is entirely due to the enthusiasm and intellectual generosity of the staff of the Politics Department, and especially of those who work in the political philosophy sector. Alex Callinicos, David Edwards, Matt Matravers, Peter Nicholson, and Jon Parkin all provided invaluable comments on my work, all took on additional teaching and administrative burdens in order that I might have research leave. None complained (not to me, anyway). I cannot thank them enough.

Catriona McKinnon, Matt Matravers, and David Miller read the entire manuscript in draft form, and gave me extremely helpful written comments on it. I thank them most warmly for all the work they did on my behalf.

Finally, this book would not have been started, much less completed, without the support and encouragement of my friend and colleague, Matt Matravers. I doubt whether he has any idea how much his intellectual companionship means to me, and it would be embarrassing for both of us were I to parade my indebtedness here. So I simply dedicate this book to Matt, who made it possible.

Susan Mendus

University of York
October 2001

Contents

Introduction

It is mostly a true book; with some stretchers, as I said before.

Huckleberry Finn

In Part III of *Justice as Impartiality* Brian Barry writes: 'it is a commonplace that anglophone moral and political philosophy has for the past decade been the scene of a running battle between defenders and critics of impartiality.' Amongst the defenders of impartiality he counts Kantians, utilitarians and (of course) himself. Amongst its critics he counts Bernard Williams and feminist care theorists. However, and within the page, Barry has concluded that this battle (the battle between impartialists and their critics) is ill-joined. He writes: 'what the opponents are attacking is not what the supporters are defending. I believe that the core contentions of the friends and foes of impartiality (as they conventionally represent themselves) are equally valid. If this is so, then there can be no contradiction between them' (Barry 1995: 191).

Barry's conclusion should surprise us, for if it is true, then at least ten years of moral and political philosophy have been largely wasted. However, if the conclusion is surprising, it is far from novel. In a 1991 issue of *Ethics* devoted to Impartiality and Ethical Theory a number of the contributors conclude that the debate between partialists and impartialists is based on a series of confusions and misunderstandings, that talk of partialism and impartialism does not help to illuminate our philosophical differences, and that there is far less and far less deep disagreement between opponents and proponents of impartialism than is commonly supposed (see, for example, Becker 1991; Baron 1991; Deigh 1991).

Yet not all concur. For some, the differences between impartialists and their critics do seem to run exceedingly deep. Bernard Williams, for example, tells us that:

the point is that somewhere...one reaches the necessity that such things as deep attachments to other persons will express themselves in the world in ways which cannot at the same time embody the impartial view, and that they also run the risk of offending against it. They run that risk if they exist at all; yet unless such things exist, there will not be enough substance or conviction in a man's life to compel his allegiance to life itself. Life has to have substance if anything is to have sense, including adherence to the impartial system; but if it has substance, then it cannot grant supreme importance to the impartial system and that system's hold on it will be, at the limit, insecure. (Williams 1981: 18)

For Williams, and famously, the demands of an impartial system of morality are ones which can threaten our ground projects, our deepest commitments to others, and, at the limit, our motivation for carrying on with life itself.

On the one hand, then, the debate between impartialists and their opponents is said to represent no more than a series of confusions and misunderstandings which have very few (if any) interesting philosophical implications. On the other hand, it is presented as being of the utmost significance, for it is concerned with the very terms on which we can find life worth living at all. My aim in this book is to show that partial concerns are indeed the ones which give life substance and make it worth living, but that those concerns can nonetheless be reconciled with impartialism. In short, I aim to show that although the differences between impartialists and their critics run very deep, reconciliation is possible, and its possibility lies in a form of impartialism which accords centrality to partial concerns.

However, before attempting the reconciliation, it is important to be clear about what exactly is being reconciled with what, and it is especially important to be clear about the different forms impartialism takes in political and moral philosophy respectively. Barry (quite correctly) characterizes the battle between defenders and critics of impartiality as one that runs through both moral and political philosophy, but if it is a single battle, it has different manifestations in the two contexts. In political philosophy, it is closely associated with the requirement to treat everyone equally by, for instance, according them equal rights or granting them equal consideration in the distribution of social and political benefits. As such, impartialist theories stand in opposition to political theories which would grant special rights to some groups on the basis of, for instance, ethnicity, birth, gender, or status. Now of course the requirement to give everyone equal consideration does not rule out all inequalities as illegitimate but, as Barry emphasizes, it does rule out unmediated claims to advantage on those grounds. So impartialist political theory is to be contrasted with theories which would give special status to members of some groups simply because they are members of that group and for no other reason. As such, it may seem to be no more nor less than the common sense of modern western democrats. But there's the rub, for (notoriously) modern western democratic societies do not consist entirely of modern western democrats. On the contrary, they are multicultural, multiracial, and multi-religious societies in which very different people must live together harmoniously. Moreover, and problematically, not all those who live within an impartialist political system will themselves subscribe to the principle of equality which, it is said, underpins impartialism, and the question which then arises is how (if at all) can impartialism be commended to those people?

In political philosophy, therefore, the task for impartialism is to show why those who are not themselves impartialist might nonetheless accept an impartialist political order, why they might accept it as genuinely just, and why they might concede that its demands take priority over the conflicting values endorsed by their own comprehensive conception of the good. This question is addressed in Chapter 1, where I emphasize the demands imposed by two requirements of impartialist political philosophy: the permanence of pluralism and the priority of justice. I argue that these demands require a careful response, for if impartialist political philosophy is to show the priority of justice to be more than a *modus vivendi*, then it must have a moral foundation. However, if impartialist political philosophy is to acknowledge the permanence of pluralism, then that moral foundation cannot be one which implies acceptance of a specific comprehensive conception of the good.

In Chapter 2 I take up the question of the moral priority of impartialism. Whereas Chapter 1 noted that priority is a vexed issue in political contexts where not everyone can be assumed to endorse impartiality as a value, Chapter 2 suggests that, even where it is endorsed, a problem about priority may persist. Following Korsgaard, I label this 'the normative problem'. It arises when partial commitments (commitments to particular people or to projects of one's own) conflict with impartial considerations, and it is expressed in the agent's self-directed question 'why should I act on the motivation to do what impartial morality dictates rather than on the motivation to act partially?' Since this question arises even (indeed especially) for those who accept the importance of impartial demands, it forces us to consider the origins and extent of impartialism's motivational power. My claim is that that motivational power derives from impartialism's ability to accommodate the partial concerns we have for particular others. Impartialism can command allegiance only when it is seen as arising from, and therefore consonant with, the partial concerns we have for things and people we care about or love. Moreover, if this is true for those who accept the importance of impartiality, it may also be the best way of commending impartiality to those who do not antecedently acknowledge its force. Chapter 3 attempts to spell out this suggestion in more detail and to show how our partial concerns for others might provide a route into impartial morality, or a way of getting it 'off the ground'. Finally, Chapter 4 gives some reasons for thinking that such a form of impartialism may also be commended as congruent with the good of the agent him or herself. In defending congruence, I ally myself with the position advanced by John Rawls in Part III of *A Theory of Justice*, and in particular with the analogy he draws there between love and justice (Rawls 1971). I try to show how the analogy may be developed in a way that supports congruence, but does not require commitment to a comprehensive conception of the good.

This book therefore takes seriously the impartialist desire to assert both the (moral) priority of impartial justice and the permanence of (moral) pluralism. It asks how impartiality can be accorded priority in a world characterized by its proliferation of different, yet reasonable, comprehensive conceptions of the good, and it suggests that that can be done by seeing impartialism as deriving both its moral and its motivational force from partial concerns themselves.

Two sub-themes recur throughout the book and ought now to be signposted. The first is the relationship between questions of motivation and questions of justification; the second is the importance of our partial concerns. On the first, I set my face against those who would make a sharp distinction between the justification of impartialist philosophy and its power to motivate. It seems to me that, especially in conditions of modernity, questions of justification and questions of motivation are inextricably intertwined. This is partly attributable to the so-called 'disenchantment' of the modern world, which dictates that we no longer have (if indeed we ever did have) recourse to anything beyond ourselves that can provide us with reason to be moral. We must therefore seek a justificatory story which is also capable of attaining motivational purchase. More generally, it is because, without motivational power, theories of morality and of politics threaten to become 'schizophrenic' (Stocker 1976) or 'dysfunctional' (Gauthier 1986: 339) or 'unstable' (Rawls 1971: 455).

On the second, I claim that if impartialist theory is to motivate, and is to do so without invoking a comprehensive conception of the good, then it must take seriously the things people do in fact care about—the partial concerns they have and, especially, their concerns for other people such as friends and family. In invoking our propensity to care about people as an important component of impartialist morality, I set myself at odds with writers such as Harry Frankfurt and Bernard Williams, who draw a sharp distinction between what we care about and the demands of morality (Frankfurt 1988, 1999; Williams 1981). I argue that caring about things has a distinctively moral dimension, but that it does not imply any particular comprehensive conception of the good. This is because caring about things gives evidence of what we value morally, but does not itself entail any particular set of moral values.

In his 1990 British Academy Lecture, the late Martin Hollis wrote: 'Old-World Ethics set Reason to discern a meaning in life which pointed beyond it. Platonists sought the Form of the Good and the Right, to which a moral life should conform. Aristotelians hoped to attune the good life to moral rhythms in the larger universe where human nature belonged. New-World ethics dispensed with all such external sources of meaning.' Having done so, it left us 'to work through the ethical implications of denying all meaning to human life external to human life itself, and yet to emerge with an account of how there can be moral reasons for action' (Hollis 1996: 109, 116). Impartialism is a very significant attempt to respond to this challenge. Impartialist moral philosophy aims to show how we can have reason, indeed compelling reason, to be moral in a world where life has no meaning beyond itself. Impartialist political philosophy aims to show how we can have reason, indeed compelling reason, to be just in a world where the very question of life's meaning is deeply, and permanently, in dispute.

My suggestion is that, in such a world, we must embrace impartialism in both moral and political philosophy, but that we must embrace a form of impartialism which takes seriously the partial concerns we have for others. This, I believe, is our best hope of showing why impartial considerations should have priority, and it is also our best hope of affirming the permanence of pluralism in good faith. What follows is an attempt to explain exactly how impartialism can execute this task: how it can command allegiance at the individual level, and how it can provide a response to the fact of pluralism which is more than a *modus vivendi* but less than the assertion of a specific, and contested, comprehensive conception of the good. It is an argument to the effect that, in a world where life has no meaning beyond itself, we can find both meaning and morality in the partial concerns we have for particular others.

1

Impartiality in Political Philosophy

My aim in this book is to explain the attractiveness of impartialist philosophy, and to show how its demands can be reconciled with the partial concerns and commitments that 'give life substance'. In order to do that, however, I must first say something (however rough and ready) about what impartialism is, and what motivates commitment to it. One powerful and recurrent theme in the literature is that impartialism reflects a commitment to equality. Thus, Thomas Nagel writes: 'the requirement of impartiality can take various forms, but it usually involves treating or counting everyone equally in some respect—according them the same rights, or counting their good or their welfare or some aspect of it the same in determining what would be a desirable result or a permissible course of action' (Nagel 1987: 215). Similarly, Brian Barry associates impartiality with equality, arguing that the whole idea of justice as impartiality: 'rests upon a fundamental commitment to the equality of all human beings. This kind of equality is what is appealed to by the French Declaration of the Rights of Man and of the Citizen and by the American Declaration of Independence. Only on this basis can we defend the claim that the interests and viewpoints of everybody concerned must be accommodated' (Barry 1995: 8). And John Rawls, too, understands impartiality as requiring that we judge 'in accordance with principles without bias or prejudice ... choosing a conception of justice once and for all in an original position *of equality*' (Rawls 1971: 190, emphasis added). Impartialist political philosophy, then, is a way of spelling out, and indeed living out, our belief in the fundamental equality of all human beings.

However, this widespread agreement about the centrality of impartiality, and about its grounding in equality, is coupled with widespread disagreement about the best way of realizing it. Famously, Rawls rejects the utilitarian suggestion that impartiality is to be attained by taking each person to count as one because, he says, such a procedure undermines the separateness of persons and reduces impartiality to impersonality. Crudely, his complaint is that utilitarianism, so interpreted, can legitimize sacrificing some people in the name of greater overall benefit. When this happens the losers do not, in fact, count as one. They are not treated equally, but may, in some circumstances, be sacrificial lambs on the altar of the greatest good. As he puts it: 'what the principle of utility asks is that . . . we accept the greater advantages of others as sufficient reason for lower expectations over the whole course of our life. This is surely an extreme demand. In fact, when society is conceived as a system of co-operation designed to advance the good of its members, it seems quite incredible that some should be expected, on the basis of political principles, to accept lower prospects of life for the sake of others' (Rawls 1971: 178).

It is for a similar reason that Brian Barry also rejects the so-called 'impartial spectator' interpretation of impartiality and, following Scanlon, urges instead an interpretation which emphasizes reasonable agreement: 'principles of justice that satisfy the [reasonable agreement] condition are impartial' he writes 'because they capture a certain kind of equality: all those affected have to be able to feel that they have done as well as they could reasonably hope to' (Barry 1995: 7). For both Barry and Rawls, the best way of under-standing impartialist commitment to the equality of all human beings is via the concept of reasonable agreement. Since the losers in such an agreement recognize that they could not reasonably have expected to do better under any alternative arrangement, the principles of justice that are delivered can properly be said to have taken everyone's interests into account, and thus to have reflected the commitment to equality that lies at the heart of impartial-ism.

Political impartialism, then, is informed by a concern for and commitment to equality: some (for example, some utilitarians) think that this commitment is best honoured by taking each to count for one, and summing the overall benefit. Others (notably contractarians) think that it is best honoured by asking what it would be reasonable for people to agree to in appropriate conditions. But whatever the best way of honouring it, impartialist political philosophers seem to be agreed that it is indeed the value of equality which underpins and explains the attractiveness of impartiality.

Moreover, this same understanding of impartiality as grounded in equality is also to be found in moral philosophy. In a 1991 *Ethics* symposium on 'Impartiality and Ethical Theory' Barbara Herman traces the origins of impartialism in ethical theory to 'the fundamental moral equality of agents' (Herman 1991: 797), and in his book, *Friendship, Altruism and Morality*, Lawrence Blum writes 'the moral point of view involves impartiality regarding the interests of all, including oneself. It involves abstracting from one's own interests and one's particular attachments to others. To be moral is to respect others as having *equal value* to oneself, and as having *an equal right* to pursue their own interests' (Blum 1980: 3, emphasis added). In both moral and political philosophy, therefore, impartiality reflects a commitment to equality, even though the way in which that commitment is to be made manifest is a matter of dispute.

The Scope of Political Impartiality

But if impartialism generally is a way of reflecting commitment to the equality of all human beings, political impartialism is restricted in at least two, and arguably three, significant ways. First, it confines itself to questions of justice, where justice is only one value amongst others (it is only a part of morality, not the whole of it). By confining itself to questions of justice, political impartialism displays a restriction in *subject matter*. Second, political impartialism construes justice as being centrally concerned with the distribution of benefits and burdens by the state. It is not, or not primarily, concerned with the ways in which individuals behave towards one another, but rather with the principles on which society as a whole should operate. Political impartialism is therefore restricted in *scope*. Finally political impartialism focuses on questions of justification, not on questions of motivation. It is interested in the legitimacy of the principles adopted by society, not with the question of what moves individuals to act justly. So political impartialism is restricted in *aim*: it is concerned with justification, not with motivation.

Or is it? It is here that controversy begins, for although the restriction on aim is widespread in political impartialism, it is by no means universal: some political philosophers see their task as being simply to justify the principles which should regulate the distribution of benefits and burdens in society, but others believe that it is equally important for impartial political philosophy to address the motivational question. This difference is an important one for my overall project because I want to suggest that questions of justification cannot be kept separate from questions of motivation, and I also want to claim that this fact has implications for the possibility of defending political impartialism outside the context of a defence of moral impartialism more generally. Broadly speaking, I will argue that any attempt to justify political impartialism necessarily raises motivational questions, and those motivational questions are ones that ultimately require us to defend political impartialism within the wider context of a defence of moral impartialism. Therefore, because of the importance of the restriction on aim to my overall project, I shall now say something about it before going on to suggest why political impartialism cannot confine itself to justificatory questions, but must also engage with questions of motivation.

Political Impartiality: Motivation and Justification

In the conclusion to Part I of *Justice as Impartiality*, Brian Barry draws a distinction between justificatory and motivational questions and, while issuing a promissory note to the effect that Volume III of his *Treatise* 'will show that some well-known arguments about the psychological impossibility of impartial justice are misguided', he nonetheless goes on to insist that his main concern in *Justice as Impartiality* is with the truth of the theory, not with its motivational efficacy. He writes: 'my object in this *Treatise* is to present the results of some twenty years of thought about what justice is and what it entails. My concern is with truth, not with popularity ... how strong the desire to behave justly actually is, when it comes into competition with other desires, I leave open. I claim only to tell you what justice is; what you do about it, if you believe me, is up to you' (Barry 1995: 115). And in 'Something in the Disputation Not Unpleasant', he reinforces this commitment to the justificatory enterprise when he says:

we live in a world that is full of other people with different conceptions of the good, and they should have a fair chance to pursue them even if we have the power to stop (some of) them. Any adequate theory of justice should, I suggest, take that thought and give it specificity. That is what I claim to have done in *Justice as Impartiality*. If somebody is totally unmoved by the elementary thought that I have expressed, then of course the theory will not speak to him. But the theory can explain why it is justifiable to do whatever is necessary to restrain such people. (in Kelly 1998: 237)

Barry's theory of justice, then, concentrates on demonstrating the truth of impartial principles. It is largely indifferent to the question of whether and to what extent we will be motivated to act on those principles once we have conceded (if we do) that they are true.

By contrast, John Rawls is deeply concerned about the question of motivation, and devotes a great deal of time to it in Part III of *A Theory of Justice*, where he writes: 'however attractive a conception of justice might be on other grounds, it is seriously defective if the principles of moral psychology are such that it fails to engender in human beings the requisite desire to act on it' (Rawls 1971: 455). Where Barry takes the robust view that we cannot expect a theory of justice to 'pick people up by the scruff of the neck and force them to behave justly, regardless of their beliefs and inclinations' (1995: 114), Rawls is concerned to show not only that his theory of justice will have motivational force, but also that, by adopting a regulative attitude towards justice, we will realize our true nature as free and equal rational beings. In short, and for the Rawls of *A Theory of Justice*, acting justly will be congruent with the good of the agent himself. This 'congruence' requirement is a very strong one (arguably too strong), and indeed it is one that Rawls has subsequently renounced precisely because he believes that it requires commitment to a comprehensive (Kantian) conception of persons. In *Political Liberalism* he writes: 'Although the distinction between a political conception of justice and a comprehensive philosophical doctrine is not discussed in *Theory*, once the question is raised, it is clear, I think, that the text regards justice as fairness and utilitarianism as comprehensive, or partially comprehensive doctrines' (Rawls 1993: xvi).

Whatever the truth on that point, the contrast between Barry and Rawls serves to highlight the fact that political philosophers are divided in their understanding of the proper aim of an impartialist political theory. Where Barry is content, at least *pro tem*, to defend his theory on the grounds that it is true, Rawls denies that this is enough for completeness, and places great weight on the ability of a theory of justice to command allegiance from those who live under it. Here, then, we have distinct views about the centrality of motivational questions to an adequate impartialist political theory, and my first aim in this chapter is to provide some reasons for thinking that justificatory questions cannot hang free of motivational ones, and that any acceptable impartialist political philosophy must respond to questions of motivation. If this is right, then the question which next arises is what that response should be and, in particular, whether and how it can be one that rests on a commitment to equality. Before addressing that question, however, I must first explain why and how justificatory questions carry motivational implications with them, and to do that I need to say something about the problems political philosophy faces in the modern world.

Political Philosophy and Modernity

In 'The Idea of an Overlapping Consensus', Rawls tells us that the aims of political philosophy depend on the society it addresses and that modern democratic societies are characterized by 'the fact of pluralism' (Rawls 1999: 421–48).They are societies in which different people have different and conflicting comprehensive conceptions of the good, different and conflicting beliefs about the right way to live morally speaking. Thus, modern democratic societies contain people of many different religious faiths, and people of no religious faith. They contain feminists, homosexuals, conservative moralists, libertarians, greens, anti-abortionists, New Age travellers, and merchant bankers, to name but a few. It is clear that these people have very different beliefs about the 'highest good' or the best way to lead one's life morally speaking. In Rawls's own terminology, they have different and conflicting comprehensive conceptions of the good. Nonetheless, and despite these conflicting comprehensive conceptions, they must live together and find principles of justice on which they can somehow agree.

However, the problem of establishing principles of justice in a world characterized by pluralism is exacerbated when we note that the pluralism of the modern world has two distinctive features: it is, Rawls says, both permanent and significant. In 'Kantian Constructivism and Moral Theory' he notes that 'diversity naturally arises from our limited powers and different perspectives; it is unrealistic to suppose that all our differences are rooted solely in ignorance and perversity or else in the rivalries that result from scarcity' (Rawls 1999: 329). And again, in *Political Liberalism*, he cites the burdens of judgement as sources of irreconcilable, yet reasonable, disagreement and concludes: 'different conceptions of the world can reasonably be elaborated from different standpoints and diversity arises in part from our distinct perspectives' (Rawls 1993: 58). In short, we cannot expect diversity to disappear, and indeed we should not consider its continued existence a disaster. On the contrary, since the persistence of pluralism is partly a function of the way in which reason operates, to conceive of it as a disaster would be like conceiving of the exercise of reason under conditions of freedom as a disaster (Rawls 1993: xxiv). So, while modernity is characterized by its proliferation of different and conflicting conceptions of the good, and while this poses a problem of political justice, we should not attempt to resolve the problem by removing the pluralism, since pluralism is the natural outcome of the operation of reason under conditions of freedom. This, then, is the first significant feature of pluralism. In conditions of modernity, pluralism is permanent.

The second feature of pluralism is that, in the modern world, it has a significance which, in other times, it lacked. This, Rawls says, is because in modernity 'belief matters', and it matters much more than it once did. He writes:

when moral philosophy began, say with Socrates, ancient religion was a civic religion of public social practice, of civic festivals and public celebrations. Moreover, this civic religious culture was not based on a sacred work, like the Bible or the Koran, or the Vedas of Hinduism. The Greeks celebrated Homer and Homeric poems were a basic part of their education, but the *Iliad* and the *Odyssey* were never sacred texts. As long as one participated in the expected way and recognized the proprieties, the details of what one believed were not of great importance. It was a matter of doing the done thing and being a trustworthy member of society, always ready to carry out one's civic duties as a good citizen—to serve on juries or to row in the fleet in war—when called upon to do so. It was not a religion of salvation in the Christian sense and there was no class of priests who dispensed the necessary means of grace; indeed, the ideas of immortality and eternal salvation did not have a central place in classical culture. (Rawls 1993: xxi)

However, and on Rawls's account, this early understanding of religion has changed in two highly significant ways: first, the medieval period saw the rise of 'salvationist' conceptions of religion; second, the Reformation period witnessed the fragmentation of religion into distinct schisms, each of which had its own view of the route to salvation. What we find, therefore, in the post-Reformation period and in the subsequent wars of religion, is a dramatically altered conception of the significance of religious belief, which comes to be, no longer a matter of indifference, but a matter of supreme importance on which depends one's prospects of attaining life everlasting. When this supreme significance is attached to religious belief, and when there are also conflicting views about which belief is the true one, the scene is set for a form of conflict which knows no compromise in principle, and Rawls now claims that the significance first accorded to belief in this period has survived into the modern world and has become a central feature of modernity (Rawls 1993: xxii). This, then, is the second significant feature of pluralism: it reflects the importance attached to individual belief as a means, indeed *the* means, to salvation.

These two features of the modern world—that it is a world in which pluralism is permanent and in which individual belief matters—set the agenda for modern political philosophy. Since the aims of political philosophy depend upon the society it addresses, and since modern society is characterized by reasonable pluralism understood as both permanent and significant, the aims of political philosophy must be to arrive at principles of justice which acknowledge pluralism as both permanent and significant. Additionally, and crucially, a theory of justice must defend the priority of justice over comprehensive conceptions of the good. It must show why impartial justice should win when it comes into conflict with reasonable comprehensive conceptions and, according to Rawls at least, it must do that in a way which defends the priority of justice as more than a mere *modus vivendi*. So it will not be enough for a theory of justice to offer pragmatic reasons, or reasons of expediency, for favouring justice; it must also explain why people would freely and willingly endorse the priority of justice when its dictates conflict with the dictates of their own comprehensive conception of the good.

Given this understanding of the aspirations of modern political philosophy, I now have two aims in this chapter: the first is to show that the distinction between motivation and justification referred to earlier is unsustainable, and that attempts to justify impartial political philosophy will unavoidably involve appeal to motivational questions. In particular, they will make claims about the nature and significance of individual belief, and those claims will undermine the restriction on aim characteristic of at least some kinds of impartialist political philosophy.

My second, and connected, aim will be to argue that the specific understanding of belief implicit in Rawls's impartialist theory is one that highlights a general tension between the permanence of pluralism and the priority of justice. The more strongly we adhere to the conception of belief that is necessary to defend the permanence of pluralism, the less able we will be to assert the priority of justice in cases of conflict. So, in the first place, the interconnection between justification and motivation has consequences for the conception of belief available to modern impartialist political philosophy, and in the second place the conception of belief available to modern impartialist political philosophy is one that cannot simultaneously support both the permanence of pluralism and the priority of justice. If, therefore, we are to defend the priority claim in a way compatible with the permanence of pluralism, we must look beyond political impartialism. We must find a defence of priority that is moral, but not comprehensively so. This, however, is the task for later chapters. My aim now is to explain exactly how questions of motivation and justification are interconnected, and how they imply a conception of belief that cannot simultaneously satisfy the permanence and priority requirements which are central to political impartialism.

Justification and Motivation

I noted earlier that Rawls takes the question of motivation to be crucial for the completeness of a theory of justice, and he argues that the theory will be 'defective' if it cannot command the allegiance of those who live under it (Rawls 1971: 455). It is for this reason that, in Part III of *A Theory of Justice*, he devotes a great deal of time to defending the principles of moral psychology which underpin justice as fairness and concludes not only that justice as fairness is stable, in the sense that it accords with plausible principles of moral psychology, but also that, where the desire to act justly is regulative of a rational plan of life, 'acting justly is part of our good' (Rawls 1971: 456).

However, and famously, in *Political Liberalism* he withdraws these claims, and indeed identifies a serious inconsistency in the argument of Part III of *A Theory of Justice*. That inconsistency, which he claims is the sole motivation for the move from *A Theory of Justice* to *Political Liberalism*, arises from the fact that, as Rawls now sees it, the defence of stability offered in Part III of *Theory* requires that members of a well-ordered society accept the two principles of justice on the basis of a comprehensive philosophical doctrine. This requirement, however, is inconsistent with the permanence of pluralism about the good and must therefore be rejected. In short, what Rawls now believes is that the argument of Part III of *Theory* is one which has motivational force only for those who subscribe to a specific, and Kantian, comprehensive conception of the good according to which our true nature consists in acting as free and equal rational beings. However, this assumption contradicts the permanence of reasonable pluralism and must therefore be renounced. In the modern world, people have very different comprehensive conceptions of the good, many of those conceptions are reasonable, and not all will imply that one's true nature is best realized by taking the principles of justice as regulative. Thus:

A modern democratic society is characterized not simply by a pluralism of comprehensive religious, philosophical and moral doctrines but by a pluralism of incompatible yet reasonable comprehensive doctrines. No one of these doctrines is affirmed by citizens generally. Nor should one expect that in the forseeable future one of them, or some other reasonable doctrine, will ever be affirmed by all, or nearly all, citizens. (Rawls 1993: xvi)

Moreover, the consequences of Rawls's recent emphasis on the permanence and reasonableness of pluralism are wide-ranging, for it was the Kantian conception which provided the account of motivation in *A Theory of Justice* and therefore, in renouncing that conception, Rawls has robbed himself of that part of his theory which rendered it stable and complete. His task in *Political Liberalism*, therefore, is to explain how justice as fairness can motiv- ate people without supposing that they subscribe to any specific moral, religious or philosophical doctrine: 'The problem of political liberalism is: How is it possible that there may exist over time a stable and just society of free and equal citizens profoundly divided by reasonable religious, philosoph- ical and moral doctrines? This is a problem of political justice, not a problem about the highest good' (Rawls 1993: xxv). Indeed, he goes further and argues that not only is political liberalism not about the highest good, it must self- consciously avoid questions of the highest good and say nothing either about the truth of conflicting, though reasonable, comprehensive conceptions or about the truth of justice as fairness itself.

So Rawls now sees his theory as political in two distinct ways: first, it is political as opposed to moral in that it does not rest upon any claim about the highest good, or the best way to lead one's life. It does not suppose that people will be motivated to comply with the principles of justice because they are committed to any specific moral ideal underpinning it. Second, it is political as opposed to metaphysical in that it makes no claims about the truth or falsity of comprehensive conceptions of the good, nor does it assert its own truth as the reason for allegiance. Rather, reasons for allegiance are to be found by each person from within his or her conception of the good, and where competing yet reasonable comprehensive conceptions converge on justice as fairness, we have what Rawls calls an 'overlapping consensus'. 'This', he concludes, 'is a better and no longer utopian way of thinking of the well-ordered society of justice as fairness. It corrects the view in *Theory*, which fails to take into account the condition of pluralism to which its own principles lead' (Rawls 1999: 490).

The conclusion of Rawls's recent work is therefore that the motivational efficacy (stability) of a theory of justice can be rendered compatible with the permanence and reasonableness of pluralism only if we understand the theory as political in the ways described. In advancing it we do not assume that those who live under it will subscribe to a particular comprehensive conception of the good (such as the Kantian conception), nor do we com- mend it on the grounds that it is true, since to do that would be to put ourselves at odds with the many reasonable philosophical doctrines which have conflicting beliefs about what is true, or even deny that there is such a thing as moral or religious truth at all. Rather, we rely on the ability of the theory to command allegiance from within different comprehensive conceptions of the good: 'it is left to citizens individually to decide for themselves in what way their shared political conception is related to their wider and more comprehensive views' (Rawls 1999: 489).

This discussion of Rawls's political theory, and of the differences between his earlier and later work, is introduced as a way of emphasizing that he is concerned about both motivation and justification. Unlike Barry, who takes motivational questions to be subsidiary to and independent of questions of justification, Rawls sees an acceptable theory of justice as standing in urgent need of motivational support. However, the transition from *A Theory of Justice* to *Political Liberalism* also suggests that Rawls sees motivational questions as being connected to justificatory ones in ways which are potentially problematic for his theory. So it is not, I think, simply the case that Rawls *chooses* to address motivational questions, nor merely that he believes those motivational questions to be significant for the completeness of his theory. Rather, they are questions which arise directly from, and are demanded by, the justificatory enterprise itself.

Perhaps this point is most obvious in his claim (quoted earlier) that *Theory* 'fails to take into account the condition of pluralism to which its own principles lead', for here he is drawing attention to the fact that the motivational story which is told in *Theory* conflicts with the justificatory story which is told in *Theory*. The justification offered in *Theory* 'leads to' the permanence of pluralism, but the motivational story told in *Theory* undermines pluralism because it has purchase only if we accept the Kantian conception. Faced with this dilemma, Rawls abandons the Kantian conception in favour of a political conception of justice as fairness and an account of motivation which invokes overlapping consensus. In doing this, he hopes to show how justice as fairness might come to have motivational force for people who do not subscribe to the Kantian conception, and it is for this same reason that he advocates adopting what he calls the 'method of avoidance', which requires that in advancing a theory of justice we make no claims about its truth, but only about its ability to command assent from people with very different comprehensive conceptions. Here, too, the avowed aim is to show how justice as fairness can have motivational force for people with very different conceptions of the good. Rawls writes:

In following the method of avoidance, as we may call it, we try, so far as we can, neither to assert nor to deny any religious, philosophical, or moral views, or their associated philosophical accounts of truth and the status of values. Since we assume each citizen to affirm some such view or other, we hope to make it possible for all to accept the political conception as true, or as reasonable, from the standpoint of their own comprehensive view, whatever it may be. (Rawls 1999: 434)

So, having renounced the Kantian conception because it contradicts the fact of pluralism to which the two principles lead, Rawls must provide an alternative account of the motivation to justice—one which acknowledges the permanence of reasonable pluralism about the good and allows each person to endorse the two principles from within his or her specific and distinctive comprehensive conception. Because he believes his earlier account to have been one which required commitment to a specific comprehensive conception (the Kantian conception), and because he thinks that commitment to be at odds with the fact of pluralism, his task now is to show how justice as fairness can be commended to those who live under it in a way which does not undermine their comprehensive conceptions. Hence, the method of avoidance or, as Raz has dubbed it, 'epistemological abstinence'. The move to avoidance or abstinence therefore constitutes Rawls's attempt to justify his theory of justice, and to show how people might be motivated to comply with it, without invoking any comprehensive conception of the good, and thus without undermining the permanence of pluralism. The crucial question now is whether abstinence can indeed discharge the motivational task previously performed by the Kantian conception.

Here, Rawls's critics express serious doubts: Brian Barry rejects the doctrine of epistemological abstinence because, he says, it will ultimately collapse into moderate scepticism (scepticism understood as involving doubt rather than denial). Indeed, he goes further and claims that scepticism is the only way of defending liberal impartialism (Barry 1995: 168–88). By contrast, Joseph Raz insists that the doctrine of epistemological abstinence contains covert claims to truth and he, too, goes further, arguing that no adequate defence of justice can avoid making truth claims (Raz 1994: 60–96). Either way, epistemological abstinence is deemed to be inadequate.

Because the doctrine of epistemological abstinence is significant for my wider project, I shall spend some time discussing it. However, it might be helpful to preface that discussion with an account of why the doctrine is significant and, especially, what is at stake in disputes about it. As we have seen, Rawls's appeal to abstinence springs from his belief that a complete theory of justice must include a motivational story, together with his belief that, since pluralism is permanent, the motivational story must not invoke any specific comprehensive conception of the good. However, and as we have also seen, Rawls's insistence on the importance of motivation is contested: some political philosophers deny the centrality of motivation and argue that it is sufficient if a theory of justice can be justified. For them, epistemological abstinence is an unnecessary intrusion into a theory of justice. Since several of these writers also claim that epistemological abstinence is incoherent, they have a double reason for objecting to it: as a response to an alleged problem of motivation, it is unnecessary, and as a claim about the possibility of refraining from making judgements about moral, religious, and philosophical views it is implausible, or even incoherent.

My own belief, foreshadowed in the earlier part of this chapter, is that motivational questions cannot hang free of justificatory ones: any acceptable justification of political impartialism will have motivational implications. Moreover, I deny that the doctrine of epistemological abstinence is incoherent. On the contrary, I believe that it can be used to underpin an account of the motivation to justice which supports the permanence of reasonable pluralism. What is less clear, however, is whether epistemological abstinence is compatible with the demand (also central to political impartialism) that justice be given priority in cases where it conflicts with comprehensive conceptions of the good, and the reason for this is that the concept of belief which underpins the doctrine of epistemological abstinence and generates the permanence of pluralism is also a concept of belief which undermines the priority of justice.

The crucial claims of the remainder of this chapter are therefore (first) that the justification of political impartialism carries motivational implications with it, and (second) that the most persuasive motivational story undermines the priority of justice. Pluralism and priority are in tension with one another in political impartialism. However, if all that is true, then we will have to look elsewhere for an account of how the permanence of pluralism can be reconciled with the priority of justice. In particular, we will have to consider the priority of impartial justice as part of a wider problem about the priority of impartial morality. That will be my task in the next chapter.

I begin, however, with two arguments against epistemological abstinence. The first is advanced by Brian Barry in *Justice as Impartiality*; the second is advanced by Joseph Raz in 'Facing Diversity: The Case of Epistemic Abstinence'. My aim here is to demonstrate that while neither of these succeeds in showing the incoherence of epistemological abstinence, both strongly suggest that the doctrine of epistemological abstinence purchases the permanence of pluralism only by rendering the priority of justice indefensible.

Epistemological Abstinence and the Costs of Scepticism

As was noted earlier, Rawls's appeal to epistemological abstinence springs from his desire to show that the motivation to justice is compatible with the permanence of pluralism. He believes that the motivational story told in *A Theory of Justice* contradicts the permanence of pluralism, and now urges that political liberalism should be strictly political in the sense that it should neither comment upon the comprehensive conceptions of the good which are endorsed by citizens of a well-ordered society, nor make claims grounded in its own truth. Each will find his or her own route to the principles of justice and, as long as those principles are freely acknowledged from within the individual's comprehensive conception, political liberalism has nothing to say about the comprehensive conceptions themselves.

However, Rawls goes on to insist that this strategy (the strategy of abstinence) must be distinguished from scepticism. Because political liberalism aims to distance itself from controversial moral, religious, and philosophical doctrines, and because scepticism is itself a controversial doctrine, political liberalism does not, and must not, be taken to imply scepticism: 'it would be fatal to the idea of a political conception to see it as skeptical about, or indifferent to, truth, much less as in conflict with it. Such skepticism or indifference would put political philosophy in opposition to numerous comprehensive doctrines, and thus defeat from the outset its aim of achieving an overlapping consensus' (Rawls 1993: 150).

So political philosophy, as now understood by Rawls, requires abstinence about controversial matters: not only does it not demand that individuals embrace a specific comprehensive conception of the good, it is also, and wherever possible, silent (abstinent) about those philosophical, religious, and moral questions on which people might reasonably disagree, including the question of whether moral and religious beliefs are susceptible of truth and falsity at all. Because Part III of *A Theory of Justice* required people to embrace the Kantian conception, it undermined competing conceptions of the good, many of which were reasonable. *Political Liberalism* therefore seeks to rectify this fault by saying as little as possible about the truth or falsity of the beliefs which prompt people to embrace justice as fairness, and since some people embrace justice as fairness while denying scepticism, justice as fairness is abstinent about scepticism too. Is this injunction to remain abstinent stable?

Barry denies that it is, and indeed he goes further, arguing that not only is scepticism necessary in order to justify impartial liberalism, it is in fact the *only* thing that can justify it. On Barry's account abstinence will collapse into scepticism, and Rawls cannot deliver on his promise to justify political liberalism without invoking any controversial doctrine. However, and for Barry, this is not a disaster because, *pace* Rawls, scepticism is not itself a comprehensive conception of the good. It is, of course, controversial, but that is a different matter. 'Scepticism', Barry writes, 'is not a view of human flourishing. It is an epistemological doctrine about the status of conceptions of what constitutes human flourishing. Scepticism is, of course, a controversial view in that some people would deny it. But there is no way of avoiding the affirmation of a position that is not universally accepted if one is to get anywhere at all. My claim is that the case for scepticism cannot reasonably be rejected' (Barry 1995: 174). So, where Rawls sees scepticism as controversial, and therefore to be avoided in the defence of justice as fairness, Barry replies that the aspiration to avoid saying anything controversial is simply hopeless and that in any case scepticism, far from being at odds with liberal impartialism, is the unique route to it.

However, Rawls's aim is not simply to defend impartialism. It is also, and as we have seen, to defend impartialism in a way consistent with the permanence of pluralism. So in assessing the argument from scepticism, we must pay special attention to its implications for pluralism, understood as both permanent and significant. Barry's argument for scepticism centres on the fact (as he sees it) that in the modern world we are no longer entitled to hold our beliefs with certainty. He acknowledges the fact of pluralism, but argues that that fact is one which itself suggests scepticism: a world which contains many different and conflicting comprehensive conceptions of the good, a world in which we cannot persuade others of the truth of our own conception, is also and thereby a world in which it is appropriate to hold our own beliefs only provisionally. By insisting on the fact of pluralism, yet refusing to endorse scepticism, Rawls implies that I might be entitled to hold a belief with certainty even though I cannot persuade others of its truth, and this, Barry says, is implausible:

I question, however, whether certainty from the inside can coherently be combined with the line that it is reasonable for others to reject that same view. The most promising case would seem to be that of a private religious revelation. Suppose that God were (as it seemed to me) to grant me a vision in which certain truths were revealed. A partisan of epistemological restraint would suggest that I might be absolutely convinced of the veridical nature of this revelation while nevertheless admitting that others could reasonably reject my evidence. But is this really plausible? If I concede that I have no way of convincing others, should that not also lead to a dent in my own certainty? (Barry 1995: 179)

For Barry, then, pluralism implies moderate scepticism (scepticism understood as doubt rather than denial), and moderate scepticism is the unique foundation of impartial liberalism. By contrast, Rawls emphasizes the controversial character of scepticism, and his concern is that if impartial liberalism implies scepticism, then impartial liberalism will be unacceptable to those (many) people who, while conceding that they cannot persuade others, nonetheless continue to hold their own beliefs with utter conviction. In assessing the doctrine of epistemological abstinence, therefore, much seems to hang on the legitimacy of continuing to believe with certainty even when we cannot persuade others. The central question seems to be: 'Are we entitled to believe with certainty even if we cannot convince others?'

Thomas Nagel thinks that we are. He writes: 'when we look at certain of our convictions from the outside, however justified they may be from within, the appeal to their truth must be seen merely as an appeal to our beliefs, and should be treated as such unless those beliefs can be shown to be justifiable from a more impersonal standpoint' (Nagel 1987: 230). And in saying this he implies that it may be legitimate to retain conviction 'from the inside' even when it is impossible to persuade those who are 'on the outside'. Crucially, he appeals to epistemological abstinence as a way of addressing the problem which arises when people do, as a matter of fact, remain certain despite their inability to persuade others, for he goes on to urge that in making decisions about the coercive use of political power, we must 'abstract' from our own beliefs: the fact that I believe something, and even that I believe it with total conviction, cannot legitimize political coercion and the imposition of that view on others who do not share it and cannot be persuaded of it. Moreover, in saying this, he indicates that, *pace* Barry, the point of invoking abstinence is not to assess the legitimacy of persistent conviction despite the inability to persuade others. Rather, the point is to ascertain what political implications follow from the fact that conviction often does persist despite an inability to persuade others. In particular, it is an attempt to show why we might be entitled to refuse to use the coercive power of the state to enforce views which are held firmly and with complete conviction.

So where Barry's argument for scepticism focuses on the fact (as he sees it) that certainty is illegitimate in cases where we cannot persuade others, the doctrine of epistemological abstinence is concerned with what follows from the fact that sometimes people do retain certainty despite their inability to persuade others. The case of religious belief is perhaps the most obvious one here, but political and moral beliefs can also be held with conviction by many (perhaps all) who nonetheless fail to persuade others. Indeed, some of the most pressing problems in modern societies arise precisely because certainty is *not* dented by failure to convert, as can be seen by considering, for example, disputes about abortion or about homosexuality, or about a whole range of political and moral convictions. My failure to persuade those who believe abortion to be murder is, of course, and from my point of view, regrettable, but it does nothing to dent my conviction that they are wrong. And neither does their inability to persuade me do anything to dent their certainty. But there's the rub: Barry's insistence that conviction *should* be shaken by inability to persuade others seems both implausible and unhelpful in such cases, for many of the problems of modern societies are generated, not solved, by the persistence of conviction despite the inability to persuade, and it is these kinds of cases that the doctrine of epistemological abstinence sets out to address. In short, then, there is reason to think that Barry's argument misses the point of the doctrine of epistemological abstinence, which is not to pronounce on the legitimacy of persistent conviction, but rather to pronounce on the legitimacy of demands for political coercion based on the fact of persistent conviction.

Moreover, and importantly, the persistence of certainty despite the failure to persuade others is not simply a psychological phenomenon for, on some interpretations, commitment to the permanence of pluralism is itself commitment to the possibility that people may *reasonably* persist in their conviction despite the fact that they cannot persuade others. Rawls writes: 'many of our most important judgements are made under conditions where it is not to be expected that conscientious persons with full powers of reason, even after free discussion, will all arrive at the same conclusion' (Rawls 1993: 58), and he goes on to emphasize that this does not mean we should be hesitant or uncertain about our own beliefs. For him, then, conviction can legitimately survive the inability to persuade others, and his defence of the reasonableness of pluralism is a defence of the reasonableness of continuing to hold at least some beliefs with certainty despite the fact that they do not find favour with others. But if this is what reasonable pluralism requires, then Barry's argument undermines reasonable pluralism, since it insists on the illegitimacy of continuing conviction in face of the failure to persuade others.

What this implies is that Barry's appeal to scepticism both misunderstands the aim of epistemological abstinence and undermines the permanence of reasonable pluralism. Where Barry insists that we *should not* remain certain if we cannot persuade others, epistemological abstinence is an attempt to confront the fact that people often *do* remain certain despite their inability to persuade others. It is an attempt to show why that certainty cannot be invoked as the justification for imposition. Additionally, Barry's appeal to scepticism undermines at least some understandings of the permanence of pluralism. In particular, it undermines those understandings which insist on the reasonableness of persistent conviction despite an inability to persuade others, for on Barry's account it is not reasonable, in such circumstances, to continue to hold a conception of the good with conviction. It is only reasonable to hold it provisionally and with some hesitation or doubt.

This last point is of great significance, for it raises the question of whether, and to what extent, conceptions of the good are in part a function of the manner in which we are entitled to hold them. Barry's argument from scepticism assumes that there is a clear distinction between conceptions of human flourishing and epistemological claims about the status of conceptions of human flourishing, and he argues that Rawls need not fear appeal to scepticism because, although scepticism is of course controversial (not everyone subscribes to it), it is not a comprehensive conception of the good, but simply a view about the epistemic status of comprehensive conceptions of the good. The foregoing argument has been an attempt to show that, even if this is correct, it is not wholly relevant, since epistemological abstinence is an attempt to justify impartialism irrespective of the state of certainty in the mind of the agent.

However, some writers concur with Barry's claim that, where we cannot persuade others, we should, and often do, hold our beliefs provisionally. For them, though, the appropriateness of doubt is part of the problem of modernity, not a route to its solution. In his book, *Sources of the Self*, Charles Taylor claims that in the modern world we are in:

a fundamentally different existential predicament from that which dominated most previous cultures and still defines the lives of other people today. That alternative predicament is one in which an unchallengeable framework makes imperious demands which we fear being unable to meet. We face the prospect of irretrievable condemnation or exile, of being marked down in obloquy forever, or of being sent to damnation irrevocably ... the form of danger here is utterly different from that which threatens the modern seeker, which is something close to the opposite: the world loses altogether its spiritual contour, nothing is worth doing, the fear is of a terrifying emptiness, a kind of vertigo, or even a fracturing of our world and body space. (Taylor 1989: 18)

On Taylor's account, one very important factor contributing to what he calls our different 'existential predicament' is precisely that we can no longer hold our own beliefs unquestioningly, but must rather hold them provisionally. The plurality of different conceptions of the good (different 'frameworks', as he calls them) has a tendency to leave us in a state of doubt even about our most deeply held religious and moral convictions, for this plurality leaves us constantly aware of the fact that our framework is but one amongst many others.

However, and as is clear from Taylor's remarks, it is this condition of doubt or uncertainty which is itself our problem. In modern societies, characterized by the fact of pluralism, the manner in which we can hold our beliefs has been seriously undermined by comparison with a world in which they functioned as unquestionable frameworks. And our different existential predicament is, for him, largely a consequence of the different epistemological status of our conceptions of the good. It is the very fact that we can no longer hold our views unquestioningly which itself contributes in large part to the sense of vertigo that Taylor describes.

To put the point more generally, Taylor's analysis suggests that the plurality of competing conceptions of the good generates uncertainty, and that a conception of the good which is held with a degree of uncertainty is, in important respects, a different conception from one which is held with complete conviction. It is not merely *what* we believe that contributes to and constitutes our ability to flourish; it is also *the way in which* we are entitled to believe it, and the problem of modernity is, in large part, the problem of being unable to hold a conception of the good unquestioningly. If this is right, then while scepticism (understood as doubt rather than denial) might not be a 'view of human flourishing', it is nevertheless something which can contribute to or detract from our ability to flourish. The religious believer who can hold a belief in God unquestioningly is in a significantly different condition from the religious believer who, living in a world characterized by pluralism, can hold that belief only provisionally. The declaration 'I know that my Redeemer liveth!' has a different status from the declaration 'I believe that my Redeemer liveth, but I am unable to persuade others and must therefore entertain doubt'. In the modern world we are entitled only to the latter, but the uncertainty which is inherent in the latter is not simply an uncertainty about a single, persistent comprehensive conception of the good. It is an uncertainty that transforms the comprehensive conception and makes it different from the conception it was when it could legitimately be held without doubt.

Taylor's argument has implications for the attempt to ground impartialism in scepticism, for it suggests that views about human flourishing are in part determined by their epistemological status, but if this is true, then (again) the argument from scepticism undermines the permanence of pluralism: by denying the legitimacy of continuing to believe with conviction, scepticism denies the legitimacy of those conceptions of the good which are individuated precisely by the fact that they are held with conviction. And this clearly restricts the scope of reasonable pluralism permitted by a form of impartialism that is grounded in scepticism.

Putting these points together, we find the following problems associated with the attempt to reject epistemological abstinence in favour of scepticism: first, the argument from scepticism misidentifies the problem, which is not to adjudicate on whether people are or are not entitled to retain certainty despite their inability to persuade others. Rather, it is an attempt to abstract altogether from the agent's state of mind when making judgements about the legitimacy of political coercion or imposition. It is an attempt to render certainty irrelevant to questions of political imposition. Second, and connectedly, the argument from scepticism gives great prominence to the question of whether the agent is entitled to certainty, but in doing this it not only misunderstands the point of epistemological abstinence, it also puts itself in tension with the permanence of pluralism since, on at least some understandings, commitment to the permanence of pluralism just is commitment to the belief that it is not unreasonable for people to carry on believing with conviction in spite of the fact that they cannot persuade others. This, indeed, seems to be Rawls's own understanding of what the permanence of pluralism requires. Finally, even if the sceptical argument is correct, that is to say, even if it is true that we are entitled to hold our beliefs only provisionally in cases where we cannot persuade others, that might constitute a further statement of our problem in modernity, not a solution to it. And indeed, this is the very point Taylor is anxious to emphasize when he refers to the 'vertigo' that can afflict us in the modern world. Taylor makes the point in psychological or phenomenological terms, but it is one which rests, ultimately, on the possibility that the content of our conception of the good is in part a function of the manner in which we are entitled to hold it and that therefore there may be no stable distinction between views of human flourishing, on the one hand, and epistemological doctrines about the status of conceptions of human flourishing on the other. The move from epistemological abstinence to scepticism therefore exacts heavy costs: scepticism, unlike abstinence, gives centrality to the legitimate state of mind of the agent, but in doing that it threatens to deny the permanence of pluralism, and since the permanence of pluralism is one of the cornerstones of liberal impartialism, the victory of scepticism, even if attained, may turn out to be a pyrrhic victory.

But if these are the costs exacted by abandoning epistemological abstinence in favour of scepticism, what are the costs exacted by abandoning epistemological abstinence in favour of truth? In the next section I shall discuss this question via an analysis of Joseph Raz's article, 'Facing Diversity: The Case of Epistemic Abstinence' (Raz 1994). Again, my aim is to indicate the importance of epistemological abstinence in defending impartialist commitment to the permanence of pluralism.

Epistemological Abstinence and The Costs of Truth

Raz's argument focuses on the impossibility, as he sees it, of advocating a theory of justice without at the same time advocating it as true. So where Barry claims that epistemological abstinence is unstable and will collapse into scepticism, Raz urges that epistemological abstinence is unstable and will imply claims to truth. Again, the point is not simply a psychological one, for Raz's contention is that, without a claim to truth, a theory of justice degenerates into a theory of stability, and Rawls has no explanation of why we should value and pursue stability. Thus, Raz writes:

My argument is simple... to recommend a theory of justice for our societies is to recommend it as a just theory of justice, that is, as a true, or reasonable, or valid theory of justice. If it is argued that what makes it the theory of justice for us is that it is built on an overlapping consensus and therefore secures stability and unity, then consensus-based stability and unity are the values that a theory of justice, for our society, is assumed to depend on. Their achievement—that is, the fact that endorsing the theory leads to their achievement—makes the theory true, sound, valid and so forth. This at least is what such a theory is committed to. There can be no justice without truth. (Raz 1994: 70)

It should be noted straight away that Raz's argument operates at a rather different level of abstraction from Barry's: where Barry is concerned to show that no conception of the good can be held with such certainty as to warrant its imposition, and that therefore moderate scepticism is demanded, Raz is not primarily concerned with the epistemological status of individual conceptions of the good, but with the status of justice as fairness itself. And, of course, it is a part of Rawls's claim that we must remain abstinent not only with respect to conceptions of the good, but also with respect to justice as fairness, which is not to be commended on the grounds that it is true, but only on the grounds that it can command allegiance via overlapping consensus. It is this which Raz claims is incoherent.

Raz's criticism of epistemological abstinence operates along two dimensions: the first is a claim to the effect that the doctrine requires governments to be indifferent to the truth of the policies they implement: 'never before has it been suggested that governments should be unconcerned with the truth of the very views (the doctrine of justice) which inform their policies and actions.' The second is that it disqualifies 'certain true beliefs from providing justification from governmental action without showing that the beliefs are suspect and unreliable' (Raz 1994: 61, 61 n. 3). I shall take these in turn.

On the first point, Raz seems to beg the question against Rawls, who denies that epistemological abstinence implies indifference to truth: 'a political conception of justice need be no more indifferent, say, to truth in morals than the principle of toleration, suitably understood, need be indifferent to truth in religion' (Rawls 1993: 150). Rather, Rawls's claim is that the policies should not be commended to those who live under them *on the grounds* that they are true. And he goes on to insist that this does not entail indifference to truth. Therefore in asserting that justice as fairness is unconcerned about truth, Raz is assuming exactly what is at stake, namely whether refraining from commending something on the grounds that it is true implies indifference to truth.

In fact, Raz's position here consists of several distinct strands and it is important to disentangle them before assessing the overall status of the 'simple argument' he claims to be advancing. It is also instructive to note that the 'simple argument' is central not only to his discussion of justice, but also to his philosophy of law, where he argues that although it is a matter of social fact what the particular laws of a society are, it is nonetheless the case that those officials who accept the laws of a society must accept them not only as legally binding but also as morally binding. So although it is a contingent fact that a particular society has the laws it does have, it is not, according to Raz, a contingent fact that the officials who accept those laws (adopt the internal point of view towards them) construe them as morally binding. He writes: 'I find it impossible to resist the conclusion that most internal or committed legal statements, at any rate those about the rights and duties of others, are moral claims' (Raz 1981: 455).

This argument about the status of committed legal statements parallels the argument about committed justice claims where, as we have seen, Raz insists that commending a theory of justice must be commending it as 'true, sound, valid and so forth'. Setting aside the difficulties inherent in the rather loose use of these disparate terms ('true, sound, valid, and so forth'), we can nonetheless discern an equivocation in Raz's argument. From the fact that those who commend something believe that it is true, it does not follow that in commending it they must be commending it *on the grounds* that it is true. In the first place, those things which I commend may constitute a subset of the things which I believe to be true, and in that case my reasons for commending them are separable from my belief that they are true. It is, however, misleading to suggest that in a case of that sort I am indifferent to truth. Insofar as I commend only things I believe to be true, I am not indifferent to truth. Truth is a necessary condition of my commending, but not thereby the reason for commending. And in fact it seems that this is exactly what Rawls is proposing in advocating the method of avoidance. So in the passage from Raz quoted at the beginning of this section, two statements which are presented as equivalent turn out to be distinct. Here is a case in which there is indeed 'no justice without truth'. I commend only those things which I believe to be true. However, it is not a case which supports the claim that 'to recommend a theory of justice for our societies is to recommend it as a just theory of justice; that is as a true, or reasonable, or valid theory of justice'. Moreover, this move is made more than once, for Raz also says: 'asserting the truth of the doctrine of justice, or rather claiming that its truth is the reason for accepting it, would negate the very spirit of Rawls' enterprise' (Raz 1994: 65). But these are quite different claims. Raz criticizes Rawls for refusing to say that the doctrine of justice is true, but all Rawls need say is that its truth must not be the reason for commending it. That it is (believed to be) true is of course a necessary condition of its being commended, but that is a different matter.

There is, moreover, a second difficulty in this argument against epistemological abstinence, a difficulty which is foreshadowed in the previous sentence, and which springs from the distinctive nature of current first-person belief statements. In both his philosophy of law and his discussion of justice Raz moves very rapidly from statements about what the speaker believes to statements about what is the case. To be more precise, he moves from claims about what is implied or entailed by my statement that I believe that p, to claims about p itself. This, however, is an illicit move. Consider the two statements: 'I believe that there will be a Third World War' and 'There will be a Third World War'. It is clear that these are different statements. They have different truth conditions. However, if I assert the former, I am also logically required to assent to the latter. The case of current first person belief statements is one in which the speaker will be aware that the two statements have different truth conditions, but will have to appeal to exactly the same evidence in answering the two questions: 'Do you believe that there will be a Third World War?' and 'Will there be a Third World War?' The reasons the speaker has for believing p are indeed the reasons she has for believing p to be true (believing is believing true), but they are not thereby the reasons for p's actually being true. Thus, in urging that justice as fairness not be commended on the grounds that it is true, Rawls need not be denying the importance of truth. On the contrary, he may be displaying a very considerable commitment to truth, for it is arguably an indication of the speaker's concern for truth, not his indifference to it, that he will acknowledge both that there may be different answers to the two questions ('Do you believe that J is the theory of justice for societies like ours?' and 'Is J the theory of justice for societies like ours?'), and that he has no access to the different evidence which would serve to deliver the different answers in the current, first-person case.

Raz's claim that epistemological abstinence is unstable, and that justice as fairness requires appeal to truth, is therefore invalid and it is so for two reasons: first, truth may be a necessary condition of commending something, but not thereby the reason for commending it. Second, reasons for believing true may be distinct from reasons for truth itself, and the believer may acknowledge that, while also acknowledging that he has no access to the different reasons that might apply in the two cases. Raz's insistence that epistemological abstinence implies that one is 'indifferent to truth' springs from a failure to observe the former distinction, and his insistence that there can be no justice without truth springs from a failure to observe the latter distinction. If these arguments hold, then the doctrine of epistemological abstinence may withstand the 'simple argument' which Raz mounts against it, and Rawls's commitment to it may yet be sustainable.

The conclusion that follows from these discussions is that neither Barry's argument from scepticism nor Raz's argument from truth can show epistemological abstinence to be unstable or incoherent. As a matter of psychological fact, people often do continue to hold their beliefs with certainty even when they cannot persuade others and, as a matter of political theory, there are some understandings of the permanence of pluralism which insist on the reasonableness of their doing so in at least some cases. It is these possibilities that political impartialism must address. Moreover, if Barry's sceptical argument is accepted, it has the effect (if not the intention) of undermining the agent's commitment to his or her conception of the good, for it requires that where we cannot persuade others we should hold our own beliefs only provisionally, and there are reasons for thinking that a conception of the good which is held only provisionally is different from a conception of the good which is held with certainty. In short, the argument from scepticism misunderstands the point of epistemological abstinence and can succeed in its own terms only by denying the permanence of pluralism.

Raz's attack on epistemological abstinence also fails to show that it is incoherent or unstable, and the alleged instability arises only because Raz neglects the distinction between truth as a necessary condition of commending, and truth as the ground of commendation. Additionally, his insistence on the necessity of invoking truth, like Barry's insistence on the necessity of invoking scepticism, has implications which are in tension with the permanence of pluralism, and to see why that is so, I now turn to the second strand of Raz's argument, the argument from reliability.

Recall that Raz objects to epistemological abstinence both because it requires governments to be indifferent to the truth of the policies they implement and because it requires certain beliefs to be disqualified from providing justification for government action without showing that the beliefs themselves are suspect or unreliable. The former argument has already been discussed, so I turn now to the latter. In making this second complaint against epistemological abstinence, Raz refers to Thomas Nagel's defence of it, and Nagel's primary concern in invoking epistemological abstinence is to show when and why we might be justified in using political power to force people to do things against their will. In particular, he is concerned to show how we might justify refusing to use the power of the state to enforce sincere and firmly held religious convictions. He writes: 'the exclusion of the appeal to religious convictions must depend on a distinction between what justifies individual belief and what justifies appealing to that belief in support of the exercise of political power... what is needed to justify the employment of political power depends on a higher standard of objectivity' (Nagel 1987: 229). And it is implicit in this that where religious belief is ruled out as an appropriate ground for the exercise of political power, that is not (or not necessarily) because the conviction has been shown to be wrong, or because it fails to meet the test of reasonableness *as individual belief*. It is, then, an implication of epistemological abstinence that my belief may be justifiable as my belief, but nonetheless not be a legitimate ground of government imposition. And it is this implication which Raz finds unacceptable.

In assessing Raz's discussion of this aspect of epistemological abstinence, we should first note what seems to me to be an interesting difference between the doctrine's defenders and its critics. This is that, whereas the critics of epistemological abstinence construe it as an attempt to solve a specific problem—the problem of justifying refusal to use the coercive power of the state in order to enforce religious belief—its defenders often take the case of religious belief to be one which draws our attention to the quite general conditions under which the use of political coercion may be deemed to be legitimate. Thus, Rawls introduces epistemological abstinence as a way of 'extending the principle of religious toleration to philosophy itself', and Nagel similarly notes that some of the disagreements in modern societies may be akin to religious disagreements. By contrast, Barry and Raz see the religious case as one which must be 'tamed' by bringing it closer to other, more 'objective', cases of conflict. This difference signifies a distinction between those who take religious belief to be the paradigm of and model for belief in modernity, and those who think that religious belief must be subsumed within an account of belief which takes factual conflict to be paradigmatic.

To spell the point out in a bit more detail, we should note that both Barry and Raz see the religious case as significant, but they see its significance as lying in the fact that it appears to pose an acute and singular problem. Thus, Barry takes the case of religious revelation to be the one in which the argument for epistemological abstinence looks most plausible, but he concludes that even in this case the inability to persuade others must generate doubt, and doubt is sufficient for moderate scepticism which in turn is sufficient for liberal impartialism. On Barry's argument, therefore, the case of religious revelation is to be assimilated, as far as possible, to other cases in which there is disagreement ('The one thing we should all agree about is that nobody is entitled to certainty'), and since epistemological abstinence will not work in the most difficult case, it will not work in any other case.

Raz, too, takes religious belief to be peculiarly problematic, and indeed he construes the argument for epistemological abstinence as one whose main aim is to 'exclude revelation and the judgement that certain beliefs are self-evident from public reliance' (Raz 1994: 91), but he concludes that in this case, as in any other, we must be willing to submit our beliefs to impartial and objective tests, weighing evidence, gathering information, and so on. The problematic nature of the religious case should not force us to abandon the search for truth, nor should it encourage us to invoke a different standard of objectivity in cases where the coercive use of political power is being considered.

However, it may be that taking factual belief as paradigmatic is not the appropriate response, and that the religious case provides us with an alternative paradigm: one in which applying objective tests, weighing evidence, and gathering information, do not resolve the matter. In other words, it may be that the case of religious conviction is the one which can best illuminate the general problem posed by the permanence of pluralism characteristic of modernity. This will, in fact, be my suggestion, but the suggestion requires a distinctive understanding of Rawls's claim that 'belief matters'—an understanding which, I shall argue, must be adopted if we are to explain pluralism as both permanent and significant, while at the same time defending the priority of justice.

To see how this comes about, I begin with Raz's objection that epistemological abstinence requires certain beliefs to be disqualified as legitimate grounds of public action even though those beliefs have not been shown to be suspect or unreliable, and the first question to ask here is what Raz means by 'unreliable'. Presumably, he has in mind cases in which the evidence for a belief is conflictual, or where the truth of the belief is under-determined by the evidence. In any event, I take it that more is required for unreliability than simply the earlier points about the general status of current first-person belief statements. Since all such statements exhibit a potential gap between reasons for belief and reasons for truth—a gap which, *ex hypothesi*, the agent cannot, at the moment, fill, then all such statements are, in some sense of the word, 'unreliable'. Raz, however, must mean more than this. In objecting to the requirement that beliefs be disqualified from providing justification for government action even though they are not suspect or unreliable, he is manifesting his commitment to the overwhelming importance of truth. For Raz, everything hangs on whether or not the belief is, in fact, true. In the terms I used in discussing Barry, Raz concentrates on the justificatory question and has nothing to say about the 'existential' condition of the agent. In particular, he remains silent as to whether an unreliable belief should force doubt in the mind of the agent. However, his justificatory claim, like Barry's, has motivational or existential implications, for if we suppose that a belief is 'unreliable' in the sense that it is under-determined by the available evidence (or even, perhaps, by all possible evidence), then that either does or it does not imply the propriety of the agent's continuing to hold the belief with certainty. If it implies that the agent must not continue to hold the belief with certainty, then Raz's argument is, in the end, simply another version of Barry's argument, and all the points made against Barry apply also to Raz.

However, if unreliability does not force doubt, then Rawls's original question remains to be answered: how are we to live together in conditions of stability and justice given that people hold different and conflicting beliefs about the highest good? And, we must now add, given that it is reasonable for them (at least some of the time) to hold those conflicting beliefs with conviction. It is, I think, implicit in Raz's account that this cannot happen. As far as he is concerned there are objective standards, and beliefs either do or do not meet those standards. This applies to religious beliefs in the same way as any other beliefs, and thus it is a general truth that:

To be personally justified in believing a proposition one must accept that one's belief is in principle subject to impersonal, impartial standards of correctness. Those who comply with this condition do subject their beliefs to valid impersonal tests. It may be that others do not see it that way, and deny the validity of those tests. But given that the tests are both valid and publicly, objectively, and impartially available, it seems impossible that others can reasonably deny the validity of those tests unless they lack information. And that lack can be remedied and therefore cannot serve as the basis of [the] theory. (Raz 1994: 94)

So what is denied here is the possibility that some beliefs (religious beliefs, for example) are such that it might be reasonable for an individual to hold them despite the fact that objective tests tell against them, or under-determine them.

At this point, it is worth noting a significant difference between Raz's conclusion and Barry's. This is that whereas Barry allows that there will be cases in which the evidence is conflictual (cases which are, as he puts it, 'a matter of judgement'), Raz appears to believe that once the tests have been applied, all will concur and therefore there will be no unreliability and presumably no reason to rule out government imposition. Now to say this is, of course, to undermine the fact of pluralism by implying that it is not, as Rawls claims, a permanent fact. Since Raz himself is not committed to pluralism, this conclusion will not, in itself, trouble him. What should trouble him, however, and what I shall attempt to show, is that the conclusion results from considerations that are highly dubious.

The first respect in which Raz's argument is dubious is in its implicit assumption that what counts as an objective test is clear and uncontroversial. There may be contexts (and religious belief looks like a plausible context) in which what counts as evidence, or what counts as an objective test, is itself a matter of deep disagreement and, for such cases, Raz's claim seems simply naive. This is an important consideration, but not one I shall pursue here.[1] Rather, I shall return to the question which formed the basis of the case against Barry—the question of whether the fact of pluralism forces doubt, since this question is, I believe, as significant for an assessment of Raz's argument as it was for an assessment of Barry's. It is also the prelude to my interpretation of Rawls's claim that the modern world is one in which 'belief matters'.

I have suggested that Barry's defence of scepticism as the foundation of liberal impartialism depends crucially on his claim that, in a world character-ized by pluralism, we must hold our own beliefs with some degree of doubt, and (following Taylor) I have also suggested that a conception of the good which is held with doubt may be a different conception from one that can legitimately be held with certainty. In these respects, the argument from

---

[1] This question is discussed in Matt Matravers and Susan Mendus 'The Reasonableness of Pluralism', in D. Castiglione and C. McKinnon (eds.), *Reasonable Tolerance: The Culture of Tolerance in Diverse Societies* (Manchester: Manchester University Press, forthcoming).

scepticism does, in fact, make reference to the existential condition of the agent. By contrast, Raz's argument makes no reference to the existential condition of the agent, and we are left to guess what his view is. Since the claim that unreliability forces doubt would render Raz's position vulnerable to exactly the same objections as have been made against Barry, let us suppose that Raz believes the unreliability of a belief to be something which need not affect the propriety of an agent's holding that belief with certainty. In this case his argument implies the problem which the doctrine of epistemological abstinence sets out to answer, since it is now the case that in modern democratic societies we are confronted by an array of conflicting beliefs, all of which are held with conviction and some of which are reasonably so held. How, then, can we be justified in using the coercive power of the state in a way which is inimical to those comprehensive and firmly held convictions?

Raz's objection to epistemological abstinence (that it requires governments to disqualify certain true beliefs from providing justification for governmental action without showing that the beliefs are suspect and unreliable) carries as its corollary the claim that governments *are* entitled to use their coercive power in cases where a belief has not been shown to be suspect or unreliable, but this is a considerable hostage to fortune since the convinced religious believer will characteristically insist that his or her belief has not been shown to be suspect or unreliable and, for that very reason, will go on to insist that the state use its coercive power to enforce the belief. Indeed, the religious believer will normally go further and insist that his or her belief is true. But this propensity only identifies the problem. It certainly does not offer a solution, as John Locke was quick to point out in his *Letter Concerning Toleration*, where he writes:

If one of these churches hath this power of treating the other ill, I ask which of them it is to whom the power belongs, and by what right? It will be answered, undoubtedly, that it is the orthodox church which has the right of authority over the erroneous or heretical. This is, in great and specious words, to say nothing at all. For every church is orthodox to itself; to others, erroneous or heretical. Whatsoever any church believes, it believes to be true; and the contrary thereupon it pronounces to be error. So that the controversy between these churches about the truth of their doctrines, and the purity of their worship, is on both sides equal; nor is there any judge, either at Constantinople, or elsewhere upon earth, by whose sentence it can be determined. (Locke 1991: 24)

For Locke, then, the claim that one has truth on one's side is inadequate precisely because each side in the dispute will lay claim to truth and, against this background, Raz's implied acceptance that governments are entitled to enforce beliefs which have been shown to be true is ineffectual in respect of religious believers, who are convinced both that their beliefs are true and that they can be shown to be true. Somewhat ironically, it is exactly the fact that believing is believing true which, in Locke's eyes, is a major part of the problem, not (as Raz claims) its solution. And the reason it is a part of the problem is because there is no agreement between the parties as to who in fact is possessed of the truth, no convergence on what counts as an objective test, and certainly no convergence on whether the test has been passed. We may agree that truth justifies intervention, but even if we do, that is useless in practical terms since we do not agree about what is true.

Raz's argument from reliability is therefore, like Barry's argument from scepticism, something of a red herring. Even if we were to agree that truth justifies, our problem is that we have no agreed method for arriving at truth, and Raz's appeal to impersonal and impartial standards of correctness will be of limited use in the truly difficult cases—cases where the standards of correctness are themselves disputed. It is the recognition of these difficulties which motivates epistemological abstinence, and it does so because, as Locke saw, all the contending parties will lay claim to truth, to certainty, and to the support of reason and objectivity in defence of their own beliefs. There is, as Locke tells us, 'no judge, either at Constantinople or elsewhere upon earth, by whose sentence it can be determined'. The solution therefore must lie in abstracting from those considerations and finding a justification for the use of the coercive power of the state which makes no reference to truth, certainty or objectively verifiable facts. In other words, it must lie in appeal to epistemological abstinence.

More generally, the point which emerges from these considerations is that the motif of religious conflict and religious toleration is one which emphasizes the dual functions that a theory of justice must fulfil in the modern world. We must justify the coercive use of political power, and we must do so in a world where belief matters, and where justificatory arguments must be acknowledged by and acceptable to those who live under the resultant political system. Specifically, the arguments which justify the coercive use of political power must not rely upon commitment to any single comprehensive conception of the good, nor must they undermine competing conceptions of the good. I have argued that both Barry and Raz, in different ways, underestimate the extent to which answers to justificatory questions may have implications for questions about motivation. Barry does this by attempting to draw a sharp distinction between scepticism as an epistemological doctrine and scepticism as a view about human flourishing, whereas Raz concentrates on the justificatory question to the exclusion of questions of motivation. My claim, however, is that neither strategy can succeed. The case of religious conflict is instructive because it provides one of the most significant manifestations of the connection between motivation and justification. What happened in the Reformation period was not simply that belief came to matter in the sense that true beliefs were deemed necessary for salvation (though they were). What happened was that hitherto unasked questions arose about the propriety of continuing to believe with conviction in the face of widespread disagreement. If continuing conviction is deemed illegitimate, then the permanence of pluralism is denied (or at least undermined), but if continuing conviction is deemed legitimate, why is it not an acceptable ground for government imposition? There is, I think, an important sense in which the attempt to solve this conundrum resulted in a distinctive understanding of belief and a distinctive account of why belief matters. So it is not merely the case that belief came to matter more than it previously had, but also that belief came to be understood differently.

The question which now arises is whether this changed conception of belief, implicit in the doctrine of epistemological abstinence, can succeed in defending both the permanence of pluralism and the priority of justice. Can it show why impartial justice should prevail in contestation with competing yet reasonable comprehensive conceptions? My contention will be that it cannot. Whereas the arguments from scepticism and from truth undermine agents' commitment to their comprehensive conception of the good, and thus implicitly deny the permanence of pluralism, the argument from epistemological abstinence undermines the priority of justice.

Summary

I began by noting that the aims of political philosophy depend upon the society it addresses and that in modern societies characterized by reasonable pluralism one very important aim of political philosophy is to show how people may live together in conditions of justice and stability while subscribing to different and conflicting comprehensive conceptions of the good. Additionally, and for Rawls, their acceptance of the principles of justice must be more than a mere *modus vivendi*, more than a pragmatic response generated by the need to attain civil peace and stability. So impartial political philosophy, if it is to be more than a merely practical response to pluralism, must somehow secure the priority of justice without undermining the permanence of reasonable pluralism. Epistemological abstinence is one attempt to address this problem. By requiring that we refrain from making judgements about conflicting yet reasonable comprehensive conceptions of the good, and by further requiring that we not commend justice as fairness on the grounds that it is true, epistemological abstinence takes seriously the permanence of reasonable pluralism in modern democratic societies.

However, Barry and Raz object to epistemological abstinence on the grounds that it is unstable. They argue that it must either collapse into

scepticism or into a commitment to truth. In assessing their arguments I have
made two claims: first that there is no good reason for thinking epistemological abstinence to be unstable; second, that Barry and Raz's criticisms of it
succeed only at considerable cost. In the case of Barry, the cost lies in an
insistence that people are entitled to hold their conceptions of the good only
provisionally, but since a conception of the good is in part a function of the
manner in which we are entitled to hold it, this transformation undermines
the permanence of pluralism. Additionally, Rawls's own commitment to the
permanence of pluralism is a commitment to the legitimacy of continuing to
hold at least some conceptions of the good *without* doubt or hesitancy, and
the argument from scepticism is straightforwardly at odds with that understanding of the permanence of pluralism.

Raz's argument also undermines the permanence of pluralism, because his
appeal to truth has the effect of diminishing the room for reasonable disagreement. Again, it should be emphasized that Raz himself is unlikely to be
perturbed by this consequence: as a perfectionist liberal, he carries no brief
for the permanence of pluralism. He should, however, be troubled by the
internal defects of his argument, for they suggest both that he has misunder-
stood the point of invoking abstinence and that he has exaggerated the power
of appeals to truth in addressing conflicts between those who hold competing
comprehensive conceptions of the good. Indeed, and as the passage from
Locke makes clear, an appeal to truth is part of the problem, and cannot
therefore be the solution to questions of toleration in a world characterized
by diversity.

Additionally, these criticisms of Barry and Raz draw attention to the fact
that in political philosophy questions of justification cannot hang free of
motivational considerations (of questions about the state of mind appropriate for those who hold controversial and contested conceptions of the good),
and what this implies is that a theory of justice, if it is to be compatible with
pluralism, but more than a mere *modus vivendi*, must show why people might
be motivated to give priority to justice in cases where it conflicts with their
comprehensive conception of the good. By concentrating on justificatory
questions, Barry and Raz demonstrate their concern with the priority of
justice but, I have argued, they purchase that priority only by making
assumptions which undermine the permanence of pluralism, and which do
so by weakening the motivational force of the agent's comprehensive conception of the good.

The crucial question now, therefore, is whether epistemological abstinence
can fare any better. The preceding arguments suggest that it certainly can
fare better in respect of the permanence of pluralism. Can it, however, fare
better in respect of the priority of justice? In the next section I shall argue that
it cannot and that, in fact, the understanding of belief which is implicit in

epistemological abstinence, and which is required to sustain the permanence of pluralism, is also an understanding of belief which undermines the priority of justice. For reasons already given, all theories of justice will have a motivational story implicit in them, but the motivational story required for the permanence of reasonable pluralism is at odds with the motivational story required for the priority of justice. What may therefore be needed for a full defence of impartial theories of justice is a defence of impartialism more generally. Since, as was noted earlier, justice is only a part of morality, not the whole of it, we may find that any defence of the priority of justice requires a defence of the priority of impartial morality. That defence is one which I shall consider in detail in the following chapters. For now, however, my aim is to substantiate the claim that epistemological abstinence does indeed rest upon a conception of belief which acknowledges the permanence of pluralism only by undermining the priority of justice.

The Costs of Epistemological Abstinence

In the preceding sections I have argued that epistemological abstinence is an attempt to demonstrate the priority of justice in a way compatible with the permanence of reasonable pluralism. It is an attempt to do justice to the twin facts that, in the modern world, belief matters and belief will naturally generate a multiplicity of conceptions of the good. But if it is true that belief matters, in what way exactly is it true? Perhaps the clearest articulation of this is given by John Locke who, in his writings on religious toleration, insists that the state must stand back from questions of truth and falsity in religious matters, partly because coerced faith is inadequate for salvation, and partly because belief cannot be coerced in any case. Locke writes: 'No man can, if he would, conform his faith to the dictates of another. All the life and power of true religion consists in the inward and full persuasion of the mind; and faith is not faith without believing' (Locke 1991: 18). So belief matters in the religious context because the faith that is required for salvation is a faith that depends crucially upon the individual recognizing and acknowledging something for himself.

Moreover, the importance of believing for oneself (of the 'inward and full persuasion of the mind') is not restricted to the religious context, but is a specific case of Locke's more general epistemology, as given in the *Essay on Human Understanding*, where he writes:

For I think we may as rationally hope to see with other Mens Eyes, as to know by other Mens Understandings. So much as we ourselves consider and comprehend of Truth and Reason, so much we possess of Real and True Knowledge. The floating of other Mens Opinions in our brains makes us not a jot more knowing, though they happen to be true. What in them was Science, in us is but Opiniatrety, whilst we give up our assent only to reverend Names, and do not, as they did, employ our own Reason to understand those Truths, which gave them reputation . . . In the Sciences, everyone has so much, as he really knows and comprehends: what he believes only and takes upon trust, are but shreads . . . Such borrowed Wealth, like Fairy-Money, though it were Gold in the hand from which he received it, will be but Leaves and Dust when it comes to use. (Locke 1975: I.iv.23)

For Locke, then, belief matters in the religious context because it is only sincere and inner belief that is pleasing to God. Moreover, the state lacks the means to coerce such belief. Hence the futility of persecution designed to save the soul of the heretic. But Locke thinks that in all other contexts, too, it is important that we come to see things for ourselves and not rely on the opinion of others, or take things on trust.

   As a piece of epistemology, Locke's story is highly implausible, for it is surely the case that, especially in science, we do take things on trust, and indeed we often (perhaps usually) have no choice but to do so. Beliefs about the way the world works, its construction and composition, rest on complex scientific considerations, and in the modern world there can be few who are in a position to 'find out for themselves' before taking penicillin, for example, or sending the car to the garage. There are, for all of us, areas in which we cannot sensibly do anything other than take things on trust. Additionally, it might be thought that, even in the area of the moral, we sometimes both can and should take things on trust. Annette Baier's recent work in moral philosophy mounts a very powerful case for the indispensability of trust in moral contexts, and Hilary Putnam has gone yet further, urging that the very distinction between what we can accept as scientific fact and what we believe to be morally right is less clear than is often supposed (Baier 1994: especially essays 6, 7, 8, 9; Putnam 1992: especially essay 5). So, as an epistemological claim, Locke's theory is suspect in three distinct ways: it is not a theory which can plausibly be defended in the area of science; it is contentious even in the area of the moral; and in any case there are reasons for thinking that the moral and the scientific are intertwined.

   However, I will not dwell on these objections, important though they are, for my main aim is not to cast doubt on Locke's claim that belief matters, but rather to establish whether there is an interpretation of it which permits both the persistence of pluralism and the priority of justice over comprehensive conceptions of the good. It is, after all, in this context that Rawls insists that the modern world is one in which 'belief matters', and what we therefore need is not a set of objections to the claim that belief matters but, if possible, a plausible interpretation of it. Here, I take Locke as a starting point both because he is insistent on the importance of belief (his is a conspicuously individualist understanding of belief) and because his account of toleration is referred to approvingly by Rawls in *Political Liberalism*. There are reasons, therefore, for thinking that the general method deployed by Locke is the one which Rawls has in mind when commending epistemological abstinence as the ground of toleration and the route to an impartialist political philosophy which can generate more than a *modus vivendi*, without requiring commitment to a specific comprehensive conception of the good.

A further feature of Locke's account which makes it consonant with Rawls's enterprise is that it is not based on scepticism. Locke is in no doubt that there is a God, and that He requires certain things of us: 'Every man has an immortal soul, capable of eternal happiness or misery; whose happiness depending upon his believing and doing those things in this life, which are necessary to the obtaining of God's favour, and are prescribed by God to that end: it follows from thence, first, that the observance of these things is the highest obligation that lies upon mankind, and that our utmost care, application, and diligence, ought to be exercised in the search and performance of them' (Locke 1991: 42). So the defence of toleration is not grounded in the belief that, if we cannot persuade others, we should hold our own opinion only provisionally. Why, then, ought we to tolerate those who do not do as God commands? Locke's answer is based ultimately in his conception of belief, and that answer has two component parts: first, he argues that coercion works by operating on a person's will. That is to say, in coercing someone we attempt to influence their decision-making via threats or inducements. Second, however, he argues that belief is not subject to the will. That is to say, I cannot alter my beliefs simply by deciding to change them, or willing that they change. It then follows that all attempts to coerce religious conformity (to alter the will of another) are strictly irrational, since they involve deploying means inappropriate for the desired end. They are an attempt to change belief by changing the will, but belief is not subject to the will. Waldron puts the matter this way:

Laws, Locke says, are of no force without penalties and the whole point of penalties is to bring pressure to bear on people's decision-making by altering the pay-offs for various courses of action so that willing one particular course of action (the act required or prohibited by law) becomes more or less attractive to the agent than it would otherwise be. But this sort of pressurizing is crazy in cases of action which men are incapable of performing no matter how attractive the pay-off or unattractive the consequences. Sincerely believing a proposition that one takes to be false is an action in this category . . . the imposition of belief, then, by civil law has been shown to be an absurdity. (Waldron 1991: 104)

Again, I am not here concerned with whether or not Locke's position is a plausible one. There are certainly reasons for doubting that it is, and some of those reasons are given by Waldron in the article quoted from above. What does concern me, rather, is the *kind* of defence of toleration which Locke's theory would support if it were true. And here there are reasons for thinking that it cannot deliver a principled defence but only, and at most, a *modus vivendi* defence.

This general point is noted by a number of commentators, but it comes in different guises. Thus, Waldron remarks that, by insisting on the irrationality of persecution, Locke ignores entirely the question of whether and why persecution is morally wrong. He writes: 'what one misses above all in Locke's argument is a sense that there is anything morally wrong with intolerance, or a sense of any deep concern for the victims of persecution or the moral insult that is involved in the attempt to manipulate their faith' (Waldron 1991: 120). Similarly, Paul Kelly concludes his discussion of Locke with the reflection that: 'In the *Two Tracts* Locke suggested that toleration would invite anarchy and disorder, in the "Essay" and *Letter* he argued that toleration of practices consistent with civil order was most likely to contribute to peace and stability. In each case what differs is the perception of the threat posed to the social order, and the policy most likely to remedy it. There is no attempt to advance a principled argument for toleration as a necessary component of the good society' (Kelly 1991: 143–4). And again, Russell Hardin claims that 'Locke did not assert fairness as a prior or trumping principle against any particular religious value. Rather, he argued for accommodation as a practical antecedent to achieving any religious value. It is the practical consideration of opposing forces that makes agreement to less than one's full theory of the good reasonable' (in Kelly 1998: 149).

What all this suggests is that Locke's defence of toleration, based as it is in an epistemological premise, cannot deliver a moral conclusion. At best, it will explain why persecution may be irrational, ineffective, or a waste of time, but it will be utterly impotent to explain its moral wrongness or injustice. The injunction to refrain from persecution, not because it is wrong, but because it is irrational, looks very much like a *modus vivendi* account, and the more so if we concede to Waldron the further claim that, even if coercion cannot operate directly on belief, it can easily operate on the epistemic apparatus surrounding belief: 'suppose the religious authorities know that there are certain books that would be sufficient, if read, to shake the faith of an otherwise orthodox population. Then, although again people's beliefs cannot be controlled directly by coercive means, those who wield political power can put it to work indirectly to reinforce belief by banning everyone on pain of death from reading or obtaining copies of these heretical tomes. Such means may well be efficacious, even though they are intolerant and oppressive, and Locke, who is concerned only with the rationality of persecution, provides no argument against them' (Waldron 1991: 116–17).

Recall that the motivation for this discussion of Locke is to try to find an interpretation of the claim that 'belief matters' which will sustain the fact of pluralism while simultaneously defending the priority of justice, and the charge which successive commentators level against Locke is that his account is unable to do the latter. As an account of belief it is suspect but, even if it were correct in that respect, it still would not deliver the right kind of defence of toleration because it cannot show why imposing one's views on those who do not concur with them is morally objectionable.

If accepted, this conclusion has important implications for the general (Rawlsian) project of attempting to defend impartial theories of justice via epistemological abstinence, for what is suggested here is that to the extent that epistemological abstinence is indeed an *epistemological* position, it cannot ground a defence of toleration as a requirement of justice. This, I take it, is the burden of all the comments referred to above. Epistemology shows us only, and at most, why a particular policy of persecution might be ineffective or irrational; it cannot show us why it might be morally wrong. So, in the modern context, if we interpret the claim that 'belief matters' as a Lockean claim about the nature of belief, then we have no more than a *modus vivendi* defence of toleration and of the priority of justice.

All of this suggests that the claim that 'belief matters' must have a moral component if it is to do the work required of it, and the work required of it is to show when and why we are entitled to use the coercive power of the state to force people to do things they do not believe in. As Nagel puts it: 'the real question is how to justify making people do things against their will' (1987: 224). Here, however, proponents of epistemological abstinence must tread carefully, because while what is needed is a moral defence of impartialism in politics, what is ruled out is any appeal to a specific comprehensive (moral or religious) conception in support of that defence. So the sense in which belief matters must be one which lends support to impartialism as morally right (not merely irrational or inefficacious), but not one which invokes specific comprehensive doctrines about the highest good or the life worth living. This is tricky because if we reject the straightforwardly epistemological interpretation of 'belief matters', then the most obvious alternative is to say that belief matters because it is, in some moral sense, important that people come to understand things for themselves, or come to see things as true by their own lights. But, on the face of it at least, to say this is to appeal to a specific conception of the person, one which is not only controversial but may also be objectionably comprehensive. Nagel formulates the difficulty in the following way:

Why isn't true justice giving everyone the best possible chance of salvation, for example, or of a good life? In other words, don't we have to start from the values that we ourselves accept in deciding how state power may legitimately be used?... to answer these questions we have to identify the moral conception involved and see whether it has the authority to over-ride those more particular moral conceptions that divide us—and if so, to what extent or in what respects. Rawls has said in a recent article that if liberalism had to depend on a commitment to comprehensive moral ideals of autonomy and individuality, it would become 'just another sectarian doctrine'. The question is whether its claim to be something else has any foundation. (Nagel 1987: 222)

Nagel's hope is that if we examine the moral values which underpin impartialism we will find that they are such as to be able to command allegiance from people with very different and conflicting comprehensive conceptions of the good. But what are those moral values, and how can they be defended other than as an aspect of a specific comprehensive conception of the good—as an aspect of Kantian autonomy, for instance, or Millian individualism? To see what is required here, consider three possible responses to what Nagel identifies as the real problem: 'how can we justify making people do things against their will?'

The epistemological answer provided by Locke is also a negative one: we can force people to *do* things against their will, but in some contexts (notably religious contexts) actions are irrelevant and what matters is belief. Since belief cannot be coerced, persecution is irrational. The sense in which belief matters here is that, if it is not sincerely held and inwardly endorsed, it will not count as the kind of belief appropriate for salvation at all. However, and as has been argued above, this interpretation of the way in which belief matters is not capable of generating an account of the moral wrong done by imposition. At most, it can show the inefficacy of imposition in specific contexts. Additionally, however, and crucially, where it does legitimize imposition, that seems to be for entirely the wrong reasons. As Waldron points out, Locke has no argument against successful, though oppressive, attempts to coerce belief.

A second answer is that forcing people to do things against their will is a moral insult. It is a denial of their status as autonomous individuals and therefore (presumably) imposition can only be justified when it does not take that form. Although something like this answer was implied by Rawls in *A Theory of Justice*, he has (as we have seen) since renounced that story because he believes it to depend upon a Kantian, and therefore comprehensive, conception of the person. But if both the argument from epistemology and the argument from autonomy are rejected, what else can be said about the legitimacy of forcing people to do things against their will?

The suggestion implicit in Nagel is that there may be a moral value which transcends the values inherent in specific comprehensive conceptions of the good and which can be deployed to justify forcing people to do things contrary to their will, or contrary to the specific comprehensive conception of the good they endorse. The idea seems to be that in cases where comprehensive conceptions of the good appear to conflict with the requirements of impartial justice there may be a further value, consonant with the comprehensive conceptions, which underpins impartial justice and legitimizes giving it priority.

Before discussing Nagel's account, it is worth noting a significant distinguishing feature of it. In the quotation given above Nagel expresses the hope that there may be a moral value which transcends or overrides 'those more particular moral conceptions that divide us', and it is implicit in this that the value which underpins impartiality is a value that can be accepted by all, independent of their comprehensive conception of the good. This account, however, is slightly different from Rawls's account, which (at least as I have interpreted it) does not suppose that there will be a single value supporting impartiality, but rather that each person will come to give allegiance to impartiality from within his or her comprehensive conception. In other words, for Rawls there will presumably be as many routes to impartiality as there are conceptions of the good, whereas for Nagel, apparently, there will be a single route to impartiality insofar as there is a single value underlying it.

Nagel himself notes a further difference between his own account and Rawls's account, and characterizes that difference (interestingly) in the following way: 'I shall not try to compare our approaches here, except to say that mine seems to depend less on actual consensus, and seeks an independent moral argument that can be offered to those holding widely divergent views' (Nagel 1987: 223 n. 7). The practical point here is this: if we are deciding whether it is legitimate to impose our views on others, we may try to show them that although imposition conflicts at a superficial level with the dictates of their comprehensive conception, it nonetheless, and at some deeper level, reflects a value to which they do in fact subscribe. This, I take it, is what Nagel is searching for in his attempt to find a 'higher order' defence of impartiality, one which will show it to 'have the authority to over-ride' particular and conflicting moral conceptions. The alternative is that we place our faith in the ability of impartial justice to secure overlapping consensus, and this will not require that each acknowledge a single value which over-rides his or her comprehensive conception, but only that impartial justice can secure allegiance from within each comprehensive conception.

The problem now, however, is that if we adopt Nagel's strategy and look for a single value which overrides specific comprehensive conceptions, then we self-confessedly make the argument for the priority of impartial justice a *moral* argument, even if not a comprehensive one. However, given that it was the contested and controversial status of moral claims that prompted appeal to the permanence of pluralism, there must be some doubt about the prospects for such an argument. By contrast, if we hope for an overlapping consensus generated from within each comprehensive conception, then it is not clear why the claims of impartial justice should have priority over the comprehensive conceptions which gave rise to them. Put differently, Nagel needs to show why and how the moral value appealed to in defence of the priority of impartiality is not a comprehensive value, whereas Rawls needs to show why and how the different values which deliver overlapping consensus also deliver the priority of justice in cases of conflict.

Rawls is comparatively silent on the question of priority, noting simply that political decisions are of 'great importance' and that there is a 'great good' in supporting the institutions of a constitutional regime. This, however, is merely an assertion of the value of justice, not an argument for its priority. By contrast, Nagel does have an argument for the priority of justice which aspires to demonstrate its ability to retain distance from any comprehensive conception. He argues that in order to justify forcing people to do things against their will we must show that impartial justice is impartial 'at a higher level'. That is to say, it must not only be impartial in the allocation of benefits and harms, but also in their identification: 'the defence of liberalism requires that a limit somehow be drawn to appeals to the truth in political argument', and he goes on 'I believe that something like Rawls's view is correct, that is, that exclusion of the appeal to religious convictions not rely on a skeptical premise about individual belief. Rather it must depend on a distinction between what justifies individual belief and what justifies appealing to that belief in support of the exercise of political power' (both quotations from Nagel 1987: 227).

Nagel's thinking is difficult to discern here, but I take it that his argument has something like the following form: if we aspire to impartiality in the distribution of benefits and burdens, then we must acknowledge that people's conflicting yet reasonable comprehensive conceptions of the good may lead them to different understandings of what counts as a benefit or a burden. In political contexts which involve the exercise of the coercive power of the state, we should be wary of forcing people to do things against their will, even (and perhaps especially) when that can be presented in the guise of benefiting them, for we may be assuming an understanding of what is beneficial which they themselves would reject. When that happens, claims to impartiality are disingenuous for we have not been impartial between competing comprehensive conceptions, but only impartial *given* a pre-existing comprehensive conception (usually, a comprehensive liberal conception, such as an autonomy-based one).

However, since we do think that forcing people is sometimes justified, we must provide a criterion of imposition which is not only impartial in the allocation of benefits and burdens, but also impartial in its identification of benefits and burdens. Attaining impartiality at this level means refraining from assessing the truth of comprehensive conceptions of the good, and also refraining from advancing our own conception on the grounds that it is true.

Again, 'the defence of liberalism requires that a limit somehow be drawn to appeals to truth in political argument'. So, to give an example, I cannot defend as impartial my decision to impose religious orthodoxy on the un-believer by pointing out that he will be benefited in Paradise, and the reasons are first that his conception of the good may not be one which sees a life in Paradise as a benefit (he may prefer a life of pleasure in this world), and second he may not believe it to be true that he will enjoy such a life by doing the things I am forcing him to do. If the former is the case, then imposition fails to be impartial since it assumes a contested conception of benefit. If the latter, then imposition is no more nor less than the assertion of the truth of my own belief against his counter-assertion. And while, as we have seen, believing is always believing true, in political contexts appeals to the truth of one's beliefs must be distinguishable from appeals to them simply as one's beliefs. There is a 'higher standard of objectivity' in cases where political coercion is on the agenda.

What, then, is this 'higher standard' of objectivity? It is, Nagel says, a standard which meets the 'Kantian requirement that we treat humanity not merely as a means, but also as an end' (1987: 238). What is obscure now, however, is whether this standard is epistemological or moral: Nagel's claim seems to be that there is a moral requirement to adopt stringent epistemo-logical standards in the exercise of political coercion. But his defence of these stringent epistemological standards is a distinctively moral—indeed Kant-ian—one, and famously (or notoriously), it was Rawls's unhappiness with appeal to the Kantian conception that prompted the move to *Political Liberalism* and to the doctrine of epistemological abstinence. So its reintro-duction here may appear slightly suspect.

The crucial point now is this: the doctrine of epistemological abstinence is introduced in an attempt to acknowledge the permanence of reasonable pluralism while also defending the coercive use of state power to force people to do things against their will. In its role as bulwark of reasonable pluralism, epistemological abstinence can, I think, be defended. Its justification of imposition does not undermine or cast doubt upon those comprehensive conceptions of the good which are not allowed to prevail politically and, for this reason, it is superior to arguments from scepticism which do covertly destabilize the agent's commitment to his or her comprehensive conception of the good. Similarly, epistemological abstinence is more successful than the argument from truth in sustaining the permanence of pluralism. However, the very features of epistemological abstinence which are required in order to bolster pluralism are also the ones which are inimical to its ability to defend the priority of justice. Where abstinence is taken as an epistemological doc-trine, it does not deliver the *priority* of justice, but only, and at best, a *modus vivendi* defence of it, and where it is taken as having a moral component it must invoke values (equality, unanimity, Kantian respect) which are contested and controversial even if not comprehensive.

In defending epistemological abstinence I argued that it has the advantage over scepticism in that it does not require us to undermine the agent's own comprehensive conception of the good, and for this reason it does not undermine the motivational power of that conception of the good in cases where the conception cannot be politically endorsed. But if abstinence succeeds as a support for pluralism by leaving motivation intact, then it cannot easily succeed as a support for priority, which requires that the motivation to pursue one's conception of the good be subordinated to the motivation to justice. So the very feature of epistemological abstinence which made it superior to scepticism (its ability not to undermine the agent's sense of certainty or conviction about his conception of the good) is also the feature which renders problematic its insistence on the priority of justice.

The route out of this *impasse* may be to insist that some motivations, such as the motivation to Kantian unanimity or equality, are implicit in all reasonable conceptions of the good. This, I take it, is Nagel's strategy, and it is the one which is suggested by his appeal to a 'higher order' impartiality, but it is also a strategy that defends political impartiality via an appeal to *moral* considerations, and that defence is fraught with difficulty, not least because it may require commitment to a comprehensive conception of the good that is not shared by all in conditions of permanent and reasonable pluralism.

What is now needed, therefore, is an examination of moral impartialism and, in particular, an examination of its presuppositions. The specific task is to ask what assumptions must be made by moral impartiality if it is to have priority in cases of conflict. If it turns out to be possible to defend the priority of moral impartiality without invoking a comprehensive conception of the good, then it may also be possible, by extension, to defend political impartiality without invoking a comprehensive conception of the good. And if that is possible, then impartial political philosophy may, after all, be both stable and complete. I turn now, therefore, to the problem of priority in impartial moral philosophy.

2

The Priority of Impartial Morality

The previous chapter began by noting that in both moral and political philosophy, impartialism is thought to be grounded in a commitment to the equality of all human beings. It expresses a belief that others have equal value to oneself, and an equal right to pursue their own interests. However, this commitment to equality is problematic for impartialist political philosophy, not least because some people or groups of people may subscribe to conceptions of the good which do not acknowledge its significance. The questions which then arise are: how can we defend the priority of impartial justice in cases of conflict, and how can we do so in a way that does not assume the truth of any comprehensive conception of the good, but which nonetheless amounts to more than a mere *modus vivendi*? It is the attempt to respond to these questions which is evident in Rawls's insistence that his political conception of justice is also a moral conception which aims at being acceptable to citizens as reasonable and rational, as well as free and equal (see, for example, Rawls 1993: 11–14). The conception of citizens as free and equal is intended to transcend, include, or otherwise accommodate different comprehensive conceptions of the good, and yet be a moral conception which can deliver a defence of political impartiality as more than a dictate of expediency.

However, and as was noted in the previous chapter, the search for such a defence of political impartialism is fraught with difficulty. Quite apart from the fact that Rawls's own defence requires that people distinguish between their personal commitments and their commitments as citizens—a distinction that not all will be willing to make—there is the additional and, I think, deeper worry as to why even those who do make the distinction should be prepared to give priority to justice, or to the political conception, when it comes into conflict with their comprehensive conception of the good. So, in the first place, there may be those who reject the distinction between the individual as private person and the individual as citizen (or who draw the distinction in very different ways), and in the second place, even those who do acknowledge the distinction may nonetheless ask why the demands made on them as citizens should take priority over the demands of their comprehensive conception. The arguments of the previous chapter suggest that epistemological considerations will yield only a *modus vivendi* defence—one which varies according to the practicalities and contingencies of the particular situation. What is needed, however, is a moral defence, but (again) not one that is allied to a particular comprehensive conception of the good.

In this chapter, I shall examine the nature of *moral* impartiality, and my aim will be to establish whether it can provide an appropriate foundation for political impartiality. If the value which lies at the heart of moral impartiality does not imply a comprehensive conception of the good, then it may be possible to deploy that value in impartialist political philosophy and thus to provide a defence of the latter which is moral but not comprehensively so. However, there is an important *caveat* to be issued here, which is that the relationship between moral and political impartiality is more complicated than has so far been acknowledged. In political philosophy, a central question is whether and why the claims of impartiality should take priority over comprehensive conceptions of the good which may not themselves acknowledge the equality of all human beings. In moral philosophy, however, a central question is how, *given* an acknowledgement of the equality of all human beings, we can justify favouring some (for instance our friends) over others, or how we can justify pursuing our own projects at the expense of other people's. So the priority question in moral philosophy assumes that the agent has some commitment to equality, but asks why that commitment should prevail, whereas the priority question in political philosophy cannot easily make such an assumption. In the political context commitment to equality must, I think, be shown, not assumed.

Given this difference, I shall proceed in two stages. In this chapter I shall address the priority question as it typically arises in moral philosophy. I shall ask whether and why we ought to privilege the claims of impartial morality when they conflict with partial considerations such as considerations of friendship: why should we care about impartial morality *more* than we care about other things? In asking this question I shall assume that we do in fact acknowledge impartial considerations to at least some extent, though whether that acknowledgement is best understood as an acknowledgement of equality is a separate, and more contentious, matter. Then, in the next chapter, I shall go on to ask why we should care about impartial morality at all— why should we acknowledge the demands that it makes on us, and what is presupposed by those demands? This will return us to the vexed issue of whether political impartialism can defend its own priority over comprehensive conceptions of the good which do not acknowledge the equality of all human beings, and while there are certainly some who deny that impartialism need take such people into consideration, that claim strikes me as untenable simply because there are many comprehensive conceptions of the good which are not, on the face of it, unreasonable, yet which show no clear commitment to equality. An acceptable defence of impartialism must,

I think, have something to say to such people, and here I ally myself with Jean Hampton, when she writes:

with apologies to Thomas Jefferson, I fear we cannot take [beliefs in the freedom and equality of all human beings] to be self-evident. Human history provides enormous evidence for their contestability; commitment to these beliefs has been (and remains) unusual rather than usual. Outside the West, social hierarchies and restrictions of freedom are commonplace (and Western societies derided for their commitments to freedom and equality); and even within Western democracies, beliefs that would limit liberty (eg within certain forms of fundamentalist religions) or challenge equality (such as racist or sexist views) are far more widespread than many would like to admit. (Hampton 1993: 304)

What Hampton suggests is that impartialist commitment to equality is commitment to a value which is highly contentious, and arguably at odds with some reasonable comprehensive conceptions of the good, but if this is true, it is worrying, since the original challenge was precisely to defend impartialist commitment to equality in a way compatible with the permanence of reasonable pluralism, and if conceptions of the good which do not acknowledge equality as a fundamental value are ruled out in advance, then impartialism's commitment to pluralism seems limited, if not disingenuous. What we must do in the long term, therefore, is to investigate whether impartialism can be defended in a way that is moral, but compatible with some degree of reasonable pluralism. What we must do in the short term is to establish what moral impartialism is and what difficulties it encounters.

Impartialists and their Critics

Assuming for the moment, then, that impartialism does indeed reflect a commitment to equality, one very obvious challenge which it faces is to show how that commitment can be squared with the fact that everyone sees some people as special: we love some more than others, are prepared to do more for our friends than for strangers, give preference to members of our family, and have a special concern for the well-being of our nearest and dearest. However, all this seems to sit ill with the ideal of equality: 'personal relationships, at least at first glance, are at odds with the ideals of impartiality and fairness, because it seems that personal relationships are partial and cosmically unfair by nature. Two people have a personal relationship only if they see each other as special, not as merely one person among many. If morality requires being impartial and fair, it seems not to leave room for close relationships, for close relationships thrive on partial treatment' (Graham and LaFollette 1989: 9, as quoted in Baron 1991: 837). Moreover, not only do we have these special relationships, we normally feel justified in having them. The affection I feel for my friends, and the fact that I am prepared to do more for them than for other people is neither a vice nor a moral outrage, and if impartial morality denounces such feelings and the actions that follow from them, then we may well conclude 'so much the worse for impartial morality'.

Characteristically, impartialists respond to this challenge by insisting that impartiality does leave room for special relationships and concern for others. It need not, and does not, see such relationships as 'cosmically unfair', but can endorse them and the actions that follow from them. I shall shortly discuss and assess the ways in which impartialism can make this accommodation to partial concerns, but first it is worth considering the arguments of one philosopher, William Godwin, who is notorious for his robust denial that special attachments are compatible with the demands of impartial morality. In Book II of *Political Justice* Godwin asks what should be done in a case where two people are trapped in a burning building and only one of the two can be saved. His example supposes that the two people are the Archbishop Fenelon and his valet, and in arguing for his conclusion that it is the Archbishop who should be saved, Godwin says:...

The illustrious archbishop of Cambray was of more worth than his valet, and there are few of us that would hesitate to pronounce, if his palace were in flames, and the life of only one of them could be preserved, which of the two ought to be preferred.... Suppose I had been myself the valet; I ought to have chosen to die rather than that Fenelon should have died.... Suppose the valet had been my brother, my father or my benefactor. That would not alter the truth of the proposition. The life of Fenelon would still be more valuable than that of the valet; and justice, pure unadulterated justice, would still have preferred that which was most valuable.... What magic is there is the pronoun 'my', that should justify us in overturning the decisions of impartial truth? My brother or my father may be a fool, or a profligate, malicious, lying or dishonest. If they be, of what consequence is it that they are mine? (Godwin 1976: 169–70).

This clarion call for impartiality did little to enhance Godwin's reputation or to rally support for his cause. Charles Lamb, his contemporary, mischievously referred to the example as one in which Godwin appears as 'counsel for the Archbishop Fenelon against my own mother', while others were less amused and declared him to be a 'desiccated calculating machine: his great head full of cold brains' (Locke 1980: 167–79). More recently, Lawrence Becker has commented upon the 'evident foolishness' of the belief that we must act with 'perfect Godwinian impartiality in every aspect of our lives' (Becker 1991: 699), and Brian Barry has suggested that if Godwin had not existed anti-impartialists would have to have invented him (Barry 1995: 225). The verdict is clear: any moral theory which delivers the conclusion that it is reprehensible to prefer one's friends and family over strangers is fatally flawed. So moral impartialism cannot be Godwinian impartialism; it must, rather, be a form of impartialism which acknowledges, and indeed endorses, our propensity to care for some people more than for others. And what this means is that its understanding of equality must be more subtle than the simple Godwinian understanding. What, though, is Godwin's understanding, and how exactly does it lead to absurd conclusions?

Here, commentators diverge, for although all are agreed that Godwin's conclusion is absurd, there is dispute as to whether its absurdity springs from his commitment to impartialism or whether it springs from his commitment to a particularly crude form of utilitarianism. Since utilitarianism is itself a form of impartialism, this may appear to be a distinction without a difference. However, since my overall task is to investigate the foundations of moral impartialism, it may be instructive, at this stage, to ask what the relationship is between Godwin's utilitarianism and his impartialism, and to see which of these is responsible for the 'evident foolishness' of his conclusion.

Impartiality and Utilitarianism

In 'Impartiality and Friendship' Marcia Baron claims that 'Godwin's extreme views are not based primarily on a conception of impartiality or on moral notions which motivate it, such as fairness or equality. They are based, rather, on his belief that we have a duty to do everything possible to promote the general weal—together with a rather crude notion of what it is to do so. The beliefs which underpin his example (and his commentary on it) are clearly not beliefs which an impartialist must accept' (Baron 1991: 842). For Baron, then, impartiality is motivated by considerations of fairness or equality; Godwinian utilitarianism is motivated by the belief that we should promote the general weal. These are different motivations, and it is Godwin's commitment to the latter which generates his absurd conclusion.

By contrast, Brian Barry insists that 'what makes Godwin the archetypal exponent of first order impartiality is not his idea that everyone should do the best thing open to him. What makes him distinctive is his idea that the best thing to do is behave with strict impartiality always and that this entails giving no weight to prior commitments or personal attachments' (in Kelly 1998: 246).

What we have here are different diagnoses of the flaw in Godwin's argument: where Baron cites utilitarianism as the source of the absurdity, Barry argues that Godwin's utilitarianism is only problematic because it involves commitment to thoroughgoing first-order impartiality. Moreover, these different diagnoses are significant both because they highlight the different ways in which a commitment to equality may be understood, and because they draw attention to the different aims which moral theories, including impartial theories, may have.

So, on the first point, Baron draws a very clear distinction between impartialist commitment to equality on the one hand, and utilitarian commitment to the promotion of the general good on the other. These, she says, are different motivations, and the absurdity of Godwin's conclusion springs from his preoccupation with the latter and has nothing to do with the former. However, some take the utilitarian aim of promoting the general good to be, in itself, a way (even the best way) of working out a commitment to equality. So the utilitarian motivation, far from being distinct from the motivation to impartiality, is in fact, and on some accounts, a way of implementing it. Indeed, Rawls notes this in his critical discussion of utilitarianism when he writes: 'some philosophers have accepted the utilitarian principle because they believed that the idea of an impartial sympathetic spectator is the correct interpretation of impartiality' (Rawls 1971: 189). Of course, he concludes that this is not, in the end, a strategy which can adequately reflect the ideal of equality, since it requires that some make great sacrifices in their own life prospects in order to ensure better prospects for others (Rawls 1971: 178). Nonetheless it is, Rawls thinks, an attempt, albeit a misguided attempt, to pay homage to the ideal of equality. Godwin's discussion of the 'famous fire cause' therefore highlights the fact that, even when all are agreed that impartialism is grounded in equality, they are deeply divided not only about what counts as an *adequate* attempt to secure equality, but also about what counts as an attempt *at all*.

The example also draws our attention to the fact that different moral theories might have different aims. In his discussion of Godwin, Barry urges that there are two approaches to ethics and that the absurdity of Godwin's conclusion springs from his failure to recognize the difference between them. He explains: 'one is the first person point of view from which an agent is asking "what ought I to do?" with the behaviour of others given as if it were the circumstances of action. The alternative is the social point of view "what morality ought there to be?" ' (in Kelly 1998: 246), and he goes on to insist that whereas impartialist theory and Godwinian utilitarianism are attempts to answer the second question, act and rule utilitarianism are attempts to answer the first. It is a mistake to confuse these two questions, and an even bigger mistake to suppose that if we give an impartialist answer to the second question (what morality ought there to be?) we are committed to giving an impartialist answer to the first (what ought I to do?). This distinction between two approaches to ethics is central to Barry's defence of impartialism, and it figures prominently in many other defences too. It is therefore worth spending some time explaining exactly what the distinction is, how it exposes the error in Godwin's account, and how it might help to deliver a form of impartialism which can accommodate the special concerns we have for friends, relatives and those whom we love.

As indicated, Barry takes the controversy between act and rule utilitarians to be one which centres on the question 'what ought I to do?' The act utilitarian urges that each of us should respond to this question by considering which particular act will best promote happiness, utility, or welfare in the specific circumstances under consideration, whereas the rule utilitarian urges that we consider which *principle* is most likely, if adopted, to promote happiness, utility or welfare. Notoriously, act and rule utilitarianism will deliver different answers to the question 'what ought I to do?' in cases where a principle which is generally justified on utilitarian grounds dictates an act that does not maximise utility in the specific circumstances. To take a well-worn example, there are good utilitarian reasons for adopting a principle prohibiting the telling of lies, since deception is not, in general, conducive to the greatest good or to human happiness. However, there can be specific cases in which telling a lie will promote more good than any other action open to the agent. So, when confronted by a madman with an axe, rule utilitarians will draw attention to the utilitarian considerations which tell in favour of adopting, and adhering to, a general principle of truth telling, whereas act utilitarians will draw attention to the fact that, whatever the general rule, this particular case is one in which the greatest good will be maximized by telling a lie. Of course, the debate between act and rule utilitarians is much more complicated than the simplistic treatment of this example implies, but the crucial point to be noted is that both act and rule utilitarians are responding to the question 'what ought I to do?' Their aim is to provide individuals with guides to action.

By contrast, impartialism is not directly concerned with the question 'what ought I to do?'. It is, rather, an attempt to delineate the grounds on which principles should be adopted. It does not necessarily have anything to say about which precise acts should be performed, for although principles have implications for action, they do not necessarily dictate specific actions for all circumstances. On the contrary, many principles are such as to leave extensive room for personal discretion and individual judgement in particular cases. Moreover, this distinction between impartiality as a requirement on principles and impartiality as a requirement on actions is significant because, if stable, it may facilitate the development of a moral theory which is impartial in the principles it proposes, but not impartial in the objectionable (Godwinian) sense that it requires each and every act to be governed by impartial considerations. The problem for moral impartialism, then, is to demonstrate its compatibility with the partial concerns we have for (some) other people, and the solution to this problem is to differentiate between impartialism as a set of prescriptions for action in everyday life (impartialism as an answer to the question 'what ought I to do?') and impartialism as an account of the grounds on which we should select moral principles (impartialism as an answer to the question 'what morality ought there to be?'). By distinguishing between these two 'levels' of impartiality we may commend *principles* on the grounds that they are impartial without being committed to the claim that each and every *act* be informed by impartiality. So, reading this distinction back onto the 'famous fire' example, we can see that Godwin's unacceptable conclusion springs partly from his belief that moral theories are attempts to answer the question 'what ought I to do?' and partly from his belief that the right answer to that question is 'always act impartially by refusing to count anyone as special'. It springs, in short from a misunderstanding of the task of moral impartialism, together with a rather odd notion of what is required to discharge that task.

This account of the flaws in Godwin's defence of impartialism now provides an answer to the question: how can moral impartialism accommodate the special concerns we have for some people? The answer is that it can do this by distinguishing between two levels of impartiality: impartiality at the level of principle selection (level 2 impartiality, as it is often called), and impartiality at the level of particular acts (level 1 impartiality), where the former does not entail the latter. This two-level response is widely adopted by proponents of moral impartialism, and indeed many claim that once the distinction between levels is acknowledged, the debate between impartialists and their critics will largely evaporate because it will become clear that impartialists can accommodate special relationships and ties of love and friendship. Thus, Barry argues that the two-level distinction enables us to see that 'what the opponents are attacking is not what the supporters are defending' and that the 'battle' between partialists and impartialists is 'ill joined' (Barry 1995: 191). Similarly, Baron urges that it is simply an error to suppose that impartialists are committed to denying the legitimacy of friendship and, like Barry, she traces that error to a failure to distinguish between different levels at which impartiality might be deemed necessary. 'Critics', she says, 'suppose that impartialists insisting on impartiality at the level of rules or principles are committed to insisting on impartiality at the level of deciding what to do in one's day-to-day activities', but this is not so, and once the two-level distinction is noted we will see that 'there is far less and far less deep disagreement between partialists and impartialists than is often supposed' (Baron 1991: 842, 857). John Deigh goes even further when he notes that discussions of impartiality give the impression that there are two 'camps' which are 'contesting the ideal of impartiality itself and not merely the way it is rendered or deployed in this or that ethical theory' (Deigh 1991: 859). In saying this, of course, he announces his belief that moral impartialism does indeed take a commitment to equality as given and aims only to establish how that commitment can best be implemented. He assumes, in moral impartialism, precisely the commitment to equality which must be demonstrated in political philosophy. And he also assumes that moral impartialism does indeed have its foundation in equality. For Deigh, then, and for others, the debate between partialists and impartialists is less significant than is often supposed. We are, it seems, all impartialists now.

Or are we? The discussion of Godwin drew attention to a significant challenge which moral impartialism faces: the challenge of showing that it does not render relationships of love illegitimate and can accommodate the fact that we feel entitled to do more for our friends and family than for strangers. The two level distinction is a way of meeting this challenge and thus vindicating moral impartialism. However, the two-level distinction is less straightforward than has so far been recognized, for it is drawn in different ways by different writers: some see it as a distinction between different areas of our lives; some see it as a distinction between different kinds of thinking; some see it as a distinction between general principles and specific acts. These differences are, I think, significant in themselves and also in their consequences for, when spelled out, they highlight a further, and more recalcitrant problem which moral impartialism faces—a problem which does not question impartialism's ability to accommodate special relationships, but which does question the priority (or lack of priority) it accords to those relationships when they conflict with the requirements of morality impartially understood.

The previous chapter concluded with a problem about the priority of impartial justice over comprehensive conceptions of the good, and I there suggested that the possibility of defending the priority of justice might depend, in part, on the possibility of defending the priority of impartial morality more generally. However, while the two-level distinction shows the compatibility of friendship and impartial morality, it does not (so far) say anything about the relationship of priority which holds between them. But since it was this question—the priority question—that prompted the discussion of moral impartialism in the first place, it is important to see how (if at all) the priority claim can be defended. And in order to do that we must say more about the two level distinction which, it is agreed on all sides, forms the foundation of any acceptable form of moral impartialism.

The Two-Level Approach

Generally understood, the two-level approach involves a distinction between the requirements which govern our choice of principles (level 2 impartialism) and the requirements which govern our decisions about day-to-day actions (level 1 impartialism). Sensible impartialists require our principles to be impartial, but they do not require that each and every action we perform be impartial. In ordinary life, or in day-to-day actions, we are entitled to make decisions on partial grounds, and acceptable moral principles (impartial principles) will leave room for discretion in such areas. They will not require thoroughgoing, level 1 impartiality. So, for example, I do not need to deploy impartial criteria in making my choice of friends, asking myself whether this person is more worthy of my friendship than that. Nor must I, before helping my friend, establish whether there are other people who are more important, or who would benefit more from my assistance. Impartial principles permit partiality in contexts such as these, and if they do not, they will fail to command allegiance.

However, the account of two-level impartiality so far given stands in need of refinement, for while we may all agree that some contexts (such as those cited above) are ones in which impartiality is not required, there are other contexts where the appropriateness of impartiality is more controversial. So, even if we can agree that impartiality operates only at the level of principle selection, we still need to know what the scope of the principles is, when it is appropriate to apply them, and when not. It is, let us suppose, clear that we are not required to apply impartial principles in our choice of friends, nor in our choice of dinner guests or theatre companions. Here, I can invite whoever I like to join me, and there is no violation of impartiality if some are invited and others excluded. But what of our choice of fellow club members? Is impartiality required here, or are we at liberty simply to declare in favour of men and against women? Or in favour of white people and against black people? Discussing these questions, Barry writes:

the boundaries [between areas] are not fixed and at any given time there is likely to be an area that is in dispute. It used to be taken as axiomatic that the choice of club members was to be assimilated for moral purposes to the choice of friends. A club that excluded Jews, blacks or women might be criticized on much the same basis as a person's choice of friends might be—as being indicative of racial or sexual prejudice. But no issue of fairness was seen to arise, any more than it could in the choice of friends. This view of the matter is open to challenge, however, and has been challenged. (Barry 1995: 16)

What this quotation suggests, and what is confirmed later, is that, for Barry, the two-level distinction is allied to a distinction between different areas of life. So, although the central claim is that second level impartiality is addressed to the question 'what principles ought there to be?', and as such is distinct from first order impartiality, which is addressed to the question 'what ought I to do?', this distinction needs supplementing by an account of how we know which areas ought to be governed by impartial principles and which not. On this latter point, Barry is less than helpful. He is anxious to emphasize that the distinction between areas is not the same as the distinction between public and private: 'contrary to a misconception frequently found amongst philosophers...we cannot say that impartiality rules in the public sphere while partiality has free reign in the private sphere' (Barry 1995: 15), but, beyond that, he has little to say except that 'it does have to be emphasized that the scope of impartiality is bounded'. He does not, however, give any idea of what it is bounded by.

It may be objected that this criticism is both trivial and misguided: all distinctions, it will be said, give rise to demarcation problems, and the distinction between areas where impartial thinking is required and areas where it is not is no exception. Indeed, it could be argued that any account which insisted upon hard and fast distinctions between areas would be suspect for just that reason: it would fail to reflect the deeply troubling and intransigent nature of many moral dilemmas. Whatever the truth of that allegation, I shall simply set it aside for now. My main concern is simply to note that, in Barry, the distinction between principles on the one hand and actions on the other depends upon a further distinction—a distinction between areas of our lives to which the principles apply, and those to which they do not. But this further distinction is under-specified and gives rise to a demarcation problem in the application of impartial morality.

Baron also invokes the two-level approach as a way of avoiding Godwinian conclusions. However, she does not appeal to a distinction between areas of our lives in which impartial principles apply and areas in which they do not. Instead, she uses the language of 'perspectives' or 'ways of thinking' and argues that the difference between impartialists and their opponents is, in the end, one of degree: impartialists are more inclined than partialists to see impartial principles as having application to their dealings with friends, family and loved ones. Partialists, by contrast, are inclined to see the differences between relationships with friends on the one hand, and strangers on the other, as stark. 'Personal relationships in their [impartialists'] views, are really quite different from what they sometimes term "impersonal" relationships; and the moral principles or considerations which should guide and inform impersonal relationships should not be expected to apply to personal relationships. This, I think, is an important source of disagreement between partialists and impartialists' (Baron 1991: 845). However, Baron goes on to ally herself with impartialism by noting that, despite appearances to the contrary, impartial considerations do apply in our dealings with friends, family and loved ones, for here, too, we should be mindful of the need to respect privacy, autonomy, and so on. Although, in some circumstances, I may feel free to borrow my friend's books without asking her permission, I should not exploit the relationship by ignoring the fact that the books are hers and that (other things being equal) she should be consulted about their use. Similarly, although I may feel at liberty, in some contexts, to speak on behalf of my friend, I should not presume to judge for her on all occasions or to act without first asking what she herself thinks. Baron concludes: 'none of this is to deny that we do behave differently towards close friends as contrasted with casual acquaintances and that we have different expectations for each. The point is that the usual moral principles of respect for privacy and autonomy, and so on, do not fail to apply to personal relationships. There are some differences in conventions and therefore in exactly how those principles do apply, but they do nonetheless apply' (Baron 1991: 847).

So, rather than conclude with Barry that there are areas of our lives in which impartiality is not required, we should instead remember that the fact that someone is my friend ought not to lead me to believe that impartial considerations are out of place, and indeed the belief that they are can be dangerously false when, for example, it is used in an attempt to legitimate unequal or exploitative relationships. This consideration is an important one, and I shall return to it later in this chapter. Here, however, I aim only to draw attention to the fact that, whereas Barry explicates the two-level approach via a distinction between areas of our lives, Baron explicates it via a distinction between ways of thinking, where it is not assumed that there is any distinctive area of our life which is exempt from impartial thinking.

Both Barry and Baron, then, invoke the distinction between two levels of impartiality in an attempt to allay the fear that impartiality might require us to deny the legitimacy of special relationships such as friendship. And both seem to believe that, having shown that impartiality can accommodate such relationships, it is vindicated against its critics. Barry is most forthright about this. He identifies anti-impartialists as 'united on one central contention, which is that there would be something crazy about a world in which people acted on an injunction to treat everybody with complete impartiality' (Barry 1995: 194). He agrees that there would indeed be something crazy about such a world, but invokes the two-level distinction to show that in fact impartialism is not committed to any such injunction. Baron also takes the ability to accommodate special relationships as central to the debate between impartialists and their opponents, and she also concludes that 'impartialists need not slight partiality' adding 'but perhaps this is the wrong way to put it, since it seems to endorse the distinction between partialists and impartialists. If the differences are not deep, perhaps the very labels "impartialists" and "partialists" should be abandoned' (Baron 1991: 857).

However, the difficulties inherent in both accounts of two-level impartiality suggest (to me, at least) that this is not the heart of the matter. The demarcation problem to which Barry's talk of areas gives rise, can (as previously indicated) be seen simply as a problem about borderlines to which all distinctions are vulnerable. Similarly, Baron's reference to perspectives or ways of thinking can leave us wondering whether and to what extent we should apply impartial thinking in a particular case, but that too can be seen as merely a matter of degree and not a matter of deep difficulty. In each case, however, the response is adequate only on the assumption that the battle between impartialists and partialists really is about the ability of impartialism to accommodate special relationships such as friendship and love. If the question were simply 'must impartialists deny the legitimacy of all acts of friendship and all special relationships?', then the two-level distinction, in either of its guises, would be a helpful response, for both Barry and Baron show clearly that impartialists need not deny the legitimacy of such relationships. And that, it might be thought, settles the matter.

My suspicion, however, is that it does not settle the matter, and that these strategies appear to dissolve the tension between impartialists and partialists only by ignoring a question which is both important and contested between them. That question, as foreshadowed in the previous chapter, concerns the priority of impartial morality in cases where its dictates conflict (or appear to conflict) with partial considerations. Whether we take the two-level distinction to rest upon differences between areas of our lives, or on differences between ways of thinking, there will (as we have seen) be cases in which it is not clear where the line is to be drawn and therefore whether a particular case is one which falls within the area of the impartial or is one in which impartial thinking is required.

Conversely, and crucially, there can also be cases where we are quite clear that impartial considerations are required, but where, nonetheless, we are tempted to act from partial concerns. So the problem is not simply that it is sometimes difficult to see exactly where the line is to be drawn. The problem is that, even when it is clear where the line is to be drawn, we may sometimes find ourselves reluctant to accede to the requirements of impartiality. Moreover, these are not necessarily cases where, as a result of weakness, we do what we know to be wrong. They can be cases in which we acknowledge what impartiality requires, but simply see partial considerations as being more important to us than the requirements of impartial morality. Just as, in the political case, people might see what impartial justice requires, and even acknowledge the legitimacy of those requirements, yet still ask 'why should I give priority to justice when its demands conflict with my comprehensive conception of the good?', so in the moral case we may see that impartial concerns are relevant, acknowledge that the demands of impartiality are legitimate, yet still ask 'why should I give those things priority over other things that matter greatly to me?'

To see what is involved here, consider the following case from Baron's 'Impartiality and Friendship':

Among the many people who live in countries where there are very long waiting lists for medical treatment, some may be able to pull strings to schedule (e.g.) surgery the very next week for a son with cancer rather than wait two or three months until his turn comes up. What should we say about the ethics of pulling strings in such a situation? (Let us imagine that very few people would be in a position to pull strings). On the one hand, it seems patently unfair to pull strings: if the others are in more or less equally dire straits, why should one's son be treated as somehow more special? Yet how can one, in such a situation, weight the considerations and decide, 'Yes, it will greatly decrease his chances of survival if he isn't operated on for two or three months, but although I could arrange to get him surgery much sooner, that would be wrong. He has to wait his turn—even if it costs him his life.'

And she concludes:

this much, I think, is clear: we expect people to want very badly to pull strings in such a situation, and we think well of them for feeling tempted to do so. We would think less highly of someone who felt no such tug at all, and who immediately and easily ruled out that course of action, recognizing that it would be unfair. Yet we see the unfairness, and for this reason we want rules to prevent, as far as possible, people from doing this thing that they are tempted to do. (Baron 1991: 855–6)

What this example suggests is that in some cases where partial and impartial considerations conflict we might, as Baron puts it, 'think well' of someone who is tempted to go against the dictates of impartial morality, and we might think less well of someone who 'felt no such tug at all'. However, this conclusion is, if true, a troubling one for moral impartialism because, at least since Kant, moral judgements have been thought to have compelling, imperatival force. The claim that someone is morally required to do x *just is* the claim that the considerations in favour of x have priority over considerations which tell against it—including considerations of friendship, familial ties, relationships of love, and so on.

So, to return to the demarcation and symmetry distinctions noted earlier, it may well be that there are cases where we are unsure whether something falls within the area of impartiality, or where we are unsure whether the case before us is one in which the impartial perspective is required. Baron's example, however, is intriguing because it is intended to provide a case in which it is completely clear that impartial thinking is required, it is completely clear that impartial thinking prohibits pulling strings for my child, but it is also completely clear that many, if not most of us would want to ask 'Why should I give priority to what impartial morality dictates rather than giving priority to the needs of my own child?' In short, the example is one in which the principles of impartial morality apply, they deliver a determinate answer, but that answer does not appear to have the motivational force characteristic of, indeed partly definitive of, impartial morality itself.

It is this problem—the problem of the normative priority of the moral—which, I believe, lies at the heart of the dispute between impartialists and their critics, and it is this problem which survives the demonstration that impartial morality can accommodate and legitimize relationships of friendship or partial concerns generally. Moreover, the question has two distinctive features: first, it is concerned not simply with practical conflicts, but with the alleged priority of the *reasons* of morality over other, partial, reasons. So it is not primarily concerned with the question 'what ought I to do?'. In the example given we are to suppose that the mother knows what she ought to do: she ought to allow her child to wait his turn in the queue. Her question is the rather different one: 'why should the reasons offered by impartial morality take priority over the reasons offered by other considerations, including my love for my child?' Second, the question does not require an answer which justifies from the third-person perspective, but one which can motivate from the first-person perspective. Again, the mother is not asking 'why is it right to allow my child to wait his turn in the queue?' but rather 'why should I endorse the motivation to do what is right from the perspective of impartial morality, rather than endorse the motivation to help my child?'

On the first point, Baron's example reveals that even when impartial morality accommodates partial considerations, it must still show why those considerations are (or should be) less weighty than impartial ones. Why is it that, in cases of conflict, the considerations offered by level 2 thinking should take priority over the considerations offered by level 1 thinking? And here we are concerned with the status of the *reasons* or *principles* offered by impartialism, not with their recommendations for action in any specific case. T. M. Scanlon makes this point when he says that: 'values can conflict in a practical sense when they give rise to incompatible demands to action, but even when no act is in view they can conflict in a deeper sense when one value involves giving certain considerations a status *as reasons* that another value rules out. Since morality involves very general requirements governing the reasons we can accept, it can conflict with many other values in this second, deeper way' (Scanlon 1998: 160, emphasis added). And similarly, Bernard Williams emphasizes that the issue is not simply one of practical conflict, but of the demands made by the system of impartiality:

the point is that somewhere one reaches the necessity that such things as deep attachments to other persons will express themselves in the world in ways which cannot at the same time embody the impartial view, and that they also run the risk of offending against it. They will run that risk if they exist at all; yet unless such things exist, there will not be enough substance or conviction to a man's life to compel his allegiance to life itself. Life has to have substance if anything is to make sense, including adherence to the impartial system; but if it has substance, then it cannot grant supreme importance to the impartial system, and that system's hold on it will be, at the limit, insecure. (Williams 1981: 18)

Both writers emphasize that the issue is not simply whether, in cases of practical conflict, one should do the thing required by impartial morality. It runs deeper than that and involves assessing what is involved in giving priority to the *reasons* of impartial morality vis-à-vis the *reasons* of friendship, loyalty, or partiality generally. So the fact that the two-level distinction enables impartialism to accommodate partial concerns is not sufficient, for what also needs to be shown is that, in cases where impartial requirements conflict with partial concerns, there are reasons for giving priority to the reasons of morality over the reasons of partiality. And that, in turn, needs to be squared with our propensity, in at least some cases, to think well of someone who is tempted to go against the requirements of impartiality.

The second significant feature of the normative question is that it is addressed to the agent him or herself. Baron's example draws our attention away from the question of what it would be right to do in the case described and towards the agent who finds herself in the situation. Again, what is significant here is that the agent is clear that this is a case in which impartial thinking is appropriate, and is also clear that impartial thinking requires that she not pull strings for her child. Nonetheless, and while seeing the force of the impartial requirement, she is tempted to go against it, and asks herself, 'Why should I endorse the motivation to do what impartial morality requires rather than endorsing the motivation to help my child?'

This first-person feature of the normative question is also noted by several writers, including Scanlon and Christine Korsgaard. Scanlon states that an acceptable moral theory must explain both the nature of moral argument and the nature of moral motivation. It must, he says, 'characterize the method of reasoning through which we arrive at judgements of right and wrong, and . . . explain why there is good reason to give judgements arrived at in this way the kind of importance that moral judgements are normally thought to have' (Scanlon 1998: 2). And he goes on to insist that the priority problem is the problem of explaining 'how considerations of right and wrong can play a certain role *in the thinking of an agent*' (Scanlon 1998: 149, my emphasis). Similarly, Korsgaard emphasizes the first-person character of the normative question when she writes:

It is easy to confuse the criteria of explanatory and normative adequacy. Both, after all, concern questions about how people are motivated to do the right thing and why people care about moral issues so deeply. And certainly a theory of moral concepts which left the practical and psychological effects of moral ideas *inexplicable* could not even hope to *justify* those effects. Nonetheless, the issue is not the same. The difference is one of perspective. A theory that could explain why someone does the right thing—

in a way that is adequate from a third-person perspective—could nevertheless fail to justify the action from the agent's own, first-person perspective, and so fail to support its normative claims. (Korsgaard 1996: 14)

The normative question therefore has two dimensions: it is concerned with the way in which reasons of morality relate to reasons deriving from other values, and it is addressed to the agent him or herself. It canvasses the possibility that the form of thinking, or the kinds of considerations, which inform impartial morality might be at odds with the form of thinking, or the kinds of considerations, which inform our concern for our friends, our family, ourselves. And it asks what can be said to the agent should that conflict arise.

Summary and Prospect

I began by asking what moral impartialism is and what difficulties it encounters. All are agreed that it is grounded in a commitment to equality and, if that is so, then its most pressing challenge seems to be to demonstrate that that commitment is not at odds with our natural and legitimate tendency to favour some people (friends, family, ourselves) over others. This challenge, I believe, can be met by distinguishing between two levels of impartiality: impartiality at the level of principle selection, and impartiality at the level of day-to-day actions and decisions. Although this two-level distinction is drawn differently by different writers, in most of its incarnations it is able to show how impartialism can accommodate partial concerns.

However, the two level distinction, by its very nature, gives rise to questions about where to draw the line between the different levels, and although this is not a disabling problem in itself, it does highlight the fact that, unlike other distinctions, the distinction between the requirements of impartiality and partiality must be rendered compatible with the priority which impartial morality claims for itself in cases where it has application. So while the two-level distinction shows that impartial morality can accommodate friendship, it does not show that reasons of friendship are completely compatible with the reasons of impartial morality, much less does it show why (from the agent's point of view) reasons of friendship must give way should they conflict with reasons of impartial morality. It is, then, the priority of the impartial which is at stake between impartialists and their critics, and that priority problem has two significant dimensions: first, it is a problem about reasons, and second it is a problem addressed to the agent him or herself.

In the previous chapter I identified a problem for impartialist theories of justice: the problem of demonstrating the priority of justice in a way which is more than a mere *modus vivendi*, but does not require commitment to a comprehensive conception of the good. I argued there that, while the doctrine of epistemological abstinence is compatible with the persistence of a plurality of comprehensive conceptions of the good, it is not easily reconcilable with the claim that justice has priority in anything other than a *modus vivendi* sense. It was for this reason that I turned to an examination of moral impartialism, in the hope of finding a defence of priority which is moral but not comprehensively so.

In the previous chapter I also argued that justifying political impartialism would inevitably raise motivational questions, and I tried to show that attempts to sever questions of motivation from questions of justification are unsuccessful. Barry's moderate scepticism undermines the agent's commitment to his or her comprehensive conception of the good, and thus (indirectly) undermines the persistence of pluralism. Similarly, Raz's argument from truth is in tension with pluralism and although, as a perfectionist liberal, Raz himself is happy with this conclusion, it cannot be a conclusion that is acceptable to political impartialists nor, in fact, is it a valid conclusion of the arguments Raz himself adduces. Political impartialism, then, faces the twin tasks of defending its own priority in cases of conflict with comprehensive conceptions of the good, and of defending that priority in a way that does not undermine the agent's commitment to his or her reasonable comprehensive conception.

Since it was the problem of priority in impartialist political philosophy which prompted the move to a discussion of impartialist moral philosophy, it is not surprising that the crucial question for moral impartialism should also be a question about priority, not simply a question about accommodation. As identified above, the normative question has two component parts: it is a question about the priority which can be accorded to the reasons of morality when they conflict with other sorts of reasons, and it is a question addressed to the agent him or her self. The appeal to reasons is analogous to political philosophy's concern to justify the priority of justice over conceptions of the good, while the appeal to the agent's own motivational state is analogous to the need to defend that priority without undermining the agent's commitment to his or her comprehensive conception of the good. The importance of these problems in political impartialism, and the need to turn to moral impartialism in order to resolve them, strongly suggests that 'what is at stake' between impartialists and their opponents is more than merely the possibility of accommodating values such as friendship, or of showing that impartiality is compatible with them. It is also a matter of showing whether there can be conflict at the level of reasons between the two sets of considerations and, if that is a possibility, of showing whether and why, from the agent's own point of view, it is the moral motivation which should be endorsed and acted upon. To repeat, however, my concern in this chapter is with those who do feel the force of impartial requirements, and who may therefore be 'torn' in cases where those requirements (appear to) conflict with other things they value. I am not yet concerned with the status of those for whom the requirements of impartial morality have no force. That will be my focus in the next chapter.

The Normative Question

The normative question, then, is the question which must be answered if impartialism is to be defended fully. What answers are available? Consider again the case in which I am tempted to pull strings to ensure that my child gets early medical treatment, even though I acknowledge that to do so would be unfair to others whose needs are equally pressing. In such a situation, the normative question has the form: 'why should I endorse the moral motiv-ation (the impartial motivation) rather than the motivation to help my child?'

In attempting to answer this question, two kinds of consideration might be adduced, and they highlight the tension between justifying priority and providing motivation identified in the previous chapter. We might put the emphasis on the word 'why?', construing that as a request for a compelling *reason*—a reason which outweighs, and therefore silences, all others. Alter-natively, we might place the emphasis on the first-person form which the question takes (why should *I* endorse the moral motivation?), where that question demands a reason *for me* and, as such, makes implicit appeal to the kind of person I am, the commitments I have and the values I endorse.

The problem which arises now, however, is that both answers bring problems in their wake: to appeal to something about the agent is (in part or in prospect) to turn moral considerations into matters of mere narcissism, or self-indulgence. It is to prioritize the agent's own sense of self above the needs and interests of others. On the other hand, to appeal to a 'trumping reason' is (at least potentially) to dissolve the problem altogether. It is to answer it in a way which evacuates the original dilemma of its force, and makes it extremely difficult to defend the thought that we can think well of someone who is tempted to go against the requirements of impartial moral-ity, or that we might think less highly of someone who felt no such tempta-tion.

What this suggests is that it will be difficult to defend the priority of impartial morality from the agent's own point of view, and indeed that will be my conclusion. It is not clear to me that in cases of the type described by Baron the agent always will have reason to give priority to what impartial morality requires. However, I believe that this is not necessarily an endorse-ment of self-indulgence, nor need it be at odds with impartialism, but can be explained by considerations internal to it. The intransigence of the dilemmas does not exhibit the conflict between partial and impartial considerations, but rather their interdependence. This, at any rate, will be my claim. Because the defence of this claim is complex, I shall approach it via a discussion of two responses to the normative question: the response given by Scanlon in *What We Owe to Each Other*, and the response given by Korsgaard in *The Sources of Normativity*. I shall identify both the virtues and the defects of their approaches as a preliminary to providing an account of my own which can, I hope, provide a better response to the normative question in both moral and political philosophy.

The Normative Question: Two Responses

The Reductivist Response

In his book, *What We Owe to Each Other*, Scanlon attempts to resolve the normative problem by arguing that, despite appearances to the contrary, there is no conflict between impartial morality and other values *at the level of reasons*. He begins by noting that 'since morality involves very general requirements governing the reasons we can accept, it can conflict with many other values' (Scanlon 1998: 160), but soon concludes that, in the specific case of friendship, there is ultimately no real conflict. Moreover, since friendship is a model for partial values generally, the demonstration that friendship does not conflict with impartiality is also strong evidence that partial values generally do not conflict with impartiality—not, at least, at the level of reasons. He writes:

the conception of friendship that we understand and have reason to value involves recognizing the moral value of friends *qua* persons, hence the moral claims of non-friends as well. No sacrifice of friendship is involved when I refuse to violate the rights of strangers in order to help my friend. *Compatibility with the demands of interpersonal morality is built into the value of friendship itself.* (Scanlon 1998: 165, emphasis added)

Scanlon's argument for this conclusion has two component parts. First, he claims that 'real' friendship, at least as we understand it, requires a recognition of the friend as a separate person in his or her own right. So the moral requirement of respect for persons does not stand in opposition to, but is a pre-requisite of friendship, properly understood. Second, he claims that, in the absence of this recognition, we would not have friendship at all because 'the moral standing [of the "friend"] would be too dependent on the contingent fact of affection' (Scanlon 1998: 164). The task for moral impartialism is to defend its own priority over other values in cases of conflict, and the example of friendship highlights the fact that values which may appear to be in conflict with impartial morality in fact depend upon it for their status as values, rather than as manifestations of desires, preferences or personal likings.

The Identity Response

The second response, which I shall call the 'identity response', is implicit in the characterization of impartiality given by Williams and quoted earlier: 'somewhere one reaches the necessity that such things as deep attachments to other persons will express themselves in the world in ways which cannot at the same time embody the impartial view, and that they also run the risk of offending against it. They run that risk if they exist at all; yet unless such things exist, there will not be enough substance or conviction to a man's life to compel his allegiance to life itself. Life has to have substance if anything is to have sense, including adherence to the impartial system' (Williams 1981: 18). Moreover, its general form is endorsed by Korsgaard, when she writes:

Personal relationships, then, as a form of practical identity, are independent *sources* of obligation, like moral obligations in their structure, but not completely subsumed under them. And the thought of oneself as a certain person's friend, or lover or parent or child can be a particularly deep form of practical identity. There is no obvious reason why your relationship to humanity at large should always matter more to you than your relationship to some particular person; no general reason why the laws of the Kingdom of Ends should have more force than the laws of the Kingdom of Two. I believe this is why personal relationships can be the source of some particularly intractable conflicts with morality. (Korsgaard 1996: 128)

Again, there are two features of Korsgaard's account which should be noted. The first is that, unlike Scanlon, she sees the obligations of friendship and the obligations of morality as having distinct (though analogous) sources. It is not, for her, true that the requirements of friendship are grounded in the requirements of morality and, for this very reason, the possibility of conflict is permanent and persistent. Second, Korsgaard sees the demands of friendship as involving one's practical identity. To be required to reject my commitments to my friend, my husband, my child in the name of impartial morality is (at the limit) to jeopardize my understanding of who I am. So this response affirms the persistence and intractability of conflicts between morality and other values. It sees them as conflicts in which one's practical identity may be at stake, but it offers no general hope of resolution.

So far, then, we have the following responses to the priority problem:

1. conflicts between morality and friendship are more apparent than real because, on inspection, the reasons of friendship turn out to be grounded in the reasons of morality. Morality is necessary for friendship, properly understood, and where a 'friendship' is not grounded in moral considerations it is not a genuine friendship at all.
2. conflicts between morality and friendship are both real and intractable. They are real because morality and friendship have distinct sources. They

are intractable because both sources involve our practical identity and there is no reason, in principle, why that part of my practical identity which flows from being moral should take precedence over that part which flows from deep personal relationships and commitments.

However, the difficulty with both these responses is that they seem to underscore, rather than answer, the problem with which we began, which was to show whether and why impartial morality should have priority in cases of conflict. The reductivist response denies that there is conflict of the kind we are interested in—namely, conflict at the level of reasons; while the identity response denies that there is any reason for thinking impartial morality to have a legitimate claim to priority. Nonetheless, each response contains important insights which can help in constructing an alternative and, I hope, richer response to the normative question. I shall therefore begin by identifying what seems to me to be true in each of the two accounts, then I shall say something about what seems to be mistaken in each, and finally I shall propose an alternative understanding of the priority problem which can, I believe, pave the way to a fuller analysis of what commitment to impartial morality implies.

The Truth in the Reductivist Account

Scanlon's resolution of the priority problem involves the claim that reasons of friendship are compatible with because grounded in reasons of morality. Again, it is important to emphasize here that he is not arguing that practical conflicts do not arise; his claim is that the deeper form of conflict—conflict between reasons—does not arise. So although there may be specific cases in which the requirements of friendship appear to conflict with the requirements of morality, it does not follow that the reasons of friendship are in conflict with the reasons of morality. And indeed, Scanlon denies that they are, noting, for instance, that friendship as we understand it involves recognizing the friend as a separate person with moral standing—as someone to whom justification is owed in his or her own right, not merely in virtue of being a friend (Scanlon 1998: 164). Here he seems to have in mind something akin to Baron's thought that considerations of respect for privacy, autonomy, and so on have application in the case of friendship, and that where they are not acknowledged it is doubtful whether the case is genuinely one of friendship at all.

As we have seen, Baron deploys this thought to bolster her contention that the differences between impartialists and partialists are largely a matter of degree, and that: 'the usual moral principles of respect for privacy and autonomy, and so on, do not fail to apply in personal relationships. There are some differences in conventions and, therefore, in exactly how those principles do apply, but they do nonetheless apply' (Baron 1991: 849). So, for her, friendship is bounded by morality in just this sense, that to be a genuine friend is not to act from reasons which are utterly at odds with the reasons of impartial morality; on the contrary it is to act in a way which is sensitive to impartial considerations, and which recognizes that our friends are separate and autonomous people and, as such, are deserving of the same respect as we show for all others. Perhaps the foundational thought here is simply that before drawing too sharp a distinction between friendship and impartiality we should remember that impartial morality serves to protect the rights of people as human beings quite generally. If we suspend those considerations when dealing with our friends, then we run the risk of treating them less well than unknown others, and it cannot be compatible with friendship to treat my friends less well than strangers.

To see how friendship can fail when not informed by impartial morality, consider the case of Nora in Ibsen's *Doll's House* (Ibsen 1965: 145–232). The two central characters of the play are Torvald Helmer and his wife, Nora. Torvald is a successful businessman who, as the play opens, is on the brink of promotion to a high-ranking position in the local bank. The promotion will bring with it wealth and status in the local community. It represents the culmination of Torvald's ambition. However, success and status have been hard won and during the early years of his marriage to Nora he suffered serious ill health. At that time, and unbeknownst to him, Nora borrowed money to pay for his medical treatment. Because women were not allowed to borrow money without a male guarantor she forged her father's signature on the loan document and has subsequently spent most of her time surreptitiously trying to earn money to pay back the debt. As the play unfolds it becomes increasingly clear that her misdeed will be discovered, Torvald's promotion will be jeopardized, and his reputation as a pillar of the community will be destroyed. In the final scene of the play Torvald does indeed discover what Nora has done. She hopes that the discovery will make him realize how much she has loved him and how much she has been prepared to sacrifice for him but, to her horror, he receives the news as proof that he has been married to a liar, a forger, and a cheat. His wife is not the innocent and guileless 'doll' he thought her to be, but a common criminal. The final scene focuses on the discussion which ensues between them, and in which their different and conflicting conceptions of what is important in life are revealed.

Throughout the play, we are presented with a vision of Nora as a bird, a plaything, a creature of light and joy, a capricious, whimsical, unpredictable child. This is the way her husband, Torvald, perceives her and it is this perception which has informed their relationship from the start. In the end, it is their undoing. When, in the final scene of the play, Nora announces that she will leave Torvald and their children, he reminds her of her duties to their children and to him as her husband. She replies that she has 'more sacred' duties—duties to herself: 'I believe that before everything else I am a human being—just as much as you are', she says, and with these words she gives voice to her deep resentment that Torvald's 'love' for her has never been informed by a recognition of her as a separate person, deserving of respect. Indeed, what she now sees is that Torvald has never really loved her at all, but has felt only affection for the 'songbird' he took her to be. She tells him 'you arranged everything to suit your own tastes, and so I came to have the same tastes as yours ... or pretended to. I'm not quite sure which ... our home has been nothing but a play-room. I've been your doll-wife here, just as at home I was Papa's doll-child. And the children have been my dolls in their turn. I liked it when you came and played with me, just as they liked it when I came and played with them. That's what our marriage has been, Torvald' (Ibsen 1965: 226). By refusing to recognize Nora as a human being first, Torvald has destroyed the basis on which their marriage could genuinely be a marriage. He has, of course, enormous affection for Nora (or at least for what he believes her to be), but that is not enough. Friendship and love, as values, must go beyond that. In particular, they must involve an acknowledgement of the other person as a human being before all else and as deserving of respect for that reason.

The case of Nora highlights what I take to be an important truth in the views advanced by Scanlon and Baron: even the most personal and intimate of relationships—the relationship of marriage—requires that each party recognize the other person as a separate and autonomous human being. In the absence of this recognition, there are reasons for doubting whether the relationship genuinely is a relationship of friendship, or of love, at all.

However, Scanlon's claim goes beyond Baron's, for whereas the latter simply asserts that friendship must be informed by considerations of impartial morality, Scanlon argues that compatibility with the demands of interpersonal morality is built into the value of friendship itself. Having insisted that 'friendship, at least as I understand it, involves recognizing the friend as a separate person with moral standing—as someone to whom justification is owed in his or her own right, not merely in virtue of being a friend', he goes on to give the following, rather curious, example:

A person who saw only friends as having this status would therefore not have friends in the sense I am describing: their moral standing would be too dependent on the contingent fact of his affection. There would, for example, be something unnerving about a 'friend' who would steal a kidney for you if you needed one. This is not just because you would feel guilty toward the person whose kidney was stolen, but because of what it implies about the 'friend's' view of your right to your own body parts: he wouldn't steal them, but that is only because he happens to like you. (Scanlon 1998: 164–5)

What is implied here is not simply that impartial considerations apply to friends, but that they are the foundation of friendship such that, where we act against impartial morality and in the name of 'friendship', it is not really friendship at all that we display. I shall return to Scanlon's example later, when discussing what I see to be the flaws in the reductivist response. For now, however, I am concerned only to point out what seems to be correct in it, and that is that it draws our attention to the fact that friendship is a value, and its status as a value cannot be explicated fully without reference to considerations of impartial morality. This is the truth in the reductivist account.

The Truth in the Identity Account

What, then, is the truth in the identity account? Korsgaard gives the following analysis of what is central to and distinctive of personal relationships (including relationships of love and friendship):

a personal relationship is a reciprocal commitment on the part of two people to take one another's views, interests and wishes into account. This kind of reciprocity leads to what Kant called 'a unity of will', for the two parties must, at least in the areas their relationship is concerned with, deliberate as one. Personal relationships are therefore constitutive of one's practical identity. (Korsgaard 1996: 127)

What is significant here is the identification of something beyond contingent affection which is partly definitive of some personal relationships Where Scanlon concludes that in the absence of a moral grounding personal relationships will become merely a matter of contingent affection, Korsgaard identifies another possibility, which she calls 'reciprocal commitment'. This goes beyond contingent affection because it can be constitutive of one's practical identity, but it is not (she says) grounded in morality. On the contrary, it has a separate source and may therefore conflict with morality.

The concept of reciprocal commitment as partly constitutive of one's practical identity is (for me at least) somewhat elusive, so let me try to explain what I take it to imply. Consider, again, the case of Nora in *Doll's House*. In discussing the truth in the reductivist response, I suggested that one source of the tragedy lies in Torvald's refusal (or inability) to recognize Nora as a separate person with moral standing—as someone to whom justification is owed in her own right, and not simply as a wife and mother. It is this which prompts Nora to conclude that Torvald has never really loved her and that their marriage has never been a true marriage.

However, there is another dimension to Nora's conclusion. This is her realization that she and Torvald have never been, in Korsgaard's words, 'reciprocally committed'. Torvald has never endorsed Nora's views, interests, and wishes. He has never seen them as his, or even as partly his. On the contrary, he has always acted from his own, independent and pre-existing, wishes. At the point in the play when Torvald realizes that his honour will be impugned if Nora's crime becomes public, he rejects her in words which make plain that his projects and values have never been informed by hers. His own ideals of the supremacy of honour, the law, and public affirmation stand untouched by Nora's ideals of loyalty to her husband and protection of her children before all else. Thus, when Torvald declares that it is unreasonable to expect him to sacrifice his honour for her ('No man would do that' he says), Nora concludes that throughout their marriage they have been 'strangers' to one another, and I take it that part of what is implied by this conclusion is that he has never modified his own ideals in the light of hers, much less has he taken her ideals as contributory to or partly constitutive of his own.

The claim that friendship involves reciprocal commitment which can lead to a Kantian 'unity of wills' refers, in part, to the fact that, in friendship, I am normally influenced by the mere fact that certain things are important to my friend: they matter to him and, for that reason alone, they matter to me too. Of course, the extent to which this is true, and indeed the precise nature of the truth, will differ according to the nature of the relationship. Where someone is my friend, I will, as Korsgaard puts it, 'take his interests and views *into account*'. I will be disposed to respond to his wishes because they are his, and because he is my friend. However, where someone is my partner or spouse, it is likely that his interests will become more or less indistinguishable from my own. I will not merely 'take them into account', I will adopt them as my own and come to see them not as exclusively his, but as mine, too, or as ours together. In the former case the desires and projects of another influence and move me; in the latter case I embrace those desires and projects for myself. It is unclear to me whether the language of a 'unity of wills' is appropriate in the former case, and I shall return to this point later, as it is important in identifying the flaws in the identity argument. However, even if a unity of wills exists only in the case of very close relationships, Korsgaard's general point persists, which is that friendship implies being moved to act by the needs and desires of the friend simply because they are her needs and desires. The fact that something is desired by or of importance to my friend serves (or should serve) to motivate me to action, and what is defective about Torvald's response in *Doll's House* is that it shows how little he has taken Nora's views into account. It demonstrates that he has never been moved by what she wants or thinks worthwhile, but has acted only from his own, independent and pre-existing, desires.

Taken together, these two features of *Doll's House* highlight the truths in the reductivist and identity responses respectively: they exemplify both the fact that friendship is a moralized concept which requires acknowledgement of the friend as a separate person, and the fact that friendship involves reciprocal commitment understood as (at least) a propensity to be motivated by the views and interests of the other person, and (sometimes) to make them one's own. However, the acknowledgment of these truths also serves to highlight the flaws in the two responses, and I now turn to these.

The Flaws in the Reductivist Account

One difficulty with the reductivist account is that, as noted earlier, it appears to dissolve, rather than resolve, conflicts between friendship and morality. By insisting not only that friendship is informed by morality, but that it is compatible with because grounded in morality, Scanlon identifies a single source of both morality and friendship, but he thereby renders the dilemmas of conflict mysterious *as dilemmas*. For if it is true, as he claims, that reasons of friendship are grounded in reasons of morality, and that conflict at the level of reasons is therefore impossible, then it is unclear why the agent ought ever to feel torn between the demands of the two. In the case described by Baron, the phenomenology of the situation is one in which the agent sees the reasons of friendship as conflicting with the reasons of impartial morality, and asks why she should give priority to morality over other things she values and (let us suppose) values more. But Scanlon's reductivist analysis precludes this as a correct understanding of the situation, and thereby implies that the agent's own perception of it is defective.

Moreover, this is a serious problem for Scanlon's account, because he insists that any acceptable moral theory must be phenomenologically accurate, and he makes much of the fact that his theory is just that (see, for example: Scanlon 1998: 155, 158, 187). Here, however, it is not clear that the theory has the virtue claimed for it: Scanlon's own kidney theft example just seems too easy, for very few people would be tempted to steal a kidney for a friend who needed one. So this is not even a *prima facie* case in which we feel inclined to give priority to the demands of friendship over the demands of morality. However, the normative question, on Scanlon's own account, is addressed to the agent, and arises when the agent is tempted to go against the demands of impartial morality and to give priority to the demands of friendship. Now there are certainly those who seem to believe that friendship does (or at least might) require us to steal a kidney for a friend, and I shall discuss their view shortly. What is most significant here, however, is that this example (the kidney theft example) does not provide a sufficiently strong case in which the agent might be pulled in both directions and where, therefore, the normative question arises.

If, however, we return to Baron's example, we do find a case in which the temptation to act against the dictates of impartial morality is (for most of us) strong, but it is not clear that Scanlon can explain whether and why this, too, is a case in which the demands of friendship are compatible with because grounded in the demands of impartial morality, and even if he can, he has no explanation of why, in that case, the agent feels torn.

One problem with the reductivist response, therefore, is that it is phenomenologically suspect. It fails to reflect or address the agent's own thinking, and since Scanlon himself emphasizes that an acceptable response to the normative question must address the agent's own thinking, it follows that if the reductivist account fails at this level, it fails overall. The agent may concede that friendship will not be genuine unless it acknowledges the claims of morality in some general sense, and yet still wonder why, in this particular case, the reasons of morality should matter more than the reasons of friendship.

However, even if this phenomenological point is moot, there remains a further difficulty with the reductivist strategy, which is that, in the strong form in which Scanlon embraces it, it requires a highly moralized understanding of friendship, one which seems to end in the assertion that cases in which morality is rejected in favour of friendship are not cases of genuine friendship at all, but merely cases of contingent affection. Scanlon never considers Korsgaard's suggestion that there can be reciprocal commitment which is more than contingent affection yet which has a source distinct from the source of impartial morality, nor does he canvass any other possibility. For him, it seems, there is no middle way between a conception of friendship as grounded in morality and a conception of friendship as a matter of contingent liking. Again, this seems dubious, not least because to say that another person is my friend is not simply to say that I like him; it is also (and as we have seen) to say that his interests and wishes motivate me. I am moved by them, and in some cases I will embrace them for myself. This propensity is distinct from liking, since it is not simply a function of the affection one feels for another, but rather a matter of the significance one accords to his views and interests, and the place they hold in one's own life. Moreover, it is also distinct from impartial morality, because there is no reason for thinking that when I am moved by the interests of my friend I am moved in a way consonant with the dictates of impartial morality. Indeed some would say that to be moved by my friend's interests only when those interests are consonant with impartial morality is not to be a true friend at all (see, for example, Stocker 1990: 226).

So, in the first place, the reductivist response seems unable to provide the requisite motivational purchase on the agent—at least in the most difficult cases—and in the second place the reductivist response succeeds only by moving too rapidly from the claim that real friendship has a moral component to the conclusion that any act of friendship not grounded in reasons of morality can only be grounded in contingent affection.

The Flaws in the Identity Account

But if the reductivist account is incapable of generating motivational purchase on the agent, the identity account struggles to generate the right *kind* of
motivational purchase for the resolution of the normative problem. It explains the agent's temptation to favour a friend by reference to the significance which the friendship has for the practical identity of the agent himself
(or herself). Thus, and famously, in the 'ground projects' cases discussed by
Williams, it can appear that what motivates the agent is a kind of self-
indulgent interest in his own projects—a concern to protect his own integrity
and practical identity above all else (see, for example, Williams 1981: essays
1, 3; cf. Hare 1982: 29). However, it is a huge exaggeration to suggest that all
cases in which I fail to fulfil an obligation of impartial morality are cases in
which my identity is threatened. There are cases (many cases) in which
obedience to the requirements of impartial morality would force me to
sacrifice something I care about very deeply, and would therefore result in
deep disappointment, but disappointment is a very long way from loss of
identity.

Moreover, even in those cases where it might plausibly be thought that the
agent's identity is at stake, this still seems the wrong kind of reason either for
us to cite or for her to invoke in defence of her decision to reject the dictates
of impartial morality. The mother who is tempted to pull strings for her child
will be so tempted because she cares for the child, not because she cares for
her own practical identity. It is of course true that, if the mother decides not
to pull strings, and the child dies, she will very likely lose her sense of who she
is and what she stands for. She may well ask, despairingly, 'what sort of
person am I such that I can leave my own child to die when I could so easily
have helped him to live?', and in asking this question she does indeed indicate
that her practical identity has been damaged, perhaps irreparably. However,
even here she is not (we must hope) holding up the preservation of that
identity as her reason for 'pulling strings', and the knowledge that that was
what motivated her would certainly not prompt us to think well of her for
being tempted.

In discussing the truths in the identity account, I concurred with Korsgaard's claim that friendship is more than contingent affection, suitably
moralized. However, by identifying the extra element as reciprocal commitment, and by construing reciprocal commitment as leading to something like
a Kantian unity of wills, Korsgaard misleads in two ways: first, she implies
that all cases in which the normative question arises are identity threatening,
but this seems an exaggeration. Second, even in those cases where the identity
of the agent is threatened by the dictates of impartial morality, it should not
be that threat which motivates action, but the threat to the friend, or the

child, or the spouse. Put differently, even where my husband's interests and my own are bound together in such a way that damage to his interests is tantamount to damage to my interests, it does not follow that my reason for ignoring the dictates of impartial morality should be that it will preserve my practical identity. At the level of motivation, appeal to a unity of wills seems mistaken.

The reductivist and identity accounts both answer to an important dimension of the normative question: the reductivist account shows why the reasons of friendship are not totally at odds with the reasons of morality, but it does so in a way which dissolves the dilemma entirely and fails to account for the agent's motivational difficulty. By contrast, the identity account answers to the agent's motivational difficulty, but does so in a way which exaggerates what is at stake in conflicts of this kind, and in any case it provides the wrong kind of motivational story. It implies a motivation which looks to the interests and identity of the agent herself, but this appears to justify what is (or may be) merely narcissistic concern for oneself, not concern for those whom one loves.

Responding to the Normative Question

I began by noting that there appears to be unanimous agreement that impartiality is grounded in the value of equality. However, in the case of political impartialism, this grounding is problematic because not all subscribe to the value of equality. Moreover, even in moral impartialism, where a commitment to equality is taken as given, there is still a difficulty in explaining its alleged priority over other things the agent values, and an even greater difficulty in explaining why we might think well of someone who was tempted to go against the demands of impartial morality. Given these difficulties, my suggestion is that instead of taking impartialism to be grounded in a commitment to equality, we should consider whether it can be grounded in our commitment to specific others whom we care about and whose needs and interests are directly motivating for us. So we do not suppose that all endorse equality, and then attempt to show how values such as friendship arise from that commitment. Instead, we begin with the partial concerns people have for those who are nearest to them, and then see whether and how those partial concerns might cast light on commitment to impartial morality.

If successful, this strategy will have the following advantages: first, it will provide a defence of impartialism which does not depend upon a contested (and arguably comprehensive) conception of the good. Second, by placing emphasis on the actual commitments we have to specific others, it will generate a more plausible motivational story in cases where people are tempted to go against the dictates of impartial morality: it will not see these as cases in which people act to preserve their own identity, but rather as cases in which they act in recognition of the needs and interests of those whom they love. Finally, it will not see our commitments to particular people as being entirely at odds with the requirements of impartial morality. Since (I shall argue) the appeal of impartial morality is in part explicable by reference to the concerns we have for particular others, impartial morality cannot be completely in conflict with partial concerns. On the contrary, it is vindicated by its ability to accommodate those concerns.

Moreover, if successful, this explanation may be capable of being reflected back onto the problem of priority as it arose in the case of political impartialism. The challenge there was to defend the priority of impartial justice in a way compatible with the persistence of reasonable pluralism, and what that meant was that the disposition to accord priority to justice should not rest on a motivational assumption which undermined the agent's commitment to his own reasonable comprehensive conception. By showing how impartialism can be grounded in our pre-existing commitments to specific people, this strategy may also enable us to see how the priority of justice can flow from comprehensive conceptions of the good, and how it can do so in a way which is more than the pursuit of stability. So my suggestion is that we begin with the partial commitments people actually have and try to show how and why they might ground a concern for the requirements of impartial morality.

It should be emphasized that throughout this chapter my focus has been (and continues to be) on cases in which the agent acknowledges the force of impartial morality. I am not here concerned with the amoralist, or with the agent who gives no weight to what impartial morality requires. Rather, I am addressing those who feel the tension between partial and impartial concerns, and my suggestion is that we can explain that tension by showing how partial concerns themselves play a role in explaining the force of impartial requirements. So whereas Scanlon sees the value of friendship as grounded in the value of impartial morality, my claim is that the value of impartial morality is (partly) grounded in friendship, or at least in those partial concerns we have for particular others.

However, this claim is complicated because, as Scanlon emphasizes, friendship is itself a moralized concept, and it would therefore be circular to draw upon the moral component of friendship in order to generate a defence of impartial morality. It seems, therefore, that we are driven, rather unpromisingly, to exactly those considerations which are usually invoked in order to show the conflict between morality on the one hand, and partial concerns on the other. I have already noted Korsgaard's appeal to reciprocal commitment understood as a willingness to take the interests of another into account, and as something which can lead to a Kantian unity of wills. Her account of reciprocal commitment as constitutive of practical identity was, I argued, overstated, and I suggested that what is in fact significant about relationships of friendship (and indeed about close relationships generally) is that they are directly motivating. So, in Baron's example, the mother's dilemma is best explained by reference to the fact that her child's needs move her immediately and directly. She has the simple thought: 'my child needs help'. That thought, however, appears to be in conflict with the thought which impartial morality presses, and which she also acknowledges: 'other children also need help, and they are no less valuable as human beings than my child'.

I believe, however, that this appearance is deceptive and that the propensity to be directly motivated by those we care for, far from being in conflict with impartial morality, lies at its foundation. Moreover, this propensity is sometimes invoked by impartialist philosophers in their characterization of the good of impartial morality. For example, having argued that moral principles are principles of rational choice and that, as such, they can be commended to non-tuists, David Gauthier nonetheless goes on, in the closing chapters of *Morals by Agreement*, to emphasize that participation with others is a source of enrichment in our lives, and that:

Morality takes on a different coloration when viewed in relation to participation. For asocial seekers and strivers morality could be no more than a needed but unwelcome constraint. But for those who value participation, a morality of agreement, although still a source of constraint, makes their shared activity mutually welcome and so stable, ensuring the absence of coercion or deception. (Gauthier 1986: 337)

And he adds:

Our concern here is not with empirical moral psychology . . . we do not suppose that actual moral feelings represent the outcome of a prior valuing of participation . . . . Rather our argument is that, if we are to consider our moral affections to be more than dysfunctional feelings of which we should be well rid, we must be able to show that they would arise from such a valuing and awareness. (Gauthier 1986: 338–9)

Similarly, Rawls appeals to 'natural affections for particular persons' as a prerequisite for the sense of justice. Unlike Gauthier, he is ambivalent as to whether these affections are a part of the developmental story only, or whether they are also necessary in the account of later moral motivation, but he nonetheless concludes that 'it would be surprising if these attachments were not to some degree necessary' for later moral motivation (Rawls 1971: 486).

Although these writers use different terms ('natural affection', 'valuing participation'), each appeals to the positive value we find in associating with others, and each insists that that value need not be undermined by commitment to impartial morality. On the contrary, and for Gauthier at least, impartial morality must be shown to be consonant with the value we find in associating with others, lest it become 'dysfunctional'. Moreover, Gauthier is clear that this is not a claim of empirical psychology, but a part of the philosopher's task of rational reconstruction: moral feelings must, he says, be capable of being seen as an 'appropriate extension of . . . concern for others in the context of valued participatory activities' (Gauthier 1986: 339). They must be compatible with the value we find in associating with particular people, and if they cannot be understood as an 'appropriate extension' of that value, they will not command allegiance.

If, then, we begin with the value we find in associating with particular people, how does that help to illuminate the value of impartial morality for those who do find it valuable? Earlier I emphasized the directly motivating character of relationships of love and friendship, and I suggested that it is this which accounts for our being tempted to go against the dictates of impartial morality, rather than any concern for our own identity. So, in discussing the Baron example I objected to the claim that it is the practical identity of the mother which is crucial in the case where she is tempted to pull strings for her child, and suggested instead that what is crucial is that the mother acts directly from her care for and concern about her child. She has the unmediated thought: 'my child needs help', and it is that thought which moves her to act.

This directly motivating or unmediated quality of acts done from friendship has been emphasized by a number of writers: Harry Frankfurt claims that 'it is merely a tautology that a lover takes the fact that a certain action would be helpful to his beloved as a reason for performing the action. His taking it as a reason for action is not the outcome of an inference' (Frankfurt 1999: 176). Similarly, Dean Cocking and Jeannette Kennett argue that 'the interests of the other in friendship, whether serious or slight, are not, in general, filtered through one's antecedent tastes and interests or subjected to rational or moral scrutiny' (Cocking and Kennett 2000: 285), and in support of their position they cite Elizabeth Bennet's reproach to Mr Darcy: 'A regard for the requester would often make one yield readily to a request, without waiting for the arguments to reason oneself into it.' In friendship, then, the needs, wants and interests of the friend motivate directly, and the mere fact that something is in my friend's interest or is important to her provides sufficient reason for action. No further argument or inference is needed. Indeed, many writers go on to claim that the provision of a further reason, and particularly of a moral reason, can serve to undermine the act as an act of friendship at all. Michael Stocker considers a case in which a friend visits you in hospital but, when thanked for his visit, replies that he 'always tries to do what he thinks is his duty, what he thinks will be best'. Stocker continues:

You at first think he is engaging in a polite form of self-deprecation, relieving the moral burden. But the more you two speak, the more clear it becomes that he was telling the literal truth: that it is not essentially because of you that he came to see you, not because you are friends, but because he thought it his duty, perhaps as a fellow Christian or Communist, or whatever, or simply because he knows of no one more in need of cheering up and no one easier to cheer up. (Stocker 1976: 462)

The moral which Stocker draws is that, if the friend makes reference to his duty, then 'the wrong sort of thing is said to be the proper motive'. Although friendship is indeed a moralized concept, and although there are obligations of friendship, it does not follow that a friend will or should be motivated by those obligations. On the contrary, she will normally act from the immediate recognition that this is what the friend needs.

The problem now, however, is that this characterization of close personal relationships as directly motivating seems to undermine the claim that we can reconcile impartial morality and friendship, for not only is it the case that acts of friendship or of love are performed without interference from other considerations, it is also the case that, where other considerations, including moral considerations, are allowed to intrude, they can detract from the value of the act as an act of friendship or of love. Indeed, those who appeal to the directly motivating character of friendship usually do so precisely in order to highlight the contrast with impartial morality. Thus Frankfurt emphasizes the gulf which separates what we care about from what morality demands when he writes: 'suppose that someone does know what he is morally obliged to do. He may nonetheless choose deliberately to violate this obligation—not because he thinks it overridden by a stronger one, but because there is an alternative course of action which he considers more important to him than meeting the demands of moral rectitude ... what is most important is distinguishable from the question concerning what is morally right' (1988: 81–2). Similarly, Cocking and Kennett conclude that 'the good of friendship does not sit well within the moral framework [because] the nature of our commitment to, and interest in, our friends is inherently likely to lead us into moral danger' (2000: 296); while Stocker famously deploys his example of the hospital visit to demonstrate the 'schizophrenia' of modern ethical theories. Such theories, he insists, sometimes require us not to be moved by what we value, and not to value what moves us (1976: 454), and in saying this he is emphasizing that the direct motivation provided by friendship and love is distinct from, and potentially in conflict with, the motivation to do what is morally right. So on all these accounts, friendship and morality appear to be distinct and sometimes irreconcilable sources of motivation.

But if all this is true, how can impartial morality be construed as an extension of directly motivating personal relationships? Recall that my aim is to respond to the normative question, where that question is a question about the relationship between reasons of morality and reasons of a more partial nature, and where it is also a question addressed to the agent's own thinking. We need to explain why the agent might feel torn between the claims of morality and more partial concerns, and we need to do that in a way which neither denies the dilemma altogether by denying the value of friendship when it conflicts with the requirements of impartial morality (as does the reductivist account), nor provides the wrong kind of motivational story, by insisting that it is the agent's own practical identity that is at stake (as does the identity account).

My suggestion is that this can be done by accepting, in general outline, the motivational story told by Frankfurt, Cocking and Kennett, and Stocker. Although, as we have seen, all these writers take their motivational story to be one which demonstrates the incompatibility of friendship and impartial morality, I believe that, when fully elucidated, it in fact shows the reverse. My argument begins with an example introduced by Cocking and Kennett in their article, 'Friendship and Moral Danger'. The example is taken from the film *Death in Brunswick*, and is as follows:

Carl, the main character of the film, is no saint. Weak, vain, disorganized, he is a severe disappointment to his mother. He drinks too much, and he works as a cook in a seedy nightclub in Brunswick where he falls foul of the owners by falling in love with a young barmaid. One night, Mustapha, his drug-dealing kitchen hand is badly beaten up in the back alley by the nightclub heavies. Carl is warned to keep his mouth shut; Mustapha is told that Carl is responsible for the beating. So late that night, Mustapha staggers into the kitchen and lunges at Carl, who is holding a long-pronged fork. Mustapha impales himself on the fork and dies. In a panic, Carl calls his best friend, Dave, an easy-going family man. Against the protests of his wife, June, Dave dresses and drives to the nightclub to see what is up. His initial response when shown the body is that the police must be called. Carl begs him not to, saying that he could not cope with going to jail. Faced with Carl's fear, Dave takes charge and helps Carl move the body. They take it to the cemetery where Dave works, he breaks into a coffin in an open grave, stamps on the putrefying corpse inside to make room for Mustapha, and re-closes the coffin. Later, they deny all knowledge of Mustapha's disappearance to his distressed widow and son. (Cocking and Kennett 2000: 279–80)

Cocking and Kennett now use the example to highlight what they see as the contrast between moral acts and acts of friendship. They note that, when Dave helps Carl to move the body, he does something which is morally wrong by any reasonable standards. However, they deny that his action also constitutes a failure of friendship. Indeed, they go further and suggest that, in a situation like this, it might be thought a serious failure of friendship to refuse to help Carl dispose of the body (2000: 280). This last claim strikes me as doubtful, and I am far from clear that friendship does require the performance of such a seriously wrong act. That, however, is beside the point. Different people will doubtless have different intuitions about the case. What is crucial is that Cocking and Kennett take companionate friendship to be characterized by the propensity to have one's interests and attitudes 'directed, interpreted and drawn' by the friend, and this implies the direct motivation which, I have agreed, is central to friendship. They then use the *Death in Brunswick* example to show that the sources of friendship and the sources of morality are distinct and potentially in conflict with one another, for what is required of Dave as a friend is that he be directly and immediately moved by Carl's request, not that he subject that request to moral scrutiny. Moreover, not only is it true that Dave may be a less good friend if he does subject the request to such scrutiny, it is also true that refusal to do so is testimony to the strength of his friendship. Thus, they conclude that a friend's willingness to lie for me 'is surely proof of friendship rather than something that might undermine the friendship. After all, she [the friend] takes the moral burden of telling the lie *for me*' (Cocking and Kennett 2000: 288, emphasis original).

In the light of these kinds of considerations Cocking and Kennett conclude both that acts of friendship have a distinct source from acts of morality and that our major moral theories cannot accommodate friendship (2000: 296). The requirement that, in friendship, we refrain from subjecting our friend's request to moral scrutiny is a requirement which seems to lead ineluctably to the conclusion that morality and friendship are distinct sources of action, and indeed that what is necessary for being a good friend can be in direct conflict with what is necessary for being morally good.

However, it is not clear to me that this conclusion follows quite as straight-forwardly as Cocking and Kennett imply, nor that the requirements of friendship and the requirements of morality are as deeply opposed as they would have us believe. To see this, let us accept that friendship is directly motivating in the sense that it precludes moral scrutiny of the friend's request but, having accepted that, let us consider the *Death in Brunswick* case from the point of view of Carl rather than Dave. In other words, let us consider what is involved in Carl's request for help, rather than what is involved in Dave's acceding to or refusing the request. By considering the case from the perspective of the person who asks the favour, rather than from the perspective of the person who is the recipient of the favour, we can, I believe, discern a connection rather than a conflict between friendship (understood as directly motivating) and impartial morality.

Suppose that Dave refuses to help Carl move Mustapha's body. His reason for refusing will presumably be that it would involve committing serious moral wrongs. In the case described it would involve desecrating a corpse, interfering with a grave, and illegally disposing of a body. However, in giving these reasons for refusing, Dave indicates that he has subjected Carl's request to prior moral scrutiny. He is not directly motivated by the thought 'Carl needs help', but is motivated by Carl's needs only insofar as those needs are permissible within an impartialist framework. And, as we have seen, one significant feature of relationships of friendship and love is precisely that they are not subjected to this kind of moral filtering. Acting from friendship just is acting from the direct motivation to help one's friend, and allowing other (moral) considerations to intrude can undermine the act as an act of friendship. It is therefore true that, in refusing to help Carl, Dave may be thought to display a failure of friendship and, whatever the spectator's view of the situation, it is certainly likely that Dave himself will see his own refusal in this light, will be reluctant to refuse, and will feel badly if he does refuse. What follows from this, however, is not that morality cannot accommodate considerations of friendship. On the contrary, what follows is that considerations of friendship themselves prompt considerations of morality, for if we place ourselves in Carl's position, we see that what he is doing is asking a friend to commit serious moral wrongs, and we also see that the friend, as a friend, will be very reluctant to consider those wrongs in deciding whether to accede to the request. However, the very fact that my friend will be reluctant to submit my request to moral scrutiny, and the very fact that to do so would be at odds with friendship, should make me reluctant to make the request in cases where acceding to it involves committing moral wrongs. The directly motivating character of friendship can itself prompt moral considerations, and we see how it can do that if we take up the perspective of the person making the request, rather than the perspective of the person who is the recipient of the request.

The point is a familiar but important one: we are sometimes more reluctant to ask favours of our friends than we are of strangers, and one reason for this is that we know it will be more difficult for them to refuse and to cite the moral impropriety of the request as the reason for refusing. Moreover, we do not need to restrict ourselves to dramatic cases in order to see the force of this point. There are many everyday contexts in which the fact that a friend will be disposed to act in direct response to one's request may cause one to hesitate. Suppose that, in order to gain promotion, I need publications in prestigious journals, and suppose that a very good friend of mine is the editor of such a journal. I have a paper which I would like published, but I know that the paper is quite weak. At the very least it needs extensive revision, and at worst it is not publishable. Not, at any rate, in that journal. However, I also know that it would be awkward for my friend to refuse to publish my work: we have known each other a long time, and I have (let us suppose) done a number of favours for him in the past. To turn down my paper now would be embarrassing for him. In this situation, I might refrain from sending the paper to my friend precisely because he is my friend. I might think: 'although I need publications, I will not send the paper to Jim because to do so would put him in a difficult position, whereas any other editor could feel free to refuse without awkwardness.' Of course, I need not think this, and of course there are any number of contexts in which we will turn to our friends for help. That, after all, is part of what friendship is. That fact, however, should not disguise the converse truth, which is that we may properly be reluctant to ask a friend in cases where the request involves something we know to be morally dubious, and our reluctance, I suggest, springs precisely from the knowledge that friendship is directly motivating.

So, in the example just given, the directly motivating nature of friendship prompts moral considerations. It prompts (or should prompt) me to hesitate before asking my friend to do something I know to be morally dubious. It also, I think, explains the familiar thought that, even if refusing a friend's request signals a failure of friendship, it is also true that making the request can signal a failure of friendship because it can indicate a willingness to exploit the fact that the friend (unlike others) will be very reluctant to subject one's request to moral scrutiny, and even more reluctant to refuse for that reason.

In discussing the *Death in Brunswick* example, Cocking and Kennett write: 'one might think it a requirement of close friendship in these circumstances that Dave helps Carl move the body, and that he fails Carl in a serious way if he does not. Certainly, Carl invokes the friendship in asking for help and regards Dave's action as testimony to the strength of their friendship' (2000: 280). But there's the rub. It is indeed true that Carl invokes the friendship in asking for help. He relies upon Dave's unwillingness to submit his request to moral scrutiny and thereby expresses his own disregard for Dave both as a moral agent and, I suggest, as a friend, for it is a feature of friendship that one will not normally ask one's friend to do something which would not withstand moral scrutiny. I know that, as my friend, Dave will not submit my request to moral scrutiny, but it is for that very reason that, as his friend, I *should* submit the request to moral scrutiny and, in some cases, refrain from making it. So while Cocking and Kennett emphasize the failure of friendship which is implied by refusing the request, they ignore the failure of friendship which might equally be implied by making the request. And this latter failure suggests a connection, rather than a conflict, between friendship and the claims of impartial morality.

In fact, it suggests two connections: it is reminiscent both of Baron's claim that impartial principles do not fail to apply in the case of friendship, and of Gauthier's claim that moral affections must be capable of being seen as an appropriate extension of concern for others in the context of valued participatory activities. On the first, and as was noted earlier, Baron insists that impartial principles apply to the case of friendship, and although conceding that there will be differences in the way in which they apply to dealings with friends and dealings with strangers, she concludes that 'they do nonetheless apply' to friends (Baron 1991: 847). But the *Death in Brunswick* example shows not only that the principles apply to friendship, but that friendship itself can prompt them, or act as the catalyst for them. Since Carl knows that, as a good friend, Dave will not subject the request to moral scrutiny, it is incumbent on Carl to do that. The very fact that (as a good friend) Dave will not raise these questions should itself prompt Carl (as a good friend) to raise them on his behalf. So the *Death in Brunswick* case, when considered from Carl's perspective, shows how friendship, understood as directly motivating, can act as the catalyst for moral considerations.

On the second point, Gauthier insists that we must be able to see our moral affections as an 'appropriate extension' of the concern we have for others and here, too, the *Death in Brunswick* case is instructive for, when viewed from Carl's perspective, it shows how Carl might indeed see the constraints imposed by morality as something other than unwelcome. In the particular case, he might, if he reflects, see them as concomitants of his friendship with Dave. He might ask himself whether saving his own skin is so important as to warrant asking Dave to do things which are seriously wrong—indeed criminal. Of course, he might give himself the answer 'Yes', but even if he does, reflection on the nature of friendship *as directly motivating* should be sufficient to explain why the requirements of impartial morality are not simply dysfunctional. For now, if Carl does go ahead and ask Dave to help him move the body, he will see that he is thereby testing their friendship in a way that might well be exploitative of the friend. And if he does not ask Dave to help him move the body, that will be because his friendship with Dave will have prompted him to acknowledge the requirements of impartial morality. Either way, though, it is friendship itself which makes sense of his ability to see morality as something other (and more) than an alien imposition.

I have identified the normative question as the question which lies at the heart of the debate between impartialists and their critics. Even if impartialist moral philosophy can show that the special concern we have for some people is legitimate, it encounters difficulties in showing why the dictates of impartial morality should take priority over those special concerns in cases of conflict. However, in raising the normative question I am not supposing that it is, in any non-tautological sense, true that morality ought always to triumph. Indeed, I have objected to Scanlon's argument precisely on the grounds that it delivers the priority of morality in a way which makes the agent's own sense of conflict inexplicable. Additionally, I have urged that an appropriate response to the normative question must give some account of why we might 'think well' of someone who was tempted to go against the requirements of impartial morality and act on behalf of her friend, her lover, or her child (and why we might think less well of someone who felt no such temptation). So the challenge posed by the normative question is not the challenge of showing that morality ought to triumph. It is the challenge of showing what the dilemma consists in from the point of view of the agent.

My response to this challenge is to suggest that we see impartial morality as grounded in the relationships we have with specific people whom we care about and whose interests and wishes are directly motivating for us. This foundation, unlike the foundation in equality, can be appealed to as something which is familiar to and endorsed by most, if not all, people. For reasons adduced by Hampton, and referred to earlier, an impartialism which is grounded in equality will not be acceptable to all people: equality is a controversial value to which not all subscribe and therefore the attempt to use it as the foundation of impartialism is likely to be seen as an illicit appeal to a comprehensive conception of the good.

Nonetheless, and for reasons given in the previous chapter, the priority of impartiality requires a moral defence if it is to amount to anything more than a *modus vivendi*. The special relationships we have with some people, and the directly motivating character of those relationships, may seem to be an unpromising starting point because such relationships are normally thought to have a motivational source which is distinct from, and potentially in conflict with, impartial requirements. However, this appearance is not wholly accurate and the directly motivating character of personal relationships is, I have suggested, a significant source of impartial considerations. This is not simply because friendship is a moralized concept (there are obligations of friendship); it is also because the recognition that my friends are directly motivated by my interests and wants itself prompts moral considerations. It prompts me to ask how much I can legitimately ask of them, *given* that they are directly motivated by my wishes. So it is not merely the case that relationships of friendship include moral considerations (because friendship is itself a value); it is also the case that, understood pre-morally, relationships of friendship act as the catalyst for moral considerations and bring them to the forefront of one's mind.

If, then, we take these directly motivating relationships as foundational to impartial morality, how do they help to provide a response to the normative question? Recall that the normative question is concerned with the way in which reasons of morality relate to reasons arising from partial considerations, and it is also a question addressed to the agent's own thinking. It arises when the agent asks, 'Why should I be moved by the reasons of impartial morality rather than by the needs of my friend?' Here I have argued that reasons of morality are grounded in reasons of friendship: those who feel the force of the requirements of impartial morality will be prompted to do so, in part, by reflection on the nature of the friendships they have and value. So, if Carl sees the wrong inherent in asking Dave to help him move the body, that will be partly explicable by reference to the directly motivating character of his relationship with Dave. Reasons of friendship ground reasons of morality.

How, then, does this help to respond to the normative question, understood as a question addressed to the agent's own thinking? How does it help to answer (from the first-person perspective) the question, 'Why should I be moved by the reasons of impartial morality rather than by the needs of my friend?' It seems to me that, in some cases, there is no reason to be offered, but that in itself is instructive. I have objected to Scanlon's resolution of the normative problem because it threatens to remove the dilemma altogether. By insisting that friendship is compatible with because grounded in impartial morality, Scanlon ultimately denies that there can be any conflict between friendship and morality. By contrast, if we take reasons of morality to be grounded in reasons of friendship, then the dilemma is explicable: it arises when and because we are required, in the name of impartial morality, to marginalize those directly motivating relationships which themselves explain (in part) the appeal of impartial morality. So when we insist that morality requires the mother not to give priority to her child, or that morality requires Dave not to move Mustapha's body, we thereby insist that they ought not to be directly motivated by the needs of those whom they love. But the propensity to be directly motivated by another is itself a crucial feature in explaining the attraction of impartial morality, at least for those who do find it attractive.

The troubling cases are, therefore, troubling because they are ones in which I am required to set aside, in the name of morality, those very attitudes towards others which enable me to see the force of morality's demands in the first place. These considerations, moreover, form the basis of a response to the question 'how we can think well of someone who is tempted to go against the dictates of impartial morality?' We can think well of such a person, and less well of someone who feels no such temptation, because the temptation is evidence that the person is capable of having those relationships which are a condition of being moral.

Conclusion

The aim of this chapter has been to establish what is at stake between impartialists and their critics, and I have suggested that what is at stake is something more than the mere ability of impartialism to accommodate the special relationships we have with some other people. Any sensible form of impartialism will distinguish between a requirement of impartiality at the level of principle selection and a requirement of impartiality in day-to-day actions, and that is enough to show that impartiality need not rule out all special relationships as illegitimate or 'cosmically unfair'.

However, the two-level distinction encounters difficulties in cases where the normative priority of morality is in question, and I have argued that it is this problem (the problem of normative priority) which lies at the heart of the battle between impartialists and their opponents. Moreover, it is not surprising that the question of priority should be the crucial one for impartialist moral philosophy, since we saw in the previous chapter that it is this question which is also crucial for impartialist political philosophy. Indeed, the discussion of moral impartialism was prompted precisely by the need to defend the priority of justice in cases where its dictates conflict with people's commitments to their own comprehensive conception of the good. In such cases we need to explain the relationship which holds between impartial and partial reasons, and we need to do that in a way which addresses the agent's own thinking.

My proposal has been that we can best respond by showing how impartial considerations flow from and are implied by the partial concerns we have for particular people. By beginning here, I do not assume anything which is controversially or comprehensively moral. Unlike the attempt to ground impartiality in equality, the appeal to what people in fact care about, and what they find directly motivating, is morally minimalist. It is not, however, devoid of moral content, because the concerns we have for particular people can themselves imply moral considerations and constraints. They do not, of course, lead us to adopt the kind of concern for all others which we have for those whom we love. That is not the point. The point rather is to indicate that even those allegedly pre-moral or non-moral concerns we have for some other people do not stand in stark opposition to impartial morality, but are explanatory of its force. They constitute the conditions under which we see the appeal of impartial morality, and it is for this reason that impartial morality should be reluctant to assert its own priority over them too categorically.

In reaching this conclusion I have drawn upon, but also revised, the strategies commended by the reductivist and identity accounts. Following Scanlon, I agree that friendship is a moralized concept, but I do not see friendship as compatible with because grounded in morality. Rather, morality is compatible with because grounded in friendship (or at least in relationships of love understood as directly motivating). My strategy also differs from Korsgaard's because it takes the central feature of personal relationships to be their directly motivating character, not their role as a source of practical identity. Although this directly motivating character appears to set personal relationships in opposition to morality, in fact it is a significant feature in its defence, for the recognition that others are directly motivated by our needs and interests itself prompts impartial considerations. The knowledge that my friend will be directly motivated by my wishes, interests, and needs informs what I can properly ask of her and thus moves me in the direction of impartial considerations. So if we begin with what people actually care about, we can move from that to an explanation of the appeal and motivational force of impartial morality. And we can also say something about why the troubling cases are troubling.

However, my account now requires completion in three significant respects: the normative question takes as given the fact that people feel the force of the requirements of impartial morality, but this feature of the moral argument (that it supposes some commitment to what impartiality demands of us) is not a feature which political impartialism can call upon. As has been noted already, political impartialism must defend the priority of justice against those who have comprehensive conceptions of the good which, while reasonable, do not contain any clear commitment to equality. So having shown that concern for others is compatible with, and indeed can prompt, impartiality, we now need to ask whether it *must* prompt impartiality. And this task, which is central to the next chapter, requires a more detailed account of what concern for others involves beyond the propensity to be directly motivated by them. Second, and since my aim is to move to impartial morality from consideration of things people care for, we need to ask what would be the position of someone who had no partial concerns. What kind of commitment to impartial morality would be possible for such a person? Finally, we need to ask whether, and on what conditions, impartial morality can itself be directly motivating: can it, like friendship, be amongst the things people care about and which move them directly? In the next chapter, I will address these questions. I will ask what is involved in caring for someone, what restrictions apply to what we can care for, and whether morality itself can be an object of care.

such as friendship figure in the explanation of the attraction of impartial morality itself such that, when we are asked to ignore the interests of our friend in the name of impartial morality, we are, in effect, being asked to ignore those directly motivating relationships which themselves explain the appeal which impartial considerations have for us.

However, my overall aim is not simply to argue for the significance of partial concerns in responding to the normative question, but also to argue for their significance in the genesis of impartial morality. What I mean by this is that partial concerns have an important role to play in explaining how someone who is not moved by the requirements of impartial morality might come to be moved by them, or to see their force. More specifically, my claim is that impartialism, at both the moral and the political level, can arise from our partial concerns. In the moral context this means that it can arise from the commitments we have to particular people such as our friends and family; in the political context it means that it can arise from our comprehensive conceptions of the good—our commitments to religious beliefs or ideals of human existence. I have already given reason for thinking that, where someone antecedently feels the force of the requirements of impartial morality, that will be in part explicable by reference to his partial concerns for particular others. Impartialism, I have argued, cannot reject the significance of partial concerns without undermining its own motivational foundation. But the stronger claim—the claim that those partial concerns can themselves generate impartial considerations—still stands in need of defence.

In this chapter, therefore, my primary concern will be to defend the claim that our partial concerns and relationships can ground impartial morality and thus help to get it 'off the ground'. However, in order to mount this defence, I must say more about those partial concerns, and especially about what is implicit in my appeal to care or to love for others. In my discussion of the normative problem, I emphasized the directly motivating character of relationships such as friendship, and the appeal to direct motivation was prompted (in part) by the worry that grounding impartiality in equality is, in effect, grounding it in a comprehensive, or at least highly contested, conception of the good. In order to avoid that difficulty I suggested that a move to the directly motivating character of what we care about might provide a way of commending impartialism to those who hold conceptions of the good which do not themselves acknowledge the value of equality. It might, in short, provide a foundation for impartialism which is 'thinner' than the appeal to equality, but is also other-directed. However, it might now be thought that the partial concern we have for others, if understood simply as directly motivating, is too thin, for on the face of it people can be directly motivated by, and can care about, all sorts of things, and there is no *prima facie* reason for thinking that the things they care about will be capable of generating a concern for impartiality. Indeed, one of the central problems for political impartialism is precisely that comprehensive conceptions of the good (partial concerns) are often at odds with impartial justice. They provide us with stark examples of cases in which people care very deeply about things which conflict with the requirements of impartiality.

So I now need to be more explicit about what is meant by care, and about the conditions it must satisfy if it is to give rise to morality generally and to impartial morality in particular. I also need to clarify what is meant by saying that caring about things can ground or 'give rise' to impartial considerations, and here I should emphasize that it is no part of my claim that caring about things necessitates or entails impartialism. There is, to my mind, no rationally compelling argument which can be presented to the resolute egoist or amoralist, much less to the individual who holds a conception of the good which conflicts with impartialism. The most that can be done is to indicate that, insofar as people care about specific things, they already have, as it were, the tools necessary for allegiance to impartialism, and the gap between the things they care about and the demands of impartiality are therefore less great than may initially be thought. Since the status claimed for the argument is important, it is worth dwelling on it a little further and relating it to the overall project of the book.

I began by noting that impartialism is widely thought to reflect a commitment to equality. Political impartialism, however, is restricted in two, and arguably three, distinct ways: its subject matter is restricted to questions of justice; its scope is restricted to the basic structure of society; and its aim is (often) restricted to questions of justification. So political impartialism characteristically aims to justify the priority of justice in cases where questions about the distribution of goods arise at the societal level. However, the restriction on aim is difficult to sustain. Since political impartialism insists on the priority of justice when it comes into conflict with competing conceptions of the good, it must defend that priority to people who do not themselves subscribe to a conception of the good which includes a commitment to equality. In the first chapter I argued that epistemological arguments are unable to meet this challenge: because the justificatory and the motivational tasks are intertwined, arguments from scepticism and truth purchase the priority of justice only by undermining the permanence of pluralism, while arguments from epistemological abstinence can defend the permanence of pluralism, but have no defence of the priority of justice. If, therefore, the priority of impartial justice is to be defended in a way compatible with the permanence of pluralism, that must be on grounds which are moral, but not comprehensively so.

This conclusion prompted the move, in Chapter 2, to a discussion of the priority question in impartial moral theory, and the aim there was to see whether and how the priority of the moral can be defended in a way which does not undermine the agent's partial commitments. The challenge to political impartialism is to defend the priority of justice without undermining the agent's commitment to his or her comprehensive conception of the good. Analogously, the challenge to moral impartialism is to defend the priority of the moral without undermining the agent's partial concerns and particular loyalties. Here my claim was that impartialists should not rest their case on the value of equality, but should rather begin with the partial concerns we have for particular people. Although these concerns can appear to be (and can in fact be) in conflict with the requirements of impartial morality, they are also central to an explanation of its appeal, for if we begin with people who do feel the force of impartial morality, we will find that an account of their feeling its force requires reference to the partial concerns they have for others. Partial concerns are a crucial component in explaining the appeal of impartial morality—for those who do find it appealing.

But what of those who do not find it appealing? What is to be said to them? In addressing this question it is important to bear in mind that there are several ways in which people might fail to find impartial considerations appealing. First, of course, there is the amoralist, who is normally characterized as the person who denies that there is anything he ought to do. He is, in Bernard Williams's phrase 'the man without morality' (Williams 1972: 17–26), and since the amoralist is without morality, he is, *a fortiori*, without impartial morality. Second, there are people who fail to find impartial morality appealing, but who do find some other kind of morality appealing. The crucial category for my purposes is those people who have comprehensive conceptions of the good which conflict with the dictates of impartial justice—in short, any of the people, or groups of people, signalled by Hampton when she writes:

Outside the West, social hierarchies and restrictions of freedom are commonplace (and Western societies derided for their commitments to liberty and equality); and even within Western democracies, beliefs that would limit liberty (eg, within certain forms of fundamentalist religions) or challenge equality (such as racist or sexist views) are far more widespread than many would like to admit. (Hampton 1993: 304).

As Hampton indicates, it is not difficult to find examples of people who challenge western commitment to equality. In his autobiography, *An Indian Summer*, James Cameron reflects on the gross inequalities which are licensed, and even endorsed, by Hinduism, according to which one has an obligation to accept one's station in life and perform the duties appropriate to it. This belief in *dharma* is, says Cameron, intrinsic to the whole principle of caste. He explains:

It is the *dharma* of the wind to blow, and that of the rain to fall; it is the *dharma* of a stone to be hard and a leaf to be soft. It is likewise the *dharma* of a Brahmin to be respected, and that of a sweeper to be despised. There is no getting away from it. The sacred Bhagavadgita, which cannot properly be questioned, says: 'Even should one's *dharma* seem to be mad, its performance brings blessings more than the assumption and pursuit of another's *dharma*.' (Cameron 1974: 42)

There is here no acceptance of the value of equality in anything like the sense required by impartialist political philosophy, and certainly no belief that the equality of all human beings is a 'self-evident' truth.

Nor is it simply in non-Western societies that appeal to the equality of all human beings can prove problematic. Mark Twain's novel, *Huckleberry Finn*, provides a graphic description of a society (nineteenth-century Missouri) in which black people are seen, not as human beings at all, but as property, and Twain uses this fact to draw attention to the possibility of endorsing equality at the theoretical level, while nonetheless denying it at the level of practice. When Huck lies to Aunt Sally in telling her that the cylinder head of the boat blew up, she responds:

'Good gracious! Anybody hurt?'
'No'm. Killed a nigger.'
'Well, it's lucky; because sometimes people do get hurt.' (Twain 1950: 374)

And again, when he helps Jim the black slave to freedom, Huck is stricken by 'conscience' and reproaches himself with the words:

'What had poor Miss Watson done to you, that you could see her nigger go off right under your eyes and never say one single word? What did that poor old woman do to you that you could treat her so mean?...Thinks I, this is what comes of my not thinking. Here was this nigger which I had as good as helped to run away, coming right out flat-footed and saying he would steal his children—children that belonged to a man I didn't even know; a man that hadn't ever done me no harm' (Twain 1950: 259–60).

I shall revisit the case of Huckleberry Finn later in this chapter, because I believe it provides material in support of my claim that our partial concerns for others can give rise to impartial morality. It also, of course, raises questions far more complex than my rather simplistic description so far suggests, but I shall leave those complexities aside for now. The example is introduced here simply to illustrate the point that, if we take impartial morality to be grounded in a commitment to equality, then we appeal to a value which, far from being self-evident, is both contestable and contested.

Can an appeal to the partial concerns which we have for particular people, projects, or causes do any better in explaining how impartial morality might be commended to those who do not antecedently find it appealing? This is the central question of this chapter, and I address it in two stages: first I consider whether partial concerns can give rise to moral considerations at all; then I consider whether partial concerns can give rise to distinctively impartial moral considerations. I begin with the case of the amoralist, understood as the man who is without morals.

The Amoralist

In his book, *Morality: An Introduction to Ethics*, Bernard Williams asks what is necessary to 'get morality off the ground', and his response to this question begins with a discussion of the amoralist. Having argued that we cannot sensibly think of the amoralist as entirely devoid of concern for others (such a person would be a psychopath and 'the idea of arguing him into morality is surely idiotic'), Williams goes on to ask whether any headway could be made with someone who does have some concern for others, but whose concerns are partial and unpredictable. He writes:

one might picture him [the amoralist] as having some affections, occasionally caring for what happens to somebody else. Some stereotype from a gangster movie might come to mind, of the ruthless and rather glamorous figure who cares about his mother, his child, even his mistress. He is still recognizably amoral, in the sense that no general considerations weigh with him, and he is extremely short on fairness and other considerations . . . [but] this man is capable of thinking in terms of others' interests, and his failure to be a moral agent lies (partly) in the fact that he is only intermittently and capriciously disposed to do so. But there is no bottomless gulf between this state and the basic dispositions of morality. (Williams 1972: 24–5)

If, then, the amoralist cares for particular people and is capable of thinking in terms of their interests, he is also someone who, in Williams's opinion, has the necessary tools for entry into morality:

The model [of the amoralist] is meant to suggest just one thing: that if we grant a man with even minimal concern for others, then we do not have to ascribe to him any fundamentally new kind of thought or experience to include him in the world of morality, but only what is recognizably an extension of what he already has . . . It does not follow from this that his having sympathetic concern for others is a necessary condition of being in the world of morality, that the way sketched is the *only* way 'into morality'. It does not follow from what has so far been said, but it is true. (Williams 1972: 26)

Concern for others—an ability and willingness to take the interests of at least some other people into account—is, then, a precondition for entry into morality. Where it is absent, we are dealing with a psychopath; where it is present, no fundamentally new kind of thought is needed for morality. Or so Williams claims.

However, Williams does not explain exactly what he is supposing in supposing the amoralist to have a 'minimal concern for others', nor does he elaborate on the fault which is exhibited when he shows this concern 'only intermittently and capriciously'. Rather, he simply asserts that some such concern for others is a promising starting point and then goes on to suggest that if we could extend that concern to 'less immediate persons who need help, we might be able to do it for less immediate persons whose interests have been violated and so get him [the amoralist] to have some primitive grasp on notions of fairness' (Williams 1972: 25–6).

Although I am sympathetic to Williams's general strategy, I nevertheless feel that the argument he presents is far too quick, and too ambiguous, to do the work required of it. There are two specific areas in which it stands in need of refinement, both of which are important to the overall aim of establishing whether partial concerns can indeed get morality off the ground. The first, and most obvious, problem lies in Williams's silence about what exactly is involved in 'caring for what happens to somebody else'; the second, and connected, problem springs from an ambiguity in his appeal to capriciousness. To anticipate slightly, my reservations are that, on the first point, Williams does not say enough about care or concern to enable us to see how it can get morality off the ground, and indeed that under some interpretations it is unable to deliver on that promise. On the second point, my reservation is that his references to capriciousness are ambiguous in a way that threatens to undermine his argument. However, these claims stand in need of justification, so I shall now be more specific about them. I will begin with the ambiguity in the concept of capriciousness and then use the considerations adduced there to raise more general questions about how care must be understood if, as I believe, it is to be capable of 'getting morality off the ground'.

Agency and Capriciousness

Williams argues that the problem with the amoralist is that, while he has the concern for others which is a precondition of being moral, he applies this concern only intermittently and capriciously. And he goes on to speak in terms which imply that 'capriciousness' here refers to the amoralist's unwillingness (or inability) to extend his concern to less immediate people. He simply happens to love his mother, his child, or his mistress and, for that reason, is responsive to their needs, but (as it turns out) he does not love anyone else and therefore their needs and interests are of no consequence to him. This man, we might say, is capricious in the objects of his care or concern.

Now this certainly is one form of capriciousness, but it is not the only form, for we can also imagine a man who is only intermittently disposed to help even his mother, his child and his mistress depending, let's say, on whether he happens, at that particular moment, to feel sympathetic towards them. So he is not capricious simply in the sense that his care extends to a very restricted range of people; he is also capricious in his behaviour towards those people. Does this man have enough for morality? There are two reasons for doubting whether he does: one is external to my overall project, and the other internal to it.

The external reason is that this sort of capriciousness in one's dealings with others raises doubts about whether one is an agent at all and not simply (to use Harry Frankfurt's term) a 'wanton' (Frankfurt 1988: 11–25). The internal reason is that my overall project is to explain the relationship between impartial justice and conceptions of the good, where conceptions of the good are things to which people are committed, if not across their entire life, then certainly across significant portions of it. A conception of the good is not simply a fleeting preference on which one may or may not act depending on one's feelings at the time, but is normally something which organizes and shapes one's life over an extended period, and the important contrast in political philosophy is therefore between impartial justice and a conception of the good understood as reliable, regular, and of persistent importance to the agent. It is certainly not just a momentary whim. However, since that is the important contrast, the amoralist, understood as devoid of persistent objects of care, is irrelevant.

Moreover, and independent of that internal consideration, there are reasons for doubting whether the person who is capricious in this sense has enough even for agency, much less for entry into morality. These reasons are provided by Frankfurt in a series of influential articles which centre around questions of agency and morality, and in which Frankfurt also makes intriguing and controversial claims about the relationship between morality and what we care about. It is therefore worth spending some time explaining his position in an attempt to see whether it can illuminate the central question of this chapter: can caring about things get morality off the ground?

In 'Freedom of the Will and the Concept of a Person' Frankfurt argues that one essential difference between persons and other creatures is that persons alone are able to form 'second-order desires'. In addition to having desires and preferences, they are, he says, 'capable of wanting to be different in their preferences and purposes... No animal other than man appears to have the capacity for reflective self-evaluation that is manifested in the form of second-order desires' (Frankfurt 1988: 12). And he goes on to elaborate on this point by drawing a distinction between, on the one hand, simply having a second-order desire and, on the other, wanting that desire to be, or to inform, one's will. The latter he refers to as a second-order volition and concludes that 'it is having second-order volitions, and not having second-order desires generally that I regard as essential to being a person' (1988: 16). The reason for this, according to Frankfurt, is that it is possible for someone, while having second-order desires, to be unconcerned about whether he is moved by those desires. Such a man Frankfurt refers to as a 'wanton' and he concludes that 'what distinguishes a rational wanton from other rational agents is that he is not concerned with the desirability of his desires themselves. He ignores the question of what his will is to be. Not only does he pursue whatever course of action he is most strongly inclined to pursue, but he does not care which of his inclinations is the strongest' (1988: 17). To be a person, then, rather than a mere wanton, is to have second-order volitions, and what that implies is a concern that some of one's second-order desires, and not others, inform one's will. To be a person is to be interested in which of one's desires 'win out'.

Reading this back onto the case of the amoralist, it seems that if he is understood as capricious in the sense that he acts for his mother, his child, or his mistress when, and only when, he is more strongly inclined to do this than to do anything else, then he is merely 'wanton'. To be someone with whom we can get morality off the ground, he must be understood as reflective about his desires in the way described. So, not only must he want to help his mother or his child; he must also want his will to be informed by that desire. Frankfurt illustrates this distinction between a person and a mere wanton via a contrast between the wanton addict and the unwilling addict. He writes:

The wanton addict cannot or does not care which of his conflicting first-order desires wins out. His lack of concern is not due to his inability to find a convincing basis for preference. It is due either to his lack of the capacity for reflection or to his mindless indifference to the enterprise of evaluating his own desires and motives. There is only one issue in the struggle to which his first-order conflict may lead: whether the one or the other of his conflicting desires is stronger. Since he is moved by both desires, he will not be altogether satisfied by what he does no matter which of them is effective. But it makes no difference *to him* whether his craving or aversion gets the upper hand. He has no stake in the conflict between them and so, unlike the unwilling addict, he can neither win nor lose the struggle in which he is engaged. When a *person* acts, the desire by which he is moved is either the will he wants or a will he wants to be without. When a *wanton* acts, it is neither. (Frankfurt 1988: 18–19)

So, if the amoralist is capricious in the sense that he has no stake in which of his desires wins out, then he does not have enough for agency and therefore, we must infer, he cannot have enough for moral agency. To be a person, I must be concerned about what *I* do, where that is something more than observing which of my desires turns out to be strongest.

Moreover, and reading this point back onto the argument of the previous chapter, we can see that the propensity to be directly motivated by those whom we care about is not, in itself, a sufficient condition for personhood (in Frankfurt's somewhat technical sense of that word). Direct motivation is, I have argued, a significant feature of friendship or love, and one which can in part explain why the normative problem is indeed a problem for those who feel the force of the requirements of impartiality, but it is not the answer to our present question: 'what conditions must be satisfied if someone is to be capable of feeling the force of moral requirements in the first place?'

It is perhaps considerations of this sort which lead Williams to conclude that in order to be capable of morality the amoralist must help others *in their need*: 'the thought he [the amoralist] has when he likes someone and acts in this way is "they need help", not the thought "I like them and they need help"' (Williams 1972: 25). In saying this Williams is indeed implying that if the amoralist is to be capable of entry into morality, he must not simply react to the needs of those whom he happens, at that moment, to like or to feel sympathy for. Rather, he must endorse his first-order desires and attempt to incorporate them into his will. He must, in other words, form second-order volitions. So this proviso 'thickens' the concept of care and makes it something more than the brute tendency to be directly motivated by others or to feel sympathy for them. Minimal concern now implies both a recognition of others' needs and a concern to be the sort of person who acts from the recognition of those needs.

The crucial point therefore is that if concern for others is to be capable of getting morality off the ground it must be understood as something more than the propensity to be directly motivated by another. Certainly it cannot be capricious in a sense which implies that the agent simply acts on whichever desire is stronger at the moment, for that form of capriciousness is incompatible even with agency. But how much more is needed? In particular, is Frankfurt's requirement of reflective endorsement (the requirement that the agent be concerned about which of his desires shall inform his will) either necessary or sufficient to facilitate the move from caring about things to distinctively moral considerations?

Reflective Endorsement and Morality

Frankfurt's claim is that to be a person is to be concerned about the desirability of one's desires, and he is clear that what this implies is being concerned about the kind of person one is. In the long passage quoted above he explicitly links having second-order volitions with self-evaluation and defines a person (as distinct from a wanton) as someone who 'identifies' with certain desires: 'when a person acts, the desire by which he is moved is either the will he wants or a will he wants to be without. When a wanton acts, it is neither', and he is emphatic that what distinguishes a person from a mere wanton is that the former 'has a stake' in which desire wins out: there is something which *he* wants and which transcends the specific desires of any given moment, or moments.

However, Frankfurt goes on to deny that second-order volitions need manifest a distinctively moral stance: 'it may not be from the point of view of morality that the person evaluates his first-order desires' (Frankfurt 1988: 19 n.), and he repeatedly expresses discontent with the 'pan-moralistic' approach that many modern philosophers take to questions of practical reason, arguing that 'philosophers need to pay more attention to . . . issues that have to do with what people are to care about, with their commitments to ideals, and the protean role in our lives of the various modes of love . . . than the problems concerning obligation and virtue that compose most of the standard repertoire of contemporary moral philosophy' (Frankfurt 1999: x). For Frankfurt, then, to be a person is to be concerned about the desirability of one's desires, but this does not necessarily mean that one is concerned to have *morally* better desires. What it means is that one is concerned to act on desires which express the will one wishes to have, and which are, in that sense, 'authentic', or genuinely one's own. It is to be concerned about who one is, and that concern is distinct from a concern to be responsive to the requirements of morality, or to meet one's moral obligations.

This consideration returns us to Williams's insistence that the thought which is needed in order to get morality off the ground with the amoralist is the thought 'they need help', not the thought 'I like them and they need help'. If caring is to get morality off the ground, then it must, Williams claims, be 'other-directed'. Frankfurt, however, insists that caring is self-directed in the sense that it is essentially a matter of who we ourselves are. Of course it is true that, in caring about someone, it is *the other person* I care about. But, for Frankfurt, caring is essentially a matter of asserting who I am, not a matter of responding to others' needs. So when Williams argues that caring provides a route into morality, he is referring to caring *about others*. By contrast, when Frankfurt discusses the importance of what we care about, he is taking caring to be essentially a matter of who we ourselves are, and of what matters to us, where the things that matter to us may or may not be the needs and interests of others, and even where they are the needs and interests of others, our caring about them is separate and distinct from any moral consideration. Put bluntly, where Williams takes caring about others to be an embryonic form of moral concern, Frankfurt takes caring about others to be a statement of who we are.

These different understandings of what is implied by caring about things are further complicated if we turn to the work of Charles Taylor. In his book, *Sources of the Self*, as well as in earlier articles, Taylor agrees with Frankfurt that second-order volition is a condition of personhood, but he then goes on to associate second-order volition with what is, if not strictly moral, then at least in some general sense, ethical. Thus, in 'What is Human Agency?' he begins by allying himself with Frankfurt's general claim about the conditions of personhood. He writes 'I agree with Frankfurt that this capacity to evaluate desires is bound up with our power of self-evaluation, which in turn is an essential feature of the mode of agency we recognize as human' (Taylor 1985: 16). However, he then suggests an alternative analysis of what that mode of agency is—an analysis which is couched in terms of 'strong evaluation', where strong evaluation is a matter of judging ethically in the very general sense that it involves judgements of what is higher or lower, noble, or base. For Taylor, the concepts in terms of which we evaluate strongly are 'articulations' of the intrinsic value of things which are external to us and towards which our desires and feelings implicitly direct us. So it is not simply the case that strong evaluations serve as statements of who I am or of what I wish my will to be. They are also articulations of what I believe to be valuable and how I 'orient' myself towards what is valuable.

There is, it must be said, some equivocation in Taylor's account. Concluding his discussion in 'What is Human Agency?' he writes: 'the question at issue concerns which is the truer, more authentic, more illusion-free interpretation, and which on the other hand involves a distortion of the meanings things have *for me*' (Taylor 1985: 27, emphasis added). Here, the emphasis appears to be on what has meaning for or what matters *to the agent* but, in reading this passage, it is important to be clear that, for Taylor, the meaning things have for me is partly given by the tradition within which I find myself. It is not, as for Frankfurt, a matter of stating what I myself find important or valuable (see Taylor 1989). Thus, Taylor's account is conspicuously cognitivist, for he construes agency and strong evaluation as less a matter of authenticity or of 'getting in touch with our true feelings', and more a matter of recognizing what is genuinely right, or valuable, or noble. This point is made explicit in 'Self-Interpreting Animals' where he writes 'the tenor of this [strong] evaluation is perhaps something like this: that spite, revenge, returning evil for evil, is something we are prone to, but that there is a higher way of seeing our relations with others; which is higher not just in producing happier consequences—less strife, pain, bad blood—but also in that it enables us to see ourselves and others *more broadly, more objectively, more truly*. One is a bigger person, with a broader, more serene vision, when one can act out of this higher standpoint' (Taylor 1985: 67, emphasis added).

Crudely put, then, Taylor sees agency as linked to the capacity for strong evaluation, and strong evaluation points us in the direction of what is (or is believed to be) truly nobler or higher. Frankfurt, by contrast, sees agency as linked to the capacity to identify with certain things wholeheartedly, or to care about things, where the things we care about are not necessarily valuable (or even believed to be valuable) in themselves, but rather attain importance for us in virtue of the fact that we care about them. So although both views insist on the importance of second-order evaluation for agency, they are divided in their understandings of what such evaluation implies. Taylor sees it in terms which are broadly cognitive (it involves directing ourselves to what is nobler or truer); Frankfurt understands it as a statement of who we are and what we stand for, and he resists the suggestion that what I stand for is to be linked to claims about what is superior in evaluative terms, much less in moral terms.

The significance of these differences, from my point of view, lies in their different implications for the possibility of showing whether caring about things can indeed get morality off the ground. By emphasizing the connection between caring and self-evaluation, and by insisting that what we care about is a matter of what we find important, not a matter of what we believe to be valuable, Frankfurt's analysis appears to foreclose on the possibility of finding a route from caring to morality. Indeed, it is an important part of his argument that discussions of practical reason pay too much attention to what morality requires, and not enough attention to the things people care about. In saying this he implies that there are distinct areas of enquiry (morality, on the one hand, and what we care about, on the other), and that there is no necessary connection between the two—no clear route from the one to the other. However, while I concur with his general suspicion of 'pan-moralism' in discussions of practical reason, I also believe that we cannot divorce caring from morality in quite the clear way Frankfurt does.

In the next section, therefore, I shall identify some of the difficulties with his account—difficulties which suggest that, despite appearances to the contrary, caring about things does have a distinctively evaluative dimension and one which can facilitate a move into morality. Moreover, I shall argue that it is Frankfurt's own concept of caring which itself facilitates this move. So my strategy will be first to outline and endorse the understanding of care which is found in Frankfurt, and second to show that, so understood, caring about things can in fact serve to get morality off the ground. Before doing that, however, it might be worth recapping on the considerations which have been adduced so far.

My central question in this chapter is: 'can caring about things get morality off the ground?', and in order to answer this question I need to consider what is involved in caring about things. Taking my cue from Bernard Williams, I began by considering whether the amoralist, understood as a man who cares about some people, albeit capriciously and intermittently, has enough for entry to morality. Here I suggested that he would not have enough if he were thought to be capricious in the sense that he acted simply on whatever desire happened to weigh most strongly with him at the time. Both agency and morality demand more than that. But how much more?

Williams argues that caring about others involves responding to them *in their need*, and that this other-directedness, even if restricted to specific individuals, can nevertheless be extended to provide a route into the moral world. It gives us everything we need for entry into morality. Frankfurt, by contrast, argues that caring is not centrally a matter of being other-directed, but is rather a matter of self-evaluation. It involves discovering what matters *to us*, and although the needs of specific others may matter to us, the fact that they matter is distinct from morality, for morality is essentially a matter of our relationships with others, while caring is a matter of our relationship with ourselves. The two areas of enquiry are therefore distinct, and potentially in conflict.

Taylor concurs with Frankfurt's claim that caring about things is a matter of their importance to us, but he argues that what is important to us just is to be guided by what is truer, higher or nobler. Caring about things implies evaluation, but the evaluation is not simply self-evaluation. It is evaluation of a distinctively ethical kind, for we are, in Taylor's view, essentially strong evaluators. We search for something beyond, or above ourselves by reference to which we can make sense of our lives (Taylor 1985: 33; 1989: 27). The point at issue, therefore, seems to be whether the self-evaluation which is implicit in caring about things is also ethical or moral evaluation. In coming to care about some things, or some people, rather than others, do we also stand on the threshold of morality, or do we simply state who we are?

Let us agree that if we are to get morality off the ground with the amoralist, then we must think of him as someone who has a concern for others which is more than simply capricious in the sense described. He must not respond to the needs of his mother or his child simply because his desire to help them is, at that moment, stronger than any other desire he has. Rather, he must endorse the desire to help them in the sense of wishing that desire to inform his will. Is it the case that, when he does this, he is also orienting himself towards what he believes to be good? In other words, is it also the case that he is entertaining a distinctively, if embryonically, moral thought? *Pace* Frankfurt, I believe that he is, but I also believe that the route from caring to morality is rather less direct than the one which either Williams or Taylor imply. In the next section therefore I shall explain and largely endorse Frankfurt's concept of care before going on to show how that very concept might provide us with a route into morality.

However, one *caveat* is in order first of all. This is that it is no part of my aim to show that caring necessitates morality. For reasons which I hope will become clear both in this chapter and the next, I do not believe that the objects of our care can be restricted in such a way as to force the move to morality, much less to impartial morality. Rather, my claim is simply that if we are to get morality off the ground, we must make reference to what people care about, but clearly it does not follow from this that if we do make reference to what people care about we always will get morality off the ground.

The Concept of Care

In 'The Importance of What We Care About' Frankfurt identifies three significant features of caring about things. First, he notes that caring about things is distinct from merely desiring them, both because caring implies persistence, and (connectedly) because, in caring about things, I guide or direct myself with reference to them. He writes:

it is possible to desire something for only a moment. Desires and beliefs have no inherent persistence; nothing in the nature of wanting or of believing requires that a desire or belief must endure. But the notion of guidance, and hence the notion of caring, implies a certain consistency of behaviour; and this presupposes some degree of persistence. A person who cared about something for just a moment would be indistinguishable from someone who was being moved by impulse. He would not in any proper sense be guiding or directing himself at all. (Frankfurt 1988: 84)

Second, he argues that, although caring about things is a matter of being guided by them, it is not thereby a matter of thinking them valuable: 'to care about something differs not only from wanting it or from preferring it but also from judging it to be valuable' (Frankfurt 1999: 158). He notes that people may care about things which are not at all valuable (such as not stepping on the cracks in the paving stones) and they may also fail to care about things which are valuable: 'Each of us can surely identify a considerable number of things that we think would be worth doing or worth having for their own sakes, but to which we ourselves are not especially drawn and at which we quite reasonably prefer not to aim' (Frankfurt 1999: 106, 158; 1988: 83). More generally, he insists that caring about things is 'a personal matter', and since it is distinct from judgements of value in general, we can infer that it is distinct from judgements of moral value. Indeed, he states categorically that 'the question concerning what is most important is distinguishable from the question what is morally right' (Frankfurt 1988: 82).

Third, caring about things is not (normally) a matter of making a decision and although someone might, by making a decision, effectively bring it about that he cares about something, it 'certainly cannot be assumed that what a person cares about is generally under his immediate voluntary control' (Frankfurt 1988: 85). So, when I care about something I see it as important to me, and I am guided or directed by it over a more or less extended period. However, its importance is not a function of its antecedent value (real or imagined), for I can readily concede that some things are valuable, while not caring about them at all.

The upshot of Frankfurt's remarks here is to draw a sharp distinction between morality and what we care about, and indeed he identifies two distinct areas of enquiry: 'Ethics', he says, 'focuses on the problem of ordering our relations with *other people*. It is concerned especially with the contrast between *right* and *wrong*, and with the grounds and limits of *moral obligation*.' By contrast, what we care about is a matter of 'what to do with *ourselves*, and we therefore need to understand what is *important* or, rather, what is *important to us*' (Frankfurt 1988: 80–1). So, from the observation that people can care about all sorts of things, and that their caring about them is not based on antecedent judgements of value, Frankfurt draws the conclusions that caring is personal, that it is a matter of our relationship with ourselves and that, as such, it is distinct from morality, which does involve value judgements, and is a matter what we owe to others.

It should be clear from the above account that, for Frankfurt, a great deal hangs on the fact (and it is indeed a fact) that people can care about more or less anything, and that when they do care, that is not normally on the basis of an antecedent judgement of its value. I love my husband and care about him very much, but I do not believe him to be objectively more valuable than anyone else nor indeed do I love him *because* I deem him to be more valuable than anyone else. Conversely, there are lots of people who are very valuable but about whom I don't care in the least. Caring is, in Frankfurt's words, 'a personal matter'. Or is it? While I accept his general account of what is involved in caring (I concur with the three claims made above), I also believe that it is an account which provides us with the material needed to get morality off the ground. We can, I think, acknowledge that people can care about all kinds of things, and that their caring about those things is not based on antecedent judgements of worth, while at the same time denying that care is a personal matter in the sense of being distinct from questions of evaluation or forming an area of enquiry separate from morality. On the contrary, it seems to me that these sorts of considerations are exactly the ones which can help to get morality off the ground and in the next section I shall try to explain why that is so.

Caring, Criticism, and Evaluation

How, then, can Frankfurt's own understanding of what it is to care about things enable us to 'get morality off the ground'? How can it reveal, or imply, a connection between the kind of self-evaluation which is involved in caring, and evaluation of a more generally ethical or moral kind? I shall proceed in two stages: first, I shall try to show why care cannot be simply 'a personal matter', but must have a critical dimension. Second, I shall try to show how that critical dimension is most naturally understood as a moral one.

As we have seen, Frankfurt is anxious to emphasize that caring about something is a personal matter and that, as such, it is distinct from judgements of what is valuable. We can acknowledge that certain things are valuable without caring about them in the least, and when we do care about things it is not on the basis of an antecedent assessment of their value. This seems right, but it does not follow that caring about things is a personal matter in the sense that there can be no criticism of what we in fact care about. Nor, therefore, does it follow that there is no link between caring about things and evaluative judgements. To bring the point into sharper focus, let us agree that I can deem things to be valuable without caring about them in the least. Does the converse also hold? Is it possible to deem things to be worthless but nonetheless to care about them a great deal? Of course, we know that people do care about things that are worthless, and Frankfurt himself cites the case of the man who cares very much about not stepping on the cracks in the paving stones. But what is to be said to and about this man? In particular, can we say that he is mistaken in caring so much about what is essentially trivial? Here is Frankfurt's judgement on such a person:

No doubt he is committing an error of some kind in caring about this. But his error is not that he cares about something which is not really important to him. Rather, his error consists in caring about, and thereby imbuing with genuine importance, something which is not worth caring about. The reason it is not worth caring about seems clear: it is not important to the person to make avoiding the cracks in the sidewalk important to himself. But we need to understand better than we do just why this is so—ie what conditions must be satisfied if it is to be important to us to make something important to us which would not otherwise have had such importance. (Frankfurt 1988: 93–4)

This seems (to me at least) to be a very tortuous way of avoiding saying the most natural thing—which is that the man has indeed made a mistake: he has made something important to him when it does not merit being accorded that importance. Frankfurt, however, is highly resistant to saying this. He allows that the person cares about something which is not worth caring about, but resists the conclusion that it is not worth caring about because it is (in some objective sense) worthless. Given that one of Frankfurt's main claims is that caring about things is distinct from judging them to be valuable, it is not surprising that he resists this more objectivist explanation and instead argues in terms of the importance *to the agent* of avoiding the cracks in the sidewalk. Here, however, explanation runs out and there is (apparently) no further account of what conditions can legitimize making something important to us. This, says Frankfurt, is simply something that 'we need to understand better than we do'.

Rather than attempting to follow Frankfurt along this tortuous path, I shall instead mount a case in favour of saying the obvious thing—namely that here is a man who cares about something which is not worth caring about, and the reason it is not worth caring about is because it is indeed worthless or trivial. It must be said that many philosophers are resistant to making this move, and one obvious source of their resistance lies in the fact that we can indeed care about more or less anything, and our caring is not the result of a prior assessment of objective value or worth. In the familiar words of the poem, we love people 'for themselves alone and not their yellow hair'. And we also want others to love us for ourselves alone and not our yellow hair. Additionally, there is something suspicious about being either able or willing to give a set of reasons which justify the fact that one cares for a certain person, since to do so implies that one would care for anyone else who came along and happened to satisfy those same descriptions. Moreover, impartialist moral theorists have gone to considerable lengths to deny that their theory commits them to insisting either that we must love everyone equally, or that we must justify our loves by reference to objective standards of value. Indeed, the absurdity of thoroughgoing Godwinian impartialism lay precisely in its insistence that in the 'famous fire cause' I ought to save Fenelon because his life is more valuable. In saving my mother, my friend or my child, I do not need to deny that, by objective standards, Fenelon is more valuable. I do, however, deny that he is more important *to me*, and it is Godwin's neglect of that fact which (in part) generates his unacceptable conclusion. There is, then, considerable psychological plausibility in Frankfurt's claim that in caring about something or someone we do not do so on the basis of an antecedent assessment of its value, and any insistence that we ought to care on that basis risks Godwinian absurdity.

Connectedly, the attempt to invoke a critical dimension to care can threaten to become unacceptably 'high brow'. In one of his now famous examples, Bernard Williams tells of an imaginary Gauguin who resolves to leave his wife and children in order to devote himself to art (Williams 1981: 20–39). Williams argues that, if this Gauguin succeeds and becomes a great artist, his decision to abandon his family will be vindicated, and we must suppose that it will be vindicated because the artistic endeavour is one which is objectively worthwhile. This, certainly, is what is implied by Williams's reflection that 'we have deep and persistent reasons to be grateful' that not everyone affirms morality (Williams 1981: 23): great art is important and may (though it need not) warrant neglect of one's family. What, however, would be our verdict on someone who deserted his wife and children in order to become world onion-growing champion? What of someone who devotes his life to drawing every possible combination of colours on the Rubik cube? Or collecting all the numbers of the trains which travel the East Coast Line? Here, it is much less tempting (for me, anyway) to see such enterprises as justifying the desertion of one's spouse and children, but to say this is to imply a distinctively 'high brow' approach to the problem—one which takes the intellectual or the artistic endeavour as objectively valuable, but rejects less cerebral (or perhaps less middle-class) pursuits.

The general problem here is that if we insist (as I wish to) that there are things which are unworthy of care, then we seem duty bound to say what those things are, and why they are unworthy of care. However, in giving those reasons we must be wary of doing no more than parading our own prejudices and then claiming for them the *imprimatur* of objectivity. To put the point provocatively, middle-aged, middle-class academics will be inclined to see the creation of great art as (at least arguably) worth moral sacrifice, but maybe that just tells us what middle-aged, middle-class academics care about. As it stands, it certainly does not tell us what is worth caring about, much less does it tell us that there are some things which are objectively trivial and therefore not worth caring about. These considerations therefore tell in favour of Frankfurt's distinction between what we care about and what is valuable. We can admit that something is valuable while not ourselves caring about it at all, and we also have difficulty in justifying claims about what is valuable in a way that transcends the mere display of our own prejudices.

However, while there is indeed a difficulty inherent in finding (or even looking for) a critical dimension to care, there is also a very considerable need for it. Frankfurt himself says that 'the fact that what a person cares about is a personal matter does not entail that anything goes. It may still be possible to distinguish between things that are worth caring about to one degree or another and things that are not. Accordingly, it may be useful to inquire into what makes something worth caring about—that is, what conditions must be satisfied if something is to be suitable or worthy as an ideal or as an object of love' (Frankfurt 1988: 91). But if his earlier remarks are correct, then it is unclear on what basis we could decide that something is worth caring about—worth making important to us. If, as Frankfurt believes, caring is a matter of being guided by certain things, or investing oneself in them; if, moreover, their importance is an importance *to us* which follows from the fact that we care about them and is not antecedent to and independent of it, then it is very unclear what grounds there could be for thinking that some things are *worth* caring about. And in the end, Frankfurt does seem to admit the futility of the enterprise when he notes that all we can do is 'find what we *can* care about'. The objects of our care are not grounded in antecedent assessments of value, nor are they defensible in such terms.

In a discussion of Frankfurt's theory, Annette Baier focuses on this conclusion and identifies what I take to be a significant difficulty with it. She writes:

Frankfurt in the end suggests that all we can do is find what we *can* care about, and usually there will not be enough of such things to present us with incompatible possibilities. But isn't this too easy? Some people can care about their collection of babies' booties or women's gloves, or other such pathetic substitutes. They *can* do this, and such a care may conflict with no other possibility they see... Frankfurt's counsel to love what one can love may be all right for us the middle-aged and soured, but it is not very good advice for the young. Nor do we find it any more satisfactory if we turn from persons to care about to causes to care about. We are not content to say to Hitler, to Sadat's assassins, to fanatical Jewish groups, 'Care about what you find you can care about.' We must, somehow, be more discriminating. (Baier 1982: 96–7)

Baier's analysis of the problem identifies a very significant difficulty in the injunction to 'find what you *can* care about', for while, on a personal level, placing restrictions on what is worthy of care may appear unacceptably elitist or 'high brow', when we turn from people to causes (from, as it were, the personal to the political) it is difficult to remain phlegmatic about the adequacy of simply noting the huge variety of things which people do in fact care about. Moreover, the point has important implications for my project. Baier notes the difficulties inherent in the move from 'people to causes' and it is clear that she has in mind here the more sinister political implications of indifference in the face of those who care very deeply about ethnic purity, or about the promotion of the true religion. This is, obviously, an important consideration, but its wider implication is that care must have a critical dimension, and if it must have such a dimension at the political level, it is hard to see why it must not also have one at the level of the personal. In what follows I shall argue that care does indeed have a critical dimension both in the case of our own lives and, more obviously, in the case of ideals and causes of a more political nature.

This dimension can be discerned and defended if we distinguish between two possibilities: the possibility of caring about things which are unworthy of care, and the possibility of caring about things *while acknowledging* that they are unworthy of care. Frankfurt insists that, in caring about things, we are guided or directed by them, but we do not decide, on the basis of judgements of their value, that we will be so guided. Indeed, it seems that we do not decide this on any basis at all. We simply *find* that we care about some things. However, consequences follow from the discovery, for he goes on to note that:

a person who cares about something is, as it were, invested in it. He *identifies* himself with what he cares about in the sense that he makes himself vulnerable to losses and susceptible to benefits depending on whether what he cares about is diminished or enhanced. Thus, he concerns himself with what concerns it, giving particular attention to such things and directing his behaviour accordingly. Insofar as a person's life is in whole or in part *devoted* to anything, rather than being merely a sequence of events whose themes and structures he makes no effort to fashion, it is devoted to this. (Frankfurt 1988: 83, emphasis original).

This passage is interesting because it draws our attention to the fact that caring about things makes us, in Frankfurt's words, 'vulnerable to loss'. But what kind of loss is involved in caring about things, and can the appeal to loss be made consistent with the sharp distinction between caring and evaluation? My hunch is that it cannot and that if we consider the precise ways in which caring about things can make us vulnerable to loss, then we will see that caring implies evaluation. It is indeed true that we can care about (almost) anything, and it is also true that we do not care about things because we believe them to be objectively more valuable than anything else. But what is also true is that the vulnerability to loss which is a concomitant of caring about things is also, and characteristically, a vulnerability to ethical or moral loss. So from the fact that caring is a personal matter in the way described by Frankfurt, it does not follow and it is not true that what we care about is utterly distinct from morality, nor that the things we care about have a distinct source from morality. In the next section, I shall attempt to defend the claim that in caring about things we become vulnerable to a form of loss which is importantly and distinctively moral. Before doing that, however, it is worth pausing to recap on what the aims of this chapter are, and on what has been argued so far.

The central aim of this chapter is to show whether and how partial concerns may enable us to 'get morality off the ground'. By contrast with the previous chapter, which *assumed* a commitment to impartial morality and then attempted to explain the dilemmas faced by those who have the commitment, this chapter aims to explain how such a commitment might arise in the first place. It aims to explain the role played by partial concerns in the genesis of a commitment to impartial morality. In attempting to achieve this aim, I accept the general understanding of care proposed by Frankfurt. That is to say, I accept that people may care about a vast variety of things, and I also accept that, in caring about those things, they do not do so on the basis of antecedent value judgements. In these senses, caring is indeed a personal matter. Nonetheless, value judgements are an unavoidable concomitant of caring about things, and it is this fact which renders them more than simply personal and which is implicit in the recognition that caring about things (including people) can make us 'vulnerable to loss'. When we care, we are vulnerable, and our vulnerability is moral vulnerability. It arises most conspicuously in cases where we realize that we have invested ourselves in things that are objectively unworthy of our care. In the next section, therefore, I shall consider two cases in which someone cares about what is unworthy of care. The first is the case of Titania in Shakespeare's play *A Midsummer Night's Dream;* the second is the case of Isabel Archer in Henry James's novel, *The Portrait of a Lady*. My aim is to deploy these examples in such a way as to show how the things we care about can also be the things that get morality off the ground.

Care and Vulnerability

In Act II of *A Midsummer Night's Dream* Oberon and Titania quarrel over the ownership of a 'changeling boy'. When Titania yet again refuses to hand the boy over, Oberon resolves to punish her by making her fall in love with 'some vile thing'. Bewitched by the juice of love-in-idleness, she falls in love with Bottom, a 'rude mechanical', who is wearing an ass's head and, consumed by love, she greets him with the words:

> I pray thee gentle mortal, sing again,
> Mine ear is much enamour'd of thy note;
> So is mine eye enthralled to thy shape,
> And thy fair virtue's force (perforce) doth move me,
> On the first view to say, to swear, I love thee. (III.i)

The comic potential of the scene arises partly from the incongruity between Titania, the Queen of the Fairies, and the object of her love, Bottom, a 'rude mechanical' thinly disguised as an ass. However, there is not merely incongruity, but also bathos here, for what we (the audience) know is that Titania is in love with something coarse and ugly—something which is unworthy of her love. The poetic language in which she serenades Bottom stands in stark contrast to his own rough speech, and forces even him to conclude that 'reason and love keep little company together now-a-days'. Herein lies the bathos, for it is true (as Frankfurt insists) that we can care about, and indeed love, more or less anything, but what is also true is that there are things which are unworthy of our love despite the fact that, in love, we cannot see them to be so. So, when Oberon sees Titania serenading Bottom, he does not rejoice that she has finally found what she can care about. On the contrary, he 'pities' her 'in her dotage', and (almost) regrets the act of mischief which led him to apply the magic potion to her eyes. If we genuinely believe that all we can do is find what we *can* care about, then comedy of this kind is unavailable to us, since it depends crucially on there being things which are unworthy of our care even though we ourselves are not able to see that they are unworthy. Indeed, the comedy springs precisely from the fact that we are not able to see them as unworthy.

Moreover, the scene also shows that even though we can love what is unworthy of our love, we will nonetheless perceive the object of our love as valuable. We will invest it with values which it may well not have. Titania refers to Bottom as 'a gentleman'—even 'an angel'. 'Thou art' she says 'as wise as thou art beautiful', thus ascribing to him qualities which he conspicuously lacks. Again, the appropriate response here is not to note that all we can do is find what we can care about, for the whole force of the scene depends upon the fact that Titania has indeed, 'found what she can care about', and in so doing she makes erroneous evaluative judgements which, in their turn, serve to make her ludicrous and pitiable.

The plight of Titania in *A Midsummer Night's Dream* therefore draws our attention to the following significant facts: first, that our very ability to love or care about (almost) anything itself highlights the fact that there is a critical dimension to care. Throughout the play, mortals are presented as irredeemably 'foolish', and what makes us foolish is precisely that we can and do love (almost) anything. In Titania, this condition is a temporary one, and its catalyst is a magic potion—the juice of love-in-idleness. However, such foolishness is the natural condition for mortals, who require magic if they are to escape it. So the ability to invest almost anything with importance is not what vindicates. It is what condemns. The second point is that, if care has no critical dimension, concepts such as bathos are unavailable to the playwright, and therefore to us. It is only by seeing that Titania is indeed in love with someone who is objectively unworthy of her love that we can appreciate the dramatic force of the scene. Finally, the scene suggests that, even though we do not care about things on the basis of antecedent judgements of their value, nonetheless when once we do care about them, we also evaluate them, and our evaluations may be mistaken.

A Midsummer Night's Dream, then, highlights the fact that, without a critical dimension to care, certain kinds of comedy and bathos are not possible. By contrast, my second example—Henry James's *The Portrait of a Lady* (James 1991)—highlights the fact that, without a critical dimension to care, certain kinds of tragedy are not possible. It also enables us to see exactly why the distinction between morality and what we care about is too sharply drawn by Frankfurt. His insistence that we must simply 'find what we *can* care about' is inadequate in itself and also stands in tension with the claim that, in caring about things, we become vulnerable to loss. For the latter, I believe, implies what the former denies, namely that there is an evaluative dimension to care, and the case of Isabel Archer shows us both how badly things can go wrong if we follow Frankfurt's advice and attempt to find what we can care about, and also what kind of loss we are vulnerable to when we do care about things.

Isabel Archer, the heroine of *The Portrait of a Lady*, serves as a model of what it would be to take Frankfurt's advice and 'find what we can care about'. Moreover, and crucially, it provides an example of what would be involved in attempting to find what we can care about independent of evaluation. Frankfurt insists that, when we care, we do not do so on the basis of any antecedent value judgement. Thus, my care for my husband is not to be traced to the fact that I have assessed his value and found him to be worthy of my care, and this suggests (to Frankfurt) that what we care about is distinct from what is valuable. But what would be the position of someone who attempted to find what they could care about without recourse to any evaluative considerations? What exactly is Frankfurt telling us to do when he suggests that we find what we can care about?

The case of Isabel Archer is instructive here, for she is someone who sets out to do exactly that. As described by James, she is young and beautiful, and soon she will be rich. She is also 'full of ideas', but her upbringing has been such as to leave her with 'no guidance, no interlocutors...no help weighing and distinguishing what is important to know from what isn't' (as quoted in Pippin 2000: 130). She resolves, therefore, to 'affront her destiny': without any antecedent idea of what is worthwhile and what is worthless, she embarks on life, and her project is to find what she can care about. Isabel, we are told, 'drifts', and when asked whether she knows where she is drifting, she replies defiantly: 'No, I haven't the least idea, and I find it very pleasant not to know. A swift carriage, of a dark night, rattling with four horses over roads that one can't see—that's my idea of happiness' (as quoted in Pippin 2000: 133–4). Famously, her project ends in disaster, and it does so partly because it is a project undertaken without reference to antecedent judgements of value.

As an act of independence, even of defiance, Isabel refuses the 'good marriage' offered by Lord Warburton and instead marries Gilbert Osmond, believing him to be, like herself, a free spirit, untrammelled by convention and contemptuous of the mores of society. However, and as the novel progresses, it becomes abundantly clear that, far from being above the values of society, Osmond is in fact completely in their thrall. He has married Isabel, not because she is clever and intelligent and free-thinking, but because she is rich: 'she found herself confronted...with the conviction that the man in the world whom she had supposed to be the least sordid had married her, like a vulgar adventurer, for her money'. And in so doing, he displays, not his disregard for the values of society, but his total subservience to them.

How, then, does Isabel's predicament help us to see the connection between caring and evaluation? One obvious interpretation of the novel has it that Isabel is deceived, much as Titania is deceived. She believes Osmond to have qualities which, in fact, he lacks—much as Titania believes Bottom to have qualities which he lacks. There is certainly something in this interpretation, and indeed it is this facet of the situation which enables us to see the poignancy of Isabel's plight, just as we saw the bathos of Titania's. This, however, is not all, for James's intention in presenting us with Isabel is to show us a woman who is caught between the values of the Old World and the values of the New World, and who responds by rejecting all values. It is against this background that she attempts to find what she can care about, and it is this background (or lack of background) which explains her plight, for whereas Titania endorses certain values, but is mistaken in her belief that Bottom manifests them, Isabel has no prior values against which to judge Gilbert Osmond. On the contrary, she alights upon him as the embodiment of value. He, as it were, represents value for her, at least initially, and her mistake is therefore a rather different mistake from Titania's. Titania is antecedently committed to gentleness and to beauty (for instance), but is wrong in thinking that Bottom has these qualities. Of course, she does not love him *because* she believes him to have those qualities. The situation is simply that, having come to love him, she then sees these qualities in him. She projects them on to him. Isabel, however, eschews value altogether and therefore her mistake does not lie in the misidentification of Osmond as someone who possesses qualities she values. Rather, it lies in coming to care about the wrong thing and *thereby* coming to endorse the wrong values.

More generally, what the novel shows is that if, like Isabel, we are led simply by what we care about, independent of evaluative considerations, we risk a certain kind of moral, as distinct from cognitive, loss. Titania is deceived because Bottom does not in fact have the qualities she believes him to have. Isabel, by contrast, resolves to adopt whatever values are embodied in the person she finds she can care about and so, in caring about Osmond, she also and thereby cares about the values he in fact embraces. It is this fact which gives us a sense of how Isabel is morally, as opposed to cognitively, undone. She allows her evaluative framework to be given by what she comes to care about, and what she comes to care about is the 'serpent' Osmond.

To see how this renders Isabel morally undone, consider the final scenes of the novel: as the extent of Osmond's deceit is recognized and played out, both Isabel and Mme Merle reflect on the consequences of their having cared about (and loved) him. In her final conversation with Osmond, Mme Merle says 'I don't know how we're to end. I wish I did! How do bad people end?— especially as to their common crimes. You have made me as bad as yourself' (James 1991: 555). By investing herself in what is vulgar and sordid, Mme Merle has herself come to possess these vices. So the vulnerability to loss which is inherent in caring about things is not merely vulnerability to unhappiness. It is also, and more importantly, a vulnerability to loss of *moral* status. Note that Mme Merle's allegation is 'you have made me as bad as yourself', and in saying this she appeals not only to her own misery, and not only to her own judgement of herself, but to the moral judgement which she believes to be appropriate to her. Moreover, it is an appropriate moral judgement just insofar as she (and more clearly Isabel) has taken on Osmond's values through caring about him. The person who undertakes to find what she can care about, and who does so without reference to antecedent values, risks endorsing for herself the values of the person she cares about. If she then discovers that those values are corrupt, she also finds that she herself is corrupt. And that discovery is distinct from, and more damaging than, Titania's discovery that she was mistaken.

More generally, *The Portrait of a Lady* draws our attention to two facts: the first is that, even though we can indeed care about more or less anything, and even though we do not care about people on the basis of antecedent judgements of their value, it does not follow that care has no critical dimension. Isabel Archer's decision to 'find what she can care about' leads, inevitably, to disaster, and the disaster is directly traceable to her attempt to remain free of all evaluative judgements. Moreover, we can understand her situation *as* disastrous only because we also see that it is not, in the end, possible (either for her or for us) to remain free of all evaluative judgements. Without this dimension, the story of Isabel Archer is simply the story of someone who is disappointed because it turns out that the man she loves does not, after all, possess the qualities she thought he had. But *The Portrait of a Lady* shows us much more than this. It shows us that, even if Old World and New World values conflict, and even if we are unable to embrace either unreservedly, we still cannot do without values altogether, and if we attempt to do without them, that does not prevent our being implicated in the values possessed by what we care about.

Second, the novel draws our attention to the precise kind of loss to which we become vulnerable when we care about things, for when Isabel and Mme Merle reflect on the course their respective lives have taken, they do so in terms that are distinctively moral. What they come to realize is that, by caring about and investing themselves in 'the serpent' Osmond, they have become wicked themselves. Here, self-assessment and moral assessment are closely intertwined, and the distinction between morality (understood as involving our relations with others), and caring about things (understood as involving our relations with ourselves), is blurred. Recall that, for Frankfurt, what we care about is 'a matter of what we do with *ourselves*, and we therefore need to understand what is *important* or, rather, what is *important to us*' (Frankfurt 1988: 80–1), but the poignancy of Isabel Archer's situation is obscured if we stop there. Isabel did indeed find what was important to her, but she also found, in the end, that that thing was a serpent. In discovering what was important to her, she also discovered what her moral status was, and therein lies her tragedy.

My intention is discussing the cases of Titania and Isabel Archer has been to cast doubt on the sharp distinction Frankfurt draws between morality, on the one hand, and what we care about on the other, and I have tried to do this by showing (first) that care must have a critical dimension and (second) that in some important cases that dimension is moral. The case of Titania indicates that while it is certainly possible for people to care about almost anything, and while their caring about those things is not a reflection of antecedent judgements of value, it does not follow that caring about things is an exclusively 'personal matter'. In the absence of any appeal to what is valuable, as distinct from what the agent invests with importance, the concepts of tragedy and comedy are rendered unintelligible.

Additionally, the fact that caring about things makes us vulnerable to loss is an indication that, characteristically, care has not only a critical dimension, but a distinctively moral dimension. The loss which Isabel Archer suffers is not simply a matter of felt unhappiness, nor even of the disappointment which follows upon the realization that she has been deceived. It is a form of loss which consists in the recognition that what matters to her serves both as a statement of who she is and as a statement of what she deems to be valuable. So if we follow Frankfurt's advice and simply 'find what we can care about', we must accept that the things we care about reflect back upon us morally. Having abandoned any commitment to values, Isabel nonetheless finds that by caring about Gilbert Osmond she has, whether she likes it or not, made a statement about what her values are and what kind of person she is. Her tragedy then lies in the fact that the statement is a morally repellent one.

Summary and Prospect

The task which I faced at the end of Chapter 1 was to provide a foundation for impartiality which was moral, but not comprehensively so. I rejected appeal to equality because, although moral, it is a deeply contested, and arguably comprehensive, value. As such, it threatens to justify impartiality only by undermining its commitment to the permanence of pluralism. So what is needed is a defence of impartiality which can vindicate its commitment to the permanence of pluralism, and which can also show the priority of impartiality in a way that is moral, but not comprehensively so.

The discussion of the normative question in Chapter 2 led to the suggestion that we should seek to defend impartiality by appeal to the specific things which people care about—their partial concerns for and commitments to particular people and projects. However, although this defence could respond to the normative question (it could explain why certain dilemmas are troubling for those who already feel the force of impartial requirements), it threatened to be too thin to serve as a route into impartialism, or a way of getting morality off the ground. When understood simply as a propensity to be directly motivated by others, care has no obvious ethical or moral dimension. It is possible for people to care about (to be directly motivated by) all kinds of things, and there is, it seems, no distinctively moral or even ethical dimension to care.

If, therefore, our partial concerns are to provide a way of getting impartial morality off the ground, we must show how they suggest moral evaluation. In pursuit of this aim, I have 'thickened' the concept of care in various ways. Following Frankfurt, I have argued that care is distinct from desire in that it is temporally extended, regular and reliable. Additionally, I have concurred with his claim that the things we care about serve as statements of who we are. They indicate what we are invested in, where that investment is not explicable by reference to prior evaluation: to care about something is to assert its importance for me, but that importance need not reflect an antecedent assessment of its value. However, these attempts to 'thicken' the concept of care seemed to foreclose on the possibility of providing it with a critical, much less a moral, dimension. They suggest a gulf between the things people care about and their moral evaluations, for if caring about things is a way of investing them with importance, and not a way of expressing a judgement about their value, then a gap opens up between evaluation and the things people care about.

Against this, I have argued that caring about things does have a distinctively critical, and indeed evaluative, dimension, and that that dimension is not exclusively the dimension of self-assessment. Although it is true that the insistence on a critical dimension to care can threaten to lead in the direction of elitism, it is also true that the vulnerability to loss which is a concomitant of caring requires that the critical dimension be retained. The bathos inherent in Titania's plight when she falls in love with Bottom is explicable only by reference to the fact that she has invested herself in something which is unworthy of her care. Frankfurt of course can, and indeed does, concede as much when he notes that 'a person who cares about something thereby incurs certain costs, connected with the effort which investing himself requires and with the vulnerability to disappointment and to other losses which it imposes. In virtue of these costs, it is possible for something to be important to a person without being important enough for it to be worth his while to care about it' (Frankfurt 1988: 91 n. 3).

But the question which now arises is: 'on what grounds can it be determined that something is not worthy of our care?' As we have seen, it is here that Frankfurt's analysis grinds to a halt, and he is reduced simply to suggesting that we must 'find what we *can* care about' (Frankfurt 1988: 93 ff.). However, I have argued that the 'investment of self' which, on Frankfurt's own account, is a definitive feature of caring about things, is also a feature which implies that we must (and can) do rather more than that. The case of Isabel Archer is fully comprehensible only on the assumption that she has invested herself in someone not worthy of her care, and that she has come to see that that is what she has done. If we deny the critical dimension of care, we cannot appreciate the facts which James wishes to draw to our attention. Of course, it does not follow that in the first-person case the agent herself is able to see the tragedy, the poignancy, or the farce, of her own situation, nor does it follow that we must ourselves subscribe to the values she endorses. All that follows is that we can have the reactions we do have to these cases only on the assumption that there is some distinction between what is worthwhile and what is worthless, even if the agent does not initially see it herself, and even if, when she does see it, she endorses values other than the ones we ourselves believe to be correct.

Finally, and most importantly, the case of Isabel Archer gives us some insight into the kind of loss which can be consequent upon caring about things. Here, I have argued that the loss may be more than mere unhappiness, or disappointment. It may be moral loss: a form of loss which puts in question the value system to which the agent has committed herself and, as a result, she may feel not simply deceived or disappointed, but morally undone. Moreover, this kind of loss is most easily discernible in cases (such as the case of Isabel Archer) where the agent attempts to eschew evaluation altogether and, following Frankfurt, to find what she can care about. Far from highlighting the distinction between care and morality, the case of Isabel Archer shows us that, in the end, the things we care about serve not only as statements of who we are, but as statements of what we value.

My aim in presenting these examples has been to show how caring about things can provide us with the tools necessary to get impartial morality off the ground. However, the most that has so far been demonstrated is that, insofar as we care about things (where caring is understood as satisfying the conditions referred to above), then that care will imply evaluative judgements of some sort. Nothing follows to the effect that those evaluative judgements will be ones which imply impartiality and, as indicated at the outset, I am doubtful that any conclusive argument can be provided which takes us from caring to impartial morality. Because I believe that this is so, my argument now will take a different tack. Rather than attempting to show that caring about things, or people, entails impartiality, I will attempt to show that our propensity to care about things is best accommodated by, and reflected through, a moral theory which is impartialist and which takes our partial concerns as foundational.

In the previous chapter, I made reference to David Gauthier's claim that 'if we are to consider our moral affections to be more than dysfunctional feelings of which we should be well rid, we must be able to show how they would arise from such valuing and awareness [the valuing and awareness of participation with others]' (Gauthier 1986: 339), and Gauthier continues: 'we must be able to show that a person, reflecting on his moral feelings, would consider them an appropriate extension of his concern for others in the context of valued participatory activities'. Similarly, John Rawls insists that the moral sentiments are 'a normal part of human life', and in *A Theory of Justice* (though not in *Political Liberalism*) he deems it to be 'crucial' to stability to show that the sense of justice is congruent with the good of the agent who adopts it. The question of congruence will be taken up in the next chapter. My ambition here is the more modest one of showing how an impartialism which is grounded in the specific things we care about can be more stable (less 'dysfunctional') than moralities which do not accord centrality to those things. In other words, I want to show that a form of impartialism which is grounded in what we care about is also a form of impartialism that the agent can reflectively endorse. By contrast, a morality which is not impartialist in this way threatens to make our moral affections dysfunctional. The remainder of this chapter therefore attempts to show that grounding morality in what we care about renders it more stable and more capable of securing allegiance than forms of morality which have a different grounding. The next chapter attempts to show that grounding morality in what we care about renders it congruent with our own good.

Impartiality and the Case of Huckleberry Finn

At the beginning of this chapter I referred to Jean Hampton's insistence that, when impartialism is grounded in an appeal to equality, it is grounded in a value which is highly contested and, concurring with her, I gave the example of Mark Twain's *Huckleberry Finn*. Set in nineteenth-century Missouri, *Huckleberry Finn* tells how a young white boy (Huck) helps a black slave (Jim) to freedom, and throughout the novel Twain emphasizes that Jim is, in the eyes of his society, a piece of property. He is owned by Miss Watson and when Huck helps him to freedom, Huck steals some *thing*—a thing, moreover, which rightfully belongs to someone else. In short, Twain describes a society in which the equality of all human beings is not acknowledged (Twain 1950).

Of course, this description of the case is too simplistic for, as the earlier quotations from the novel indicate, those who subscribe to the morality of the society may protest that it does indeed acknowledge the equality of all people. It is simply the case that black people are not people. They are property. Hence Aunt Sally's relief that, when the cylinder head blew up, 'no-one was hurt'. It just 'killed a nigger'. This consideration, however, simply serves to highlight Hampton's anxiety, which is that the concept of equality cannot do the justificatory work required of it. The endorsement of equality at the level of moral ideal does not rule out its denial at the level of political and moral practice, for if we take a commitment to equality to preclude institutionalised slavery, then we must concede that there are many societies (including nineteenth-century Missouri) which do not endorse the ideal in that sense. However, if we take a commitment to equality to be compatible with institutionalized slavery, then it is hard to see what substance there is to the ideal. What exactly are we proposing when we propose an impartialist theory, grounded in equality, but compatible nonetheless with slavery? In short, if equality is understood as a substantive moral ideal, then it is not one to which all subscribe, but if it is understood as a more abstract principle, to which all can subscribe, then it appears to be too thin to do the work required of it, for it has nothing to say against societies which license the unequal treatment of different races. The problem is the recurrent one of providing a foundation for impartialism which is consistent with both the priority of justice and the permanence of pluralism, and it is not clear that an appeal to equality can resolve that problem satisfactorily.

The question which now arises is whether an appeal to impartialism grounded in what we care about can fare any better. My suggestion will be that it can in the sense that it is better able to show our commitment to morality to be more than merely dysfunctional. If we commit to a form of impartialism which takes our partial concerns seriously, then we will be better able to retain that commitment in cases where the dictates of morality conflict with other concerns. By contrast, a form of morality which is non-impartialist, either in the sense that it denies the value of equality or in the sense that it endorses that ideal only in the very abstract sense referred to above, will be more liable to be perceived by the agent as dysfunctional. The advantage, then, of an impartialist morality grounded in what we care about is that it is more stable because less likely to generate moral affections which appear dysfunctional from the point of view of the agent. In short, it offers a way of demonstrating the priority of justice. Additionally, it will be consistent with the permanence of pluralism because, although moral, the appeal to what we care about is less restrictive than the appeal to equality. That, at any rate, will be my claim, and in order to make the claim good, I shall contrast the case of Huck, when he helps Jim to freedom, with a case discussed in the previous chapter—the case of the mother who is tempted to pull strings for her child.

The latter case, to recall, is the case of someone who lives in a society where the demands of impartiality are acknowledged, and who herself acknowledges those demands, but is nonetheless tempted, in this instance, to act on behalf of her child and in disregard of morality. In discussing that example I emphasized that it is to be understood as one in which the mother is clear that this is a case where impartial thinking is called for, and is also clear that impartial thinking requires that she not pull strings for her child. Nonetheless, she is tempted to pull strings and she asks herself the question: 'why should I endorse the motivation to morality rather than the motivation to help my child?' I also emphasized that this question (the normative question) has two distinctive features: it is a question about the way in which the reasons of impartial morality relate to reasons of a more partial kind, and it is a question which must be answered by reference to the agent's own thinking.

Compare, now, the case of the mother with the case of Huckleberry Finn. Here, too, the requirements of morality conflict with partial considerations, although of course in this case the morality in question is the morality of a profoundly racist society. It is, nonetheless, a morality which Huck accepts. Like the mother in the earlier example, he sees his situation as one in which the demands of morality apply, like her he feels the force of those demands and, like her, he is tempted to go against them. So in both cases the agent knows what he or she ought to do (what morality demands) and in both cases the agent asks the normative question: 'why should I give priority to the claims of morality rather than to the needs of my friend or my child?' Thus, as the raft sails down the Mississippi, bringing Jim closer and closer to freedom, Huck reflects:

Jim said it made him all over trembly and feverish to be so close to freedom. Well, I can tell you it made me all over trembly and feverish, too, to hear him, because I begun to get it through my head that he *was* most free—and who was to blame for it? Why, *me*. I couldn't get that out of my conscience, no how nor no way ... It hadn't ever come home to me, before, what this thing was that I was doing. But now it did; and it stayed with me and scorched me more and more. (Twain 1950: 259)

Huck, then, is clear that the dictates of morality apply, and he is also clear that they preclude helping Jim to freedom. Nonetheless, he is tempted to help Jim and therefore he asks himself the normative question. What response does he have to this question, and how does his response differ from the one available to the mother? My answer to this question is intended to highlight the difference between a form of morality which is grounded in our partial concerns, and one which is not. In the previous chapter, I argued that insofar as the mother can recognize the demands of morality as grounded in her partial concerns, she need not reject her moral feelings as dysfunctional. My aim now is to show that insofar as Huck cannot recognize the demands of morality as grounded in his partial concerns, he will reject his moral feelings as dysfunctional. And this, of course, is exactly what he does. Having helped Jim to freedom, Huck 'feels bad and low' because, he says, 'I knowed very well I had done wrong'. However, he continues:

Then I thought a minute, and says to myself, hold on—s'pose you'd a done right and give Jim up; would you feel better than what you do now? No, says I, I'd feel bad—I'd feel just the same way I do now. Well, then, says I, what's the use you learning to do right, when it's troublesome to do right and ain't no trouble to do wrong, and the wages is just the same? I was stuck. I couldn't answer that. So I reckoned I wouldn't bother no more about it, but after this always do whichever comes handiest at the time. (Twain 1950: 263)

Reflecting on his moral feelings, Huck concludes that they are indeed 'dys-functional'. He has cultivated them, but he now sees that in doing so he was a fool and that he would be better off without them. It is a trouble to do right, but no trouble to do wrong and 'the wages is the same'. He therefore resolves to abandon morality and 'do whatever comes handiest at the time'. What we now need to understand is why Huck deems his moral feelings to be dysfunc-tional, and whether he would think them less so if the morality in question were more firmly grounded in the partial concerns he has for others—if, that is to say, he could understand the demands of his morality in something like the way the mother can understand the demands of her morality.

In discussing the case of the mother who is tempted to pull strings for her child, I argued that her predicament arises from the fact that, in this case, she is required to marginalize those directly motivating concerns which them-selves explain the appeal of impartial morality in the first place. *Ex hypothesi* she sees the demands of morality as legitimate, but her propensity to do that is traceable to the fact that they are demands that take seriously the partial concerns she has for others. This is (in part) why she is able to give them allegiance. Of course, in the specific case, she struggles to give them allegiance because, in the specific case, they conflict with her partial concerns. Nonethe-less, we have here a form of morality which is not dysfunctional because and insofar as it is grounded in partial concerns. By contrast, the form of morality which Huck lives under and indeed acknowledges (at least to begin with) does not take his partial concerns seriously. From the perspective of the morality of nineteenth-century Missouri what Huck is doing is stealing Miss Watson's property. Against this, the fact that he cares for and about Jim counts for nothing. Here, then, the situation genuinely is one in which Huck's partial concerns are 'at war' with the dictates of morality, and they are so because his concern for Jim is not merely overridden, but rejected, by the morality to which Huck subscribes. On seeing this, he resolves to abandon morality and 'do whichever comes handiest'.

The crucial contrast between the mother and Huck is therefore this: if the mother resolves to help her child, she can continue to feel the force of mor-ality's demands, and can continue to see her own moral attitudes as appropri-ate, even if ignored on this occasion. And the reason is quite simply that the morality has built into it a recognition of the significance of partial concerns, including concern for one's friends and family. By contrast, when Huck resolves to help Jim, he thereby resolves to abandon morality, and the reason for this is that the morality allows no room for the significance of Huck's concern for Jim. It does, of course, allow room for other partial concerns Huck has: his concern for Tom Sawyer, or for Miss Watson, for instance. Concern for Jim, however, lies outside the scope of this morality and the morality itself is dysfunctional precisely because it cannot accommodate that concern.

The comparison of the two examples is intended to show that morality's ability to command allegiance (to be other than dysfunctional) is a function of its ability to accommodate the partial concerns we have for others. However, this analysis raises a question about how we are to identify the appropriate objects of care—objects which ought properly to be included in the impartialist scheme. For although we might reject the morality of nineteenth-century Missouri on the grounds that it rules out concern for black people, we cannot believe that just anything could count as an appropriate object of care and that therefore morality ought to make room for all those many and various things that people can care about.

Suppose, for example, that Huck had not 'stolen' Jim, but instead had stolen Miss Watson's Stradivarius, and had done so because he cared about it very deeply. Here it is not plausible to suggest that the morality ought to be revised so as to include that concern. How, then, are we to decide which objects of care are to be included and which not? Two points are in order here: the first is that the analysis of care given earlier makes essential reference to its directly motivating character. To care is to be directly motivated *by the needs and interests* of others and this, in itself, suggests a limit to the objects of care which can properly be included in morality. It implies that the objects of morality will be restricted to those things which have needs and interests, and this should be sufficient to draw a distinction between Huck's theft of Jim and his theft of the Stradivarius. To say this, of course, is not to settle the matter. Far from it. It is simply to note that an insistence on the importance of what we care about, even when coupled with a recognition that people can care about almost anything, does not commit us to holding that morality must make room for all the things people might care about. My argument is only that, to the extent that a morality fails to make room for the things people care about, it risks being deemed to be dysfunctional. The question of whether, and in what circumstances, we must be prepared to live with that dysfunctionality is a separate one.

Second, however, and crucially, much of the argument of this chapter has been devoted to showing that, even though people can care about all sorts of things, there is nonetheless a critical dimension to care. So while we may accept that people do not come to care about a thing on the basis of antecedent judgements about its value, it does not follow and it is not true that our partial concerns are immune to critical commentary. Indeed, the examples of Titania and Isabel Archer were designed precisely to demonstrate that caring about things prompts critical considerations.

Putting these points together, then, we can see that the case of Huckleberry Finn is distinct from the case of the mother who is tempted to pull strings for her child, and that it is so because, while the mother can see that her morality takes seriously, indeed is grounded in, the partial concern she has for her child, Huck has no such assurance. His morality (the morality of his society) denies the significance of partial concerns for people like Jim and, for that reason, is dysfunctional for Huck. However, the recognition that a morality is dysfunctional where and because it ignores partial concerns need not drive us to the conclusion that an acceptable morality must acknowledge every partial concern people might have. For one thing, and as has been conceded from the start, people can care about almost anything and it would be impossible for any morality to accommodate all those things that people can care about. However, this is not the only significant feature of care. A further significant feature is its directly motivating and other-directed character. In caring about others, we respond directly to their needs and interests and this, in itself, suggests a restriction on the possible range of things to be considered in thinking about the relationship between partial concerns and impartial morality. It suggests that we limit ourselves to those things (characteristically people) which can have needs and interests. To put the point rather differently, the question is when and why we should be troubled if morality ignores certain of the things we care about, and my suggestion is that, since caring about things is in part a matter of other-directedness, a matter of being directly motivated by the interests and needs of the object of our care, the most worrying cases will be cases where our care is for things which themselves have needs and interests, since it is in these cases that morality will be, not simply dysfunctional for the person who cares, but also damaging to the object of care. Here, then, is one reason for thinking that some restriction can be placed on the partial concerns which must be accommodated by impartial morality. A second reason for denying that impartial morality must take every partial concern into consideration springs from the recognition that care has a critical dimension. *Pace* Frankfurt, our aim is not simply to find what we *can* care about, but also to determine whether the things we care about are worthy of that care. So grounding impartial morality in what we care about is consistent both with there being some restriction on the legitimate objects of care and with the possibility (indeed the necessity) of subjecting the things we do care about to critical scrutiny.

Conclusion

At the beginning of this chapter I said that my aim was to indicate how caring about things might enable us to get morality off the ground. Following Frankfurt, I argued that if care is to have any chance of playing that role, then it must be understood as more than simply directly motivating. It must be 'thickened' in various ways. As a first move, I suggested distinguishing between caring about things and merely desiring them or wanting them.

Caring implies reliability over time, and it also involves second-order volition. It requires not only that we reflect upon and endorse some of our desires, but also that we wish some of our desires (and not others) to inform our will. Although the need for second-order assessment is generally accepted, there is dispute as to whether it involves not merely self-evaluation but also evaluation of a more generally ethical or moral kind. Here, I suggested that self-evaluation itself implies ethical evaluation and, using the examples of Titania and Isabel Archer, I tried to indicate how the things that are important to us imply such ethical evaluation. In saying what is important to us, we also say what values we endorse, and neither comedy nor tragedy, poignancy nor bathos, can be understood without this. The question which then arose was whether those evaluative considerations need be ones which imply a distinctively impartial form of morality.

My discussion of *Huckleberry Finn* has been designed to show that the form of evaluation implicit in caring about things implies, even if it does not entail, impartiality. In particular, it implies a form of impartiality which is grounded in our partial concerns. The reason for this is that impartial morality so understood can better explain the dilemma an agent faces in cases of conflict. For the agent who feels the force of the requirements of impartial morality, there can indeed be conflict, but that conflict is between specific commitments to particular people, on the one hand, and a form of morality which itself acknowledges the value of those commitments, on the other. Indeed, the conflict is a difficult one precisely *because* impartiality contains within it a recognition of the significance of our partial concerns for particular others.

By contrast, where people care for others but live under a morality which does not acknowledge their partial concerns as morally relevant, the conflict will be differently, and less satisfactorily, understood. Concern for others will most naturally be seen as simply emotional forces which stand in opposition to morality, and if those concerns for others are endorsed at the second-order level, they will force a stand off between what matters *to me* and what is morally required *of me*. So an impartialism which is grounded in what we care about can, at the very least, acknowledge some connection between what matters to me and what is morally required of me, and in this sense it will be less dysfunctional—less alienating—than a morality which marginalizes those considerations.

Having said all that, however, it is also important to recognize the limitations of this argument. To repeat, it cannot show that caring entails impartial morality; all it can show is that any morality which hopes to command allegiance must take our partial concerns very seriously. If it sets them in direct opposition to reasons of morality, it risks being rejected because dysfunctional. The difference between the case of Huckleberry Finn and the case of the mother who is tempted to pull strings for her child is the difference between someone who has a morality that takes her partial concerns for others seriously, and someone who does not.

However, nothing follows to the effect that all partial concerns must be endorsed by impartiality: to care is, in part, to be directed by the needs and interests of the objects of our care and that in itself suggests restrictions on the range of things impartial morality must countenance. Additionally, care has a critical dimension, and therefore if we demand that impartial morality make room for the objects of our care, we must say why those things are deserving of care. Moreover, we must do that even though our own care for them is not itself based on a prior assessment of their value.

The appeal to partial concerns can therefore serve to get morality off the ground, and can do so in a way which explains the authority of moral requirements, and thereby renders morality stable. It is less contentious than the appeal to equality because the significance of partial concerns is widely, if not universally, accepted. Not all subscribe to the ideal of equality, but (almost) all have partial concerns which matter greatly to them. Additionally, the appeal to partial concerns is not one that need undermine the permanence of pluralism. Because people can care about all kinds of things, a form of morality that is grounded in what people care about does not threaten comprehensiveness. Nonetheless, and because care has a critical dimension, it is not committed to the thought that 'anything goes' and that impartialism must make room for everything people might care about. In short, then, if we ground impartial morality in what people care about, we may yet be able to maintain both the permanence of pluralism and the priority of justice. We may be able to explain how people can feel the force of moral requirements despite the fact that they have diverse, even conflicting, partial concerns or conceptions of the good. Indeed, we might be able to go further and show how impartial morality, when grounded in what we care about, is congruent with the good of the agent who adopts it. In the next, and final, chapter, I shall consider whether this is indeed a possibility, and what would follow from its being so.

4

Impartiality and Congruence

In the two preceding chapters I have argued that impartialism is best grounded in our partial concerns and that, when so grounded, it can account for the troubling nature of cases in which questions of normative priority arise. I have also argued that, so understood, impartial morality is not dysfunctional: although we may, on occasion, be tempted to go against its dictates, we do not, in general, have reason to reject it outright. Moreover, when impartial morality is seen as grounded in partial concerns it can be commended to those who do not antecedently feel its force: our partial concerns themselves provide reason to acknowledge the claims of impartial morality and indeed can constitute a way of 'getting it off the ground'.

It should be (and has been) emphasized that this defence of impartialism can have no more than persuasive force. Certainly the arguments are not ones which require commitment to impartiality on pain of irrationality, and indeed it is my conviction that no such arguments are available. The most we can hope to do is show that a form of impartialism which is grounded in partial concerns for others has plausible, even if not compelling, claims to allegiance and priority. Towards the end of the previous chapter I also suggested that such a form of impartialism might be commended as congruent with the good of the agent who endorses it, and one of my tasks in this chapter is to defend that claim more fully. However, before doing that, I need to explain why it is important to defend congruence, and that explanation must begin with a restatement of the political question which motivated this book in the first place: how, in conditions of modernity, can we reconcile the permanence of pluralism with the priority of justice?

Recall that in *Political Liberalism* Rawls tells us that us that the aims of political philosophy depend on the society it addresses, and that modern democratic societies are characterized by the fact of pluralism. They are societies in which people with very different (yet often reasonable) moral ideals must live together on terms that can be agreed to be just. Moreover, he insists that in the modern world this pluralism about ideals is permanent: 'political liberalism assumes that, for political purposes, a plurality of reasonable yet incompatible comprehensive doctrines is the normal result of the exercise of human reason within the framework of the free institutions of a constitutional democratic regime' (Rawls 1993: xvi). For this reason, we ought not to regret the persistence of reasonable pluralism, nor expect it to wither away. To regret the persistence of pluralism would be to regret that reason operates under conditions of freedom.

Nonetheless, and despite this plurality of comprehensive conceptions, people must find a way of living together on terms that all can accept as just, and their acceptance of justice can (Rawls hopes) be more than a *modus vivendi*, or accommodation to power. It can be shown to be acceptable to each from within his or her own comprehensive conception of the good, and indeed can transcend, or take priority over, specific conceptions of the good. Thus: 'the values of the political are very great values and hence not easily over-ridden: these values govern the very framework of social life—the very groundwork of our existence—and specify the fundamental terms of political and social co-operation.' And again: 'under reasonably favourable conditions that make democracy possible, political values normally outweigh whatever nonpolitical values conflict with them' (both quotations, Rawls 1993: 139). Given, then, that the modern world is characterized by pluralism about the good, the problem for political liberalism is to show why, nonetheless, people might willingly give impartial justice priority, or deem its demands to be 'such as to outweigh' their comprehensive conceptions of the good. More generally, the problem for political liberalism is to reconcile the permanence of pluralism with the priority of justice.

In Chapter 1, I discussed Rawls's response to this problem, and I argued there that while his appeal to epistemological abstinence could explain the permanence of pluralism, it could not explain the priority of justice. Indeed, I suggested that epistemological arguments generally would be impotent to demonstrate the priority of justice in any way other than as a *modus vivendi*. Crudely put, my claim was that if we wish to show why people with very different, yet reasonable, comprehensive conceptions of the good might nonetheless come to give priority to impartial justice, we must show how impartiality can be commended as *morally* prior. And, of course, we must show that moral priority to be consistent with (or at least not antagonistic to) the plurality of comprehensive conceptions of the good.

These considerations prompted the Chapter 2 discussion of the normative priority of impartial morality. Before asking how the priority of impartial justice might be commended to those who have (at least apparently) conflicting comprehensive conceptions of the good, it seemed important to establish why impartial considerations are given priority by those who do antecedently acknowledge their force. Here I argued that this, normative, question is best answered by showing that the appeal of impartial morality rests, in part, on the significance it gives to partial concerns. While partial concerns can of course conflict with the requirements of impartiality, it is also true that the impartial system as a whole gains its motivational force from, and commands allegiance because of, its recognition of the partial concerns we have for others.

In Chapter 3 I went on to argue that this understanding of impartialism could also be a plausible, even if not compelling, way of commending impartial morality to those who do not antecedently acknowledge its force. A form of impartialism that is grounded in partial concerns will enable us to get morality 'off the ground', and will also be less likely to be perceived by the agent as dysfunctional. However, the announced aim of the present chapter goes further, for what is now suggested is that such a form of impartialism will be stable because congruent with the good of the agent. It is not simply a form of morality which leaves us less alienated. It is a form of morality which is beneficial to those who adopt it.

This last claim—the claim of congruence—is a very strong one. Indeed, some have argued that it is impossibly strong, and that a moral theory cannot sensibly aspire to it. However, I wish to argue in favour of congruence, both because I believe that it is an attainable aspiration, and (more importantly) because a clear understanding of what is involved in congruence is important for the reconciliation of pluralism and priority which, after all, is the problem that motivates this book. How, then, can appeal to congruence help to reconcile the permanence of pluralism with the priority of justice? To answer this question we need to return to *Political Liberalism* and to Rawls's invocation of epistemological abstinence. Additionally, we need to set that invocation in the context of Rawls's earlier, and now discarded, theory of stability, for it is here that the significance of congruence is most evident.

Pluralism and Priority

In discussing the doctrine of epistemological abstinence, I emphasized that it reflects Rawls's conviction that modern societies are characterized by pluralism understood as both reasonable and permanent. Abstinence is, he believes, a way of acknowledging the fact that different people subscribe to different moral ideals, different religious beliefs, different understandings of the best way to lead one's life. However, this emphasis on the permanence of pluralism is prompted by the fact (as Rawls now sees it) that the view he put forward in *A Theory of Justice* was incompatible with permanence. It was, he says, 'unrealistic' because 'inconsistent with realizing its own principles under the best of forseeable conditions' (Rawls 1993: xvii). And he goes on to explain that in *Theory*:

An essential feature of a well-ordered society associated with justice as fairness is that all its citizens endorse this conception on the basis of what I now call a comprehensive philosophical doctrine. They accept, as rooted in this doctrine, its two principles of justice. Similarly, in the well-ordered society associated with utilitarianism citizens generally endorse that view as a comprehensive philosophical doctrine and they accept the principle of utility on that basis. Although the distinction between a political conception of justice and a comprehensive philosophical doctrine is not discussed in *Theory*, once the question is raised, it is clear, I think, that the text regards justice as fairness and utilitarianism as comprehensive, or partially comprehensive, doctrines. (Rawls 1993: xvi)

So what Rawls now believes is that the theory advanced in *A Theory of Justice* required people to accept the two principles of justice on the basis of their acceptance of a specific comprehensive conception of the good—a Kantian conception according to which people are essentially free and equal rational beings who express their true nature by adopting and acting on the two principles of justice commended by justice as fairness. However, in a world characterized by the permanence of pluralism, not all will subscribe to the Kantian conception. Therefore, the theory of *Theory* must be recast, and obviously it must be recast in such a way as to secure allegiance to the two principles without requiring commitment to any comprehensive conception of the good, including the Kantian conception.

Significantly, however, Rawls's initial appeal to the Kantian conception was introduced in an attempt to show why his theory of justice would be 'stable'. In other words, it was introduced in an attempt to explain why, having accepted the argument for the two principles of justice, people would then be motivated to act upon them and indeed to give them priority over other considerations. As we saw in the first chapter of this book, Rawls has always thought the demonstration of stability to be important. He has always thought that 'however attractive a conception of justice might be on other grounds, it is seriously defective if the principles of moral psychology are such that it fails to engender in human beings the requisite desire to act on it' (Rawls 1971: 455). What he now claims to have realized is that *Theory* was indeed 'seriously defective' in just this sense—that it failed to engender the requisite desire to act on the two principles. Or, at least, that it engendered that desire only in those who subscribe to the Kantian conception.

Putting together the preceding considerations, we appear to be left with the following dilemma: if the case for stability is grounded in epistemological abstinence, then the permanence of pluralism can be explained but not (I have argued) the priority of justice. However, if the case for stability is grounded in the Kantian conception, then the priority of justice can be explained but not (Rawls himself thinks) the permanence of pluralism. Moreover, this Rawlsian dilemma is a significant one for my own project. I have argued that epistemological arguments cannot demonstrate the priority of justice, and indeed that was my reason for moving to a moral defence of impartialism. However, Rawls's own intellectual history gives reason to wonder whether the move to a moral defence will also be a move to a comprehensive conception of the good, and thus will purchase priority only by denying pluralism.

Moreover, the anxiety is increased if we turn to the precise statement of the Kantian conception that Rawls gives in Part III of *A Theory of Justice*, for there are notable parallels between the argument he presents there, but now rejects, and the argument I have been advancing in defence of impartialism. In particular, my claim that impartialism is best grounded in what we care about, and in the concerns we have for particular people, echoes Rawls's claim that the sense of justice is analogous to the sense of love—indeed, that the sense of justice is 'a special case of love' (Rawls 1971: 573). So it may be that my defence of impartialism will also fall foul of the pluralism require- ment by demanding commitment to a comprehensive conception of the good.

Against this background, my strategy in this chapter will be as follows: first, I shall explain Rawls's own account of congruence and its role in supporting stability, as that is given in Part III of *A Theory of Justice*. Then, I shall examine his analogy between love and justice and show how it relates to my own defence of impartialism as grounded in what we care about. Finally, I shall try to explain how the analogy between love and justice, when suitably interpreted, can deliver priority (and indeed congru- ence) without implying commitment to a comprehensive, because Kantian, conception of the good. In short, then, I shall take seriously the defence of stability that Rawls provides in Part III of *A Theory of Justice*, but argue that he is mistaken to renounce it. If understood as a way of grounding imparti- alism in the partial concerns we have for others, it can, after all, provide us with a way of reconciling the permanence of pluralism with the priority of justice. Additionally, and connectedly, it can secure congruence without implying comprehensiveness.

Congruence and Stability

As we have seen, Rawls believes that any acceptable political philosophy must show why people would be motivated to act in accordance with its principles. Unlike some political philosophers, he does not think that polit- ical philosophy can restrict itself to questions of truth or justification, but insists that it must also engage with the problem of motivation. In my Chapter 1 discussion of epistemological abstinence, I concurred with this and indeed argued that attempts to divorce questions of justification from questions of motivation were ultimately doomed: justificatory claims, I argued, necessarily imply motivational considerations, especially in condi- tions of modernity where 'belief matters' and where there is a close connec- tion between the content and the status of our beliefs. Any acceptable political philosophy must, therefore, appeal to people's motivations and, given the importance of questions of justice, any acceptable political philosophy must show why people might be more strongly motivated to act in accordance with the dictates of justice than they are to act in accordance with countervailing considerations. Rawls dubs this 'the problem of stability' and in *A Theory of Justice* he writes:

One conception of justice is more stable than another if the sense of justice that it tends to generate is stronger and more likely to override disruptive inclinations...the stability of a conception depends upon a balance of motives: the sense of justice that it cultivates and the aims that it encourages must normally win out against propensities towards injustice. (Rawls 1971: 454)

It is important to note here that Rawls is concerned, not with single acts of justice, but with the general disposition to justice or, as he calls it, the *sense* of justice. What needs to be shown is that the sense of justice which is instilled by a particular conception is stable in the sense that it will 'normally win out against propensities to injustice'. But what could ensure that it does that? What kinds of considerations might lead me to endorse my sense of justice when it conflicts with motivations that pull in a different direction? The question is similar to the one raised in Chapter 2, where I discussed the normative priority of impartial morality, for there, as here, what is needed is a reason addressed to the agent's own thinking—a reason which shows the agent that endorsing the disposition to act justly is not dysfunctional. And the Rawls of *A Theory of Justice* believes that the best way of showing that is to show that such a disposition is congruent with the agent's own good. 'We are concerned', he says, 'with the goodness of the settled desire to take up the standpoint of justice. I assume that the members of a well-ordered society already have this desire. The question is whether this regulative sentiment is consistent with their good' (Rawls 1971: 568). And famously (or notoriously), in *A Theory of Justice*, he believes that it is. Note that, just as the normative question was addressed to those who already feel the force of the requirements of impartial morality, so the congruence question is addressed to those who already have a settled and established sentiment of justice. The additional claim here, however, is that the sense of justice will continue to be endorsed because it is congruent with the good the agent himself or herself.

This demonstration of congruence is, as one philosopher has put it, the Holy Grail: to show that the disposition to justice is congruent with our own good is to provide a compelling motivation for endorsing and nurturing it. After all, what stronger reason could there be for doing something than the recognition that it will benefit me to do it? However, the congruence requirement has been held by many to be implausibly strong and, as we have seen, Rawls himself now thinks that it must be abandoned because the demonstration of its truth implies comprehensiveness, which is at odds with the permanence of pluralism. Since, as already indicated, my own intention is to support a congruence claim, but also to defend impartialism without commitment to comprehensiveness, my task must now be to show that congruence can be secured without comprehensiveness. In particular, I must show that my account of impartialism as grounded in the partial concerns we have for others is one that can secure congruence without comprehensiveness.

To this end, I shall take my cue from the analogy between love and justice advanced in Part III of *A Theory of Justice* and attempt to show that that analogy is consonant with my own emphasis on the importance of what we care about. Additionally, and crucially, I shall attempt to show that, when suitably interpreted, the analogy between love and justice can show us how permanence and pluralism may be reconciled. First, however, I will respond in a preliminary way to the concern that the demand for congruence is unattainable and unreasonable. This is a necessary preliminary to showing why congruence need not entail comprehensiveness, for my belief is that doubts about the possibility of congruence spring, in large part, from an over-demanding understanding of what it requires. The general structure of my argument, then, is this: if we ground impartialism in partial concerns (what people care about) we can demonstrate the possibility of congruence without appealing to a comprehensive conception of the good, and we can also demonstrate the priority of justice in a way compatible with the permanence of pluralism. Moreover, the analogy between love and justice is a useful tool in securing these aims for, *pace* Rawls, it provides the means of demonstrating congruence, but need not imply comprehensiveness. First, however, a word about what exactly the congruence requirement is and how its demands can be exaggerated.

In a review article entitled 'John Rawls and the Search for Stability', Brian Barry objects to the congruence claim and cites the following example in support of his objection:

Suppose that I form the view that it would contribute to my good to take a trip around the world, and that I find that this would cost more than my resources permit. (Let us follow Rawls in assuming that I live in a just society, so that my budget limit corresponds to the one imposed by just economic institutions). Instead of simply concluding that I cannot justly take the trip (while continuing to believe that taking it would be for my good), I am told by Rawls that I must somehow persuade myself that it would not be for my good at all. (Barry 1995a: 889)

Barry's objection strikes me as misplaced. There is, I think, no reason why an appeal to congruence should imply that, on each and every occasion, the agent who acts justly will also be acting in a way which is congruent with his or her present desires, nor even with longer-term interests, as then understood. Indeed, I would go further and say that there are compelling reasons for denying that a doctrine of congruence ought to take this form. That latter claim will be defended later. For now, my main concern is to show that the requirement of congruence need not be a requirement that each and every act of justice contribute to the good of the agent in the sense suggested by Barry's example.

The reason for this, as was noted earlier, is that Rawls is not concerned with specific acts of justice, but rather with the *sense* of justice. Again: 'we are concerned with the goodness of the *settled desire* to take up the standpoint of justice. I assume that the members of a well-ordered society already have this desire. The question is whether this *regulative sentiment* is consistent with their good' (Rawls 1971: 568, emphasis added). But to show that having the regulative sentiment of justice is consistent with my good is not, or not necessarily, to show that each and every just act is consistent with my good.

To make this last point rather more perspicuous, recall the case of the mother who is tempted to pull strings for her child. In my discussion of this example I argued that one significant feature of it is that although, in the specific case, the mother sees the demands of impartial morality as in conflict with her partial concerns, she also feels the force of the impartial system because it takes seriously, and indeed is grounded in, the partial concerns she has for particular people. So although she may on a particular occasion be tempted to go against the dictates of impartial morality, and although she may even yield to that temptation, she will not see the demands of that morality as entirely alien when they can be understood as themselves flowing from a recognition of the significance which partial concerns have in her life. The troubling cases are, I suggested, troubling because they provide us with occasions on which the general consonance between morality and what we care about is threatened, and where the mother is required, in the name of impartial morality, to abandon (or marginalize) those partial concerns which themselves explain her allegiance to impartial morality itself. However, and precisely because impartial morality is grounded in partial concerns, the mother need not feel her commitment to morality to be dysfunctional. She can retain her commitment to the moral system, while recognizing that, in this specific case, that commitment is one which causes pain and suffering. So the normative question is not a question about whether, on each and every occasion, we have an overriding reason to do what morality requires. Rather, the question is about whether and why I might have reason to abandon the *disposition* to morality in cases where its dictates conflict with other things I care about. Indeed, the contrast between the case of Huckleberry Finn and the case of the mother was introduced precisely as a contrast between a case where the moral sentiment might be abandoned as dysfunctional, and a case where it need not. Both, however, were concerned with the disposition to act morally, and in both cases the question was whether that disposition might legitimately be maintained despite conflict. So the normative question only arises where there is *prima facie* conflict between our disposition to act morally, and our disposition to further the interests of those we love. Similarly, I contend, with congruence. Here, too, the interesting question is a question about whether and how, despite appearances to the contrary, our disposition to justice can be congruent with our good. It is not a question that requires us to show that each and every act is congruent with our good.

Of course, the arguments presented in discussing the normative question were designed to show only that impartial morality, when grounded in what we care about, is stable (not dysfunctional) and has comprehensible claims to priority. There was no attempt to show congruence. Nonetheless, the scope of the discussion, both there and here, ranges over the *sense* of justice, or the settled disposition to act morally, and just as we can rebut charges of dysfunctionality while also allowing that there may be some cases in which people have reason to go against the dictates of morality, so we might be able to demonstrate congruence while allowing that there are some cases in which acting morally will bring pain and suffering and, in that sense, will be in tension with the agent's perceived good. Indeed, in arguing that impartial morality need not be dysfunctional when grounded in our partial concerns, I insisted that the very absence of conflict implied by Scanlon's reductivist account was itself reason for rejecting it: a form of impartialism which denies the possibility of practical conflict is suspect for that very reason, and what needs to be shown is that, despite specific instances of conflict, the sense of justice is nonetheless one which can be endorsed as (in this case) congruent with the good of the agent. Congruence, then, takes the sense of justice, not individual acts of justice, as its scope, and what we need to know is whether having a disposition to act justly is consonant with our own good, not whether each and every act of justice is consonant with our own good.

In some ways, however, this conclusion appears to accentuate the difficulty of showing congruence without implying comprehensiveness, for if we take the scope of the discussion to be the sense of justice, then a question arises about exactly *how* the sense of justice can be congruent with the agent's good in a way that does not imply that each and every act of justice is also congruent. In the example offered by Barry, it seems that we must either suppose that taking a trip round the world is for the good of the agent, or not. If we suppose that it is, then the doctrine of congruence, even if not defeated, still stands in need of further explanation, for it is not immediately obvious *how* a doctrine of congruence can withstand the demonstration that specific acts are for the good of the agent, yet are not permitted by justice. Drawing a distinction between the sense of justice and individual acts of justice appears simply to move the problem one stage back, not (or not obviously) to solve it.

On the other hand, if we suppose that taking a trip round the world is not for the good of the agent, then it seems that we must be making implicit appeal to a conception of the agent's good that hangs free of his current desires and perceived interests. We must be supposing that, whatever the agent actually believes to be in his own interest, in fact it is the case that acting justly is what is in his interest. And that in turn implies that he has a 'real' or 'true' interest which is distinct and separable not only from his immediate wishes, but also (as in this case) from his carefully considered judgements about what is best for him. In short, it suggests a Kantian conception of the self.

It is possible, then, for those (like Barry) who deny the plausibility of a demand for congruence to resist that demand even when it is couched in terms of the sense of justice, rather than in terms of individual acts of justice. If we construe the scope of congruence as ranging over acts, then it does indeed seem 'ludicrous' to suppose that congruence can be secured, but if we construe the scope of congruence as ranging over the sense of justice, then we seem to be committed to a doctrine of the true self which implies exactly the kind of comprehensiveness which Rawls is anxious to avoid because it contradicts the permanence of pluralism. Either way, the demand for congruence looks doomed.

What is now needed, therefore, is a demonstration of the possibility of congruence which ranges over the sense of justice (the settled disposition to act justly), but which does not imply a doctrine of the real or true self distinct from, and in conflict with, the desires and preferences of the agent. It is perhaps worth emphasizing the precise way in which this task is different from, and more difficult than, the demonstration of stability given in the previous chapter: what was needed there was simply an argument to the effect that, where morality and partial concerns conflict, the agent need not feel the demands of morality as alienating. And I suggested that that could be shown by emphasizing the foundation of impartial morality in our partial concerns for others. However, the demonstration of congruence calls for a different, and superficially conflicting argument—one which shows that the reason the agent need not abandon the sense of justice is because it is for his or her own good to preserve it. So while the argument for stability works by invoking our concern *for others*, the argument for congruence requires (or seems to require) a concern *for ourselves*. And that is not only a different claim, it is a claim that is in tension with the one adduced in the previous chapter.

This, however, is exactly where Rawls's appeal to the analogy between love and justice may prove helpful, for it seems to me to offer a way of showing how congruence is possible despite the fact that some acts of justice cause suffering to the individual. It also offers a way of softening the distinction between concern for others, which was central in responding to the normative question, with concern for ourselves, which is central to congruence.

Now Rawls himself says comparatively little by way of explication of the analogy, but I believe that it is one which, when appropriately explicated, can deliver congruence without implying comprehensiveness. So I now need, first, to explain and extend the analogy between love and justice and, second, to relate it to the defence of impartialism which I have been advocating in the earlier chapters of this book. Both tasks contribute to the overall aim of showing how we can secure congruence without comprehensiveness, and thus how we can demonstrate priority without undermining the permanence of pluralism. Although what follows makes essential reference to the details of Rawls's account in *A Theory of Justice*, I should emphasize that I am not here aiming for authentic interpretation of Rawls. My intention, rather, is to show how his analogy between love and justice can inform my account of impartialism as grounded in what we care about and thus deliver congruence without comprehensiveness.

Love and Justice

Rawls's analogy between love and justice forms part of his general discussion of whether and how the disposition to act justly can be commended to each and every individual as congruent with his or her own good. This 'ancient question' arises in part because we know that people who act justly may often suffer by being just, and we also know that those who act unjustly often flourish. From Plato onwards philosophers have been mindful of the fact that injustice is not always, or obviously, damaging to the individual who practises it, and it is not without cause that the prophet asks 'Wherefore doth the way of the wicked prosper? Wherefore are all they happy that deal very treacherously?' (Jeremiah 12: 1). To this ancient question the Rawls of *A Theory of Justice* gives an ancient answer:

a just person is not prepared to do certain things, and so in the face of evil circumstances he may decide to chance death rather than act unjustly. Yet although it is true enough that for the sake of justice a man may lose his life where another would live to a later day, the just man does what, all things considered, he most wants; in this sense he is not defeated by ill-fortune, the possibility of which he foresaw.

And then, the analogy between love and justice:

The question is on a par with the hazards of love; indeed, it is simply a special case. Those who love one another, or acquire strong attachments to persons and to forms of life, at the same time become liable to ruin: their love makes them hostages to misfortune and the injustice of others. Friends and lovers take great chances to help each other; and members of families willingly do the same. Their being so disposed belongs to their attachments as much as any other inclination. Once we love we are vulnerable; and there is no such thing as loving while being ready to consider whether to love, just like that. And the loves that hurt the least are not the best loves. When we love we accept the dangers of injury and loss. In view of our general knowledge of the likely course of life, we do not think these risks so great as to cause us to cease loving. Should evils occur, they are the object of our aversion, and we resist those whose machinations bring them about. If we are loving, we do not regret our love. (Both quotations, Rawls 1971: 573)

The first point to note about the analogy between love and justice is that, as indicated earlier, it is concerned with the sense of justice, or the disposition to act justly, not with individual acts of justice. Rawls is not concerned to show that every single act of justice will bring benefit to the agent. On the contrary, he acknowledges that 'the just man might lose his life where another would live to a later day'. Nonetheless, he does not see this as at odds with the wider claim that acting from a stable sense of justice, or adopting justice as a regulative sentiment, can be congruent with the agent's good, and the reason Rawls gives for this is that, like loving, being genuinely just involves recognizing the possibility of hurt and pain. Being just *just is* a matter of accepting that our individual acts of justice might not always bring benefit, and of acting justly nonetheless. And this, of course, is precisely how we understand love, for when we love another person we accept that our love may cause us unhappiness. We know, for instance, that our love may make us vulnerable to the ill-will of the other person should he or she fail us, and we also know that we will become vulnerable to the pain consequent upon seeing the person we love damaged, hurt or unhappy. These, however, are hazards which are ineliminably involved in loving, and to refuse to accept the possibility of them (to aim to love another without risking hurt or suffering) is to refuse to love at all. Since, therefore, a willingness to accept these dangers is constitutive of love, love need not be unjustified by them.

To make the point clearer, consider a case in which the person I love falls ill and requires constant nursing care. The sight of the person I love in this condition will cause me immense distress and unhappiness. Taking care of the person may also prevent me doing things I want to do on my own account, and I may rightly reflect on the fact that by loving this person I have suffered far more than I would have done had I never loved him. None of this, however, need force me to regret loving him, much less to think that loving him was a 'bad decision'. Of course, it may cause me to think that, but it need not, and in some cases (though not all) to think such a thing would cast doubt on whether I really loved him at all.

Similarly, Rawls argues, with the sense of justice. The genuinely just man accepts that the price of being just is that, from time to time, one's very justice may be a source of pain and unhappiness, but it is no more necessary in such a case to think that cultivating the sense of justice was foolish because it brought suffering than it is to think that loving was foolish because it brought suffering. 'There is', Rawls says, 'no such thing as loving while being ready to consider whether to love, just like that', and we must infer that equally there is no such thing as being just while being ready to consider whether to be just, just like that. It is the hallmark of a genuinely just man, as it is the hallmark of someone who genuinely loves, that he does not 'test' the rationality of his sense of justice by asking, on each and every occasion, whether justice will bring more benefit than pain, and it is the hallmark of a genuinely just man, as it is the hallmark of someone who genuinely loves, that he does not declare justice to have been foolish if, on some occasions, it turns out to bring suffering he would not otherwise have incurred.

As indicated earlier, I shall use the analogy between love and justice to show how congruence may be defended without implying comprehensiveness. It is therefore important to emphasize the distinctiveness of the claim which it implies, and this can best be done by contrasting the defence of justice just given with the defence offered by Hume in *A Treatise of Human Nature*. Like Rawls, Hume is concerned with the settled disposition to justice and, like Rawls, he addresses the question of whether and how it can be commended to each individual. However, Hume's explanation of the good of justice depends upon construing it as something which, in the long run, is likely to pay off both for the individual and for society generally. So, he notes that ''tis easily conceiv'd how a man may impoverish himself by a signal instance of integrity' but nonetheless goes on to conclude that: 'However single acts of justice may be contrary, either to public or private interest, 'tis certain that the whole plan or scheme is highly conducive, or indeed absolutely requisite, both to the support of society and the well-being of every individual. 'Tis impossible to separate the good from the ill' (Hume 1888: 497).

Both Rawls and Hume, then, acknowledge that acting justly may bring pain and suffering to the individual on specific occasions, but their characterizations of the individual who suffers in this way are interestingly different. For Hume it is simply 'impossible to separate the good from the ill'—impossible to secure the benefits of the system as a whole without incurring the risk of damage on specific occasions—and therefore, since the practice of justice has overwhelming social benefits, we must, as it were, take the rough with the smooth and recognize that there can be instances where justice turns out to be disadvantageous or damaging to us as individuals. For Hume, it seems, we are simply gamblers, forced to concede that the favourite sometimes comes in last, or martyrs sacrificing ourselves on the altar of a greater social good.

For Rawls, however, we are neither gamblers nor martyrs, for having acknowledged that justice may on occasion bring suffering or even ruin in its wake, he goes on to insist that the just man is not thereby 'defeated'. Suffering and ruin are, it seems, distinct from defeat and it is an implication of Rawls's characterization of the problem that the man who retains his sense of justice and suffers as a consequence, far from being 'impoverished' is, in some way, vindicated.

However, the way in which we are vindicated in the case of love depends upon seeing love as a channel through which we express who we are. And, by analogy, Rawls implies that justice, too, can be vindicated insofar as it is expressive of who we are. Though never spelled out in any detail, Rawls's thought seems to be something like this: to love others (genuinely to love others) is precisely to be unwilling to raise the question 'will I do better for myself by continuing to love this person than by not loving him?' Similarly, to be genuinely just is to be unwilling to raise the question 'will I do better for myself by acting justly than by acting unjustly?' By contrast with Hume, who thinks that the question can be both raised and answered in the affirmative, Rawls denies that raising the question is compatible with being genuinely just. When, therefore, I find that my love for another has brought suffering to me—suffering which I would have avoided had I not loved—I will not necessarily be driven to the conclusion that it would have been better never to have loved at all. I will not perceive love as a gamble which, in this instance, failed to pay off, since such a thought may betray the fact that I never genuinely loved at all. Similarly, if the genuinely just person suffers as a result of her justice, she will not necessarily conclude that it would have been better to avoid being just, for to think that way is to raise the suspicion that one never was genuinely just. And presumably the reason will be similar in the two cases: the loves we have express who we are, and our disposition to justice also expresses who we are. Moreover, this interpretation is borne out by Rawls's conclusion that:

In order to realize our nature we have no alternative but to plan to preserve our sense of justice as governing our other aims. This sentiment cannot be fulfilled if it is compromised and balanced against other ends as but one desire among the rest... for this sentiment reveals what the person is, and to compromise it is not to achieve for the self free reign, but to give way to the contingencies and accidents of the world. (Rawls 1971: 574–5)

It is, however, with these words that Rawls appears to admit a comprehensive (Kantian) conception, for what is now suggested is that, just as love is expressive of my particular nature, so justice is expressive of my nature as a free and equal rational being. I would betray myself if I were to ask whether my particular loves were strategically beneficial, and similarly I would betray myself as a free and equal rational being if I were to ask whether justice is a good bet. The analogy between love and justice enables us to explain how congruence is possible because it suggests a way in which we may suffer without being defeated when we act from a sense of justice. However, the price of such congruence appears to be comprehensiveness and, as we have seen, Rawls believes that that price is too high.

As indicated earlier, I wish to ally myself with the defence of congruence which is implicit in the analogy between love and justice (and which is implicit in my own account of the relationship between impartiality and what we care about), but I also wish to show that that defence need not imply a Kantian conception, nor therefore need it imply comprehensiveness. In order to do this, I shall separate Rawls's argument into its component parts and deal first with the alleged Kantianism, and then with the proof of congruence. This latter part of the argument will take me back to my own account of the relationship between impartialism and what we care about, for my over-riding aim is to indicate that, like Rawls's account, that account is not in fact vulnerable to charges of comprehensiveness.

To summarize, therefore: the earlier chapters of this book have argued for an understanding of impartiality that is grounded, not in the ideal of equality, but in what we care about. The appeal to what we care about is reminiscent of Rawls's appeal to love in Part III of *A Theory of Justice*, and since Rawls has renounced that part of his theory because he believes it to imply comprehensiveness and therefore to be at odds with the permanence of pluralism, there must be a question as to whether my own account will also fall prey to that objection. My intention now is to show that grounding impartiality in what we care about (or what we love) need not, after all, imply comprehensiveness, and that both my own account and Rawls's account (suitably interpreted) can escape that charge.

The crucial move in defending this position will be one which modifies the understanding of love as an expression of who we are. As noted above, Rawls seems to take both the sense of justice and the sense of love as expressive of who we are. In particular, he takes the sense of justice to be expressive of our nature as free and equal rational beings. However, in earlier parts of this book, I have resisted the claim that our partial concerns (what we care about) are best understood as statements of who we are, or of what is important to us. They may be that, of course, but that is not all that they are. So, in what follows, I shall endorse the analogy between love and justice, but (following the arguments of earlier chapters) I shall also insist that neither love nor justice is to be understood as fundamentally a matter of expressing who we are or what is important to us. In other words, I shall argue that love and justice are indeed analogous, but that Rawls misunderstands the precise way in which they are analogous. First, however, a few words about the alleged Kantianism implicit in the analogy between love and justice.

Love, Justice, and the Kantian Conception

At first glance, the analogy between love and justice seems at odds with incipient Kantianism, and one obvious reason for this is that Kant himself was notoriously suspicious of love. In his moral theory the demands of right (justice) are opposed to the demands of love; they are certainly not to be compared with it. Moreover, the reasons for Kant's 'misamorism' are instructive in the context of an argument for congruence. Kant perceives love as essentially at odds with respect precisely because love exposes us to the ill-will of others and increases the chances of our being harmed as a result of loving them. He writes: 'the principle of mutual love admonishes men to come closer to one another; that of the respect they owe to one another, to keep themselves at a distance' (Kant 1964: 141), and he goes on to elaborate on this by claiming that the duty of love involves making another's ends my own (in so far as that is possible). However, what is problematic (indeed dangerous) about love is that, in making another's ends my own, I render myself vulnerable. Should my friend turn out to be false, or should enmity develop between us, I will risk humiliation because I have given too much of myself to the other person. I have allowed him or her too much access to me, and that knowledge may now be used as a weapon against me. Kant's advice, therefore is that we must:

so conduct ourselves towards a friend that there is no harm done if he should turn into an enemy. We must give him no handle against us. We ought not, of course, to assume the possibility of his becoming an enemy; any such assumption would destroy confidence between us; but it is very unwise to place ourselves in a friend's hands completely, to tell him all the secrets which might detract from our welfare if he became our enemy and spread them abroad; it is imprudent not only because he might thereby do us an injury if he became an enemy, but also because he might fail to keep our secrets through inadvertence. (Kant 1970: 208)

Connectedly, Kant believes that even the requirements of a 'good' friendship are in tension with considerations of respect, and he explains this by citing the case in which one friend performs a favour for another. Of this he says:

If one [friend] accepts a favour from the other, then he may well be able to count on equality in love, but not in respect; for he sees himself as obviously a step lower in so far as he is under an obligation without being able reciprocally to impose obligation ...friendship is something so delicate that it is never for a moment safe from interruptions if it is allowed to rest on feelings and if this mutual sympathy and self-surrender are not subjected to principles or rules preventing excessive familiarity limiting mutual love by the requirements of respect. (Kant 1964: 142–3)

So friendship and respect are in tension with one another, and the closeness required by friendship must be tempered by the distance necessary for respect. This is true even of a good friendship. Moreover, we have no guarantee that our friendships will remain good and, although I should not assume that my friend will become an enemy, or that he will be false and duplicitous, I should nonetheless take precautions to ensure that, should that happen, I am not damaged more than is necessary. In short, I should always protect myself against my friend, for he may not always be my friend, and even if he remains my friend, there are reasons for retaining distance between myself and him: 'excessive familiarity' undermines respect and thus undermines the equality which should exist between the two parties.

What is crucial in Kant's account is his insistence that, in cultivating a friendship or nurturing love for another, we must always remember that our own ends are distinct from, and potentially in conflict with, those of our friend. Indeed, this is the reason why friendship and love are dangerous: they enable the friend who knows our ends to subvert them, thwart them, or hold them up to ridicule. It is therefore the separateness of persons, the distinctness of their different ends, which makes love perilous and 'risky' in Kant's eyes. And although he concedes that the Idea of friendship implies that 'our love is mutual; there is complete restoration', he soon concludes that 'this Idea is valuable only for reflection; in practical life such things do not occur' (Kant 1970: 202–3). It is, then, the separateness of persons which grounds Kant's misamorism and explains (in part) his suspicion of love.

By contrast with Kant, Charles Fried proposes an understanding of love according to which:

an important and perhaps the central conception of love between persons involves a notion of reciprocity ... this must be formalized not in terms of a free renunciation of entitlements to pursue one's own interests in order to take up the beloved's interests as one's own, but rather in terms of a mutual sharing of interests ... the two lovers surely make no claims on each other, yet what they do or give must be given in mutual recognition of the firm base of each other's personality. This interest which the lovers pursue having abandoned self-interest, is not simply the reciprocal pursuit of the other's self-interest in place of one's own. That would be an absurdity. There is rather a creation of love, a middle term, which is a new pattern or system of interests which both share and both value, in part at least just because it is shared ... In this way reciprocal love represents a kind of resolution of the paradoxes of self-interest and altruism. (Fried 1970: 79)

Where Kant emphasizes the separateness of individuals, and the distinctness and difference which characterize their ends, Fried argues that one important feature of love is that it can herald the genesis of a distinct set, or system, of interests—ones which involve the abandonment of separate ends, yet not in a way that implies the submission of one person's interests to those of another, nor even the complete confidence that the other person will look after my interests. Rather, in loving another person, I cease to think in terms of my own interests and of their consonance or conflict with the interests of the person I love, and come to acknowledge an additional set of interests which are 'ours' and which help constitute my understanding of my own interest. Both Kant's warning that love renders us vulnerable to the ill will of others, and his claim that complete reciprocity is a mere Idea, ignore the possibility that there could be this creation of shared interests, or that one person might see her own interests as involving essential reference to the interests of another person whom one loves. He is therefore forced to conclude that when love goes badly, the individuals involved are simply hurt and damaged *as individuals*. They gambled that their lives would go better if they pursued a particular relationship, and the gamble failed.[1]

If, however, we take seriously the analysis offered by Fried, there is a further possibility, which is that when love goes badly we lose something beyond the mere realization of our own interests. Fried argues that people who love one another value things which are shared, and value them in part because they are shared. What is then lost when love fails is precisely that sense of what is 'ours'. Of course, such a loss is damaging to the interests of the individuals who suffer it, but it is not simply that. It is also the loss of something which transcended individual interest. By insisting that the loves that hurt the least are not the best loves, Rawls implies that we may avoid this form of vulnerability only by avoiding the commitment which facilitates the creation of shared interests such as these. Ironically, he implies precisely what one of his critics has accused him of denying—that in such cases we know a good in common which we cannot know alone (Sandel 1982: 183).

A more general point can now be made: whereas Rawls begins with a problem about justice (how it can be commended to each individual) and invokes the case of love to exemplify the fact that we do not always think that pain and suffering unjustify or 'defeat' us, Kant begins with a problem about love (how it renders us vulnerable to others) and invokes the language of right to exemplify the possibility of loving while retaining respect. The differences between their two accounts reflect a different understanding of the separateness of persons and of the ends they pursue. Having once insisted on the separateness of ends, Kant has no real escape from a conception of love as something which is potentially disastrous to the agent who practises it. Of course, it may not be disastrous if my friend actually does protect my interests, but even when he does, it is *my* interests which are being protected. My interests remain essentially mine, and essentially distinct from those of my friend. It is for this reason that friendship and love are always 'risky'.

However, if we question the assumption of separateness we may be able to present an alternative understanding of love and, by extension, an understanding of justice, which promises a 'resolution to the paradoxes of self-

---

[1] This interpretation is at odds with the interpretation given by Korsgaard and discussed in the previous chapter. However, Kant's reference to a unity of wills, of which Korsgaard makes much, occurs only in his discussion of marriage, and even there Kant expresses ambivalence about the possibility. Later in this chapter I say slightly more about the ways in which another's ends can become one's own.

interest and altruism'. If we were to come to see justice as, like love, something which involves the transformation of existing interests and the genesis of new interests, then we would be less inclined to judge every case of suffering through justice as a case of unmitigated disaster, and less inclined to think that every such case must unjustify the agent's commitment to acting justly. The problem now, however, is to explain why we should take love as primary in this way. Why ought we to construe justice as a special case of love, rather than (in Kantian fashion) seeing love as a threat to justice?

The preceding chapters of this book provide my answer to that question. I have argued that impartial morality must be understood as grounded in the partial concerns we have for others, and that unless it is understood in that way the impartial system will lack motivational force. Unlike Rawls, I claim not only that justice is analogous to love, but also that it is grounded in love in the sense that it must invoke our concern for others as central on pain of being unable to prompt us to acknowledge its dictates. However, this account of impartialism serves a function similar to Rawls's analogy between love and justice in that it aims to provide an explanation of the stability and normative priority of impartiality. My aim has been to indicate that when impartialism is grounded in our partial concerns it can defend its own claim to priority; it can do so in a way which admits the possibility of conflict but does not see that conflict as a straightforward clash of opposing forces; and it can account both for the agent's temptation to act against impartialist demands and for her recognition that those demands are nonetheless powerful and legitimate. They are not dysfunctional and the fact of conflict need not render them dysfunctional.

Rawls's analogy, however, has two further features: the first is that it aims to show stability *by showing congruence*; the second is that it takes the sentiment of justice (like the sentiment of love) to be expressive of who we are. When we nurture and endorse the settled sentiment of justice, we thereby nurture and endorse our 'true nature'. Put differently, in claiming that love is analogous to justice Rawls implies that impartial justice is itself something we can come to love, and that we will fulfill ourselves by coming to love it. Herein, obviously, lies the danger of comprehensiveness.

Since I am myself concerned to defend congruence, but also to avoid comprehensiveness, the question which now arises is whether the form of impartialism I have been advocating is one that can purchase congruence only by supposing, covertly, that we have a true or real nature which is expressed through our commitment to impartiality. I hope, now, to show that that conclusion need not follow. Additionally, and connectedly, I shall attempt to fulfil a promise made earlier in this chapter—namely to show not only that we *need not* but *must not* suppose that the doctrine of congruence requires that each and every act conform to the good of the agent. Broadly speaking, my argument will be that congruence implies comprehensiveness only if two assumptions are made: the first is the assumption of separateness, and the purpose of this section has been to cast doubt on that assumption by drawing attention to cases in which I may see the specification of my own interests as involving essential reference to the interests of others. The second is the assumption that an agent's good can be objectively specified, and the purpose of the next section is to show that that assumption, too, is questionable. Additionally, I shall argue that the questioning of separateness and objectivity, when taken together, provide the material for a defence of congruence that does not imply comprehensiveness, and also for an understanding of the priority of impartiality which does not undermine the permanence of pluralism.

Congruence without Comprehensiveness

As we have seen, there are those who allege that the doctrine of congruence is simply an absurdity and that we have no reason to suppose that acting justly will be consonant with our own good. However, the claim that it is absurd to demand congruence between morality and self-interest is most plausible if we consider a short time-slice and a fairly brute interpretation of what counts as an agent's interest. It is certainly unlikely that, at every given moment, the dictates of morality will coincide with the agent's immediate preferences or with his present understanding of his interests, and even if we interpret the congruence requirement as one which relates to longer term interests, it seems altogether possible that those interests and the requirements of morality will, from time to time, conflict. Indeed, it is in recognition of this that Hume appeals to the impossibility of 'separating the good from the ill', but nonetheless advocates justice as our best bet given the undoubted benefits of the overall system of justice. His thinking seems to be that, even in the long term, there is no absolute guarantee that justice will benefit the individual who practises it, but that it is nonetheless our best strategy in a world that is always liable to confound our expectations.

However, these doubts about congruence rest upon the covert assumption that our interests, whether long-term or short-term, are clear and determinate. Before we can even sensibly ask whether a particular act or course of action will advance our interests, we must suppose that it is possible to specify what those interests are. We must suppose that there is some standard by which we can determine whether our interests have indeed been advanced and that, obviously, requires that there be such a thing as 'what is in my interests'. In cases like the one canvassed by Barry, this assumption is quite plausible. However, once we recall that the problem of congruence ranges over the *sense* of justice and not over specific acts of justice, the assumption appears altogether more questionable for, as Rawls notes, in assessing the sense of justice: 'we are not examining the justice or the moral worth of actions *from certain points of view*; we are assessing the goodness of the desire to adopt a particular point of view, that of justice itself' (Rawls 1971: 568). So the question of congruence is not the question of whether acting justly will further my interests, where those interests are antecedently specified. Rather, the question is whether, having nurtured the kinds of interests that are the interests of a just person, I may nonetheless have cause to regret my decision.

In Book II of Plato's *Republic* we are told the story of the ring of Gyges, which made its wearer invisible. The story is used to suggest that both the just man and the unjust man will use the power of the ring to their own advantage. Neither will continue to be just in cases where it does not further his interest to be just, and where he can be sure that he will not be found out. However, the story assumes that interests are already clear and determinate, and then asks whether a just man would continue to be just given that he could further his antecedently specifiable interests better by behaving unjustly. The question of congruence, however, should not be understood on this model, for the question of congruence raises the possibility that what counts as one's interest might itself be a function of the fact that one is just. So if a genuinely just man discovers the ring of Gyges he might, because he is just, decide that he has no use for it and therefore throw it away. The question of congruence is the question of whether such a man behaves contrary to his own good.

But if this is the question, then it makes congruence implausible only on the assumption that our lives are like paths which fork and that decisions within a life are of the form: 'which of these two paths will better promote my interest?' That question, however, can be answered only if we suppose that there is such a thing as 'my interest' and that that thing admits of independent and antecedent specification. It can be answered only if we suppose that decisions within a life do not themselves alter or affect my interest, but are rather taken against the background of an antecedent understanding of what my interest is. However, the assumption is an implausible one. Taken as a whole, our lives are not (either normally or ideally) like paths which fork, and the assumption that they are misrepresents the problem of congruence and at the same time implies a misleading picture of what it is to perceive something as consonant with one's good.

The following example may help to clarify the point: as a young person I may fervently desire academic success and fame, and I may also know that marriage to this person, whom I love, will bring with it an alteration in my conception of my interests such that, in middle age, I shall be content with domesticity and scorn the ambition which now I nurture. I may see my future self as dull and complacent, while simultaneously acknowledging that my future self will look back with fond affection on what it will then perceive as the misplaced and shallow ambition of youth. From which perspective, then, am I to decide whether my interests would be better served by marrying? From which perspective should I decide whether marrying is congruent with my good? To judge exclusively from my present motivations is not only to privilege the present over possible futures in a way that itself stands in need of justification, it is also to ignore the oddity of viewing decisions within a life as parts of a 'game plan' where what counts as success is already given. So, when I play a game such as chess, I aim to win, and the question of which move I should make next is determined by that aim. I should, obviously, make whichever move will be most likely to secure victory.

In life, however, there need be no such single aim determining which move, or which decision, is the best one. Indeed, it is only rather unusual lives which are correctly characterized as lives led in the pursuit of a specific and constant aim. For most of us, aims change consequent upon earlier decisions, and what I deem to be in my interest is, in part, a function of choices I have made and decisions I have taken along the way. Thus, in the example given above, my youthful decision to marry is not (we must hope) simply a strategic decision taken in the belief that marrying will best advance my interest or best enable me to achieve my ambitions. Indeed, to have that reason for marrying would bespeak a bizarre, even corrupt, understanding of the nature of love and the significance of marriage. Rather, the decision to marry is one which itself has implications for what my interests will be. If I decide to marry, I thereby resolve to mould my life in a certain way. I now express my concern to be a certain sort of person—someone for whom professional success is not tantamount and not the measure of success overall. If not, not. Similarly in the case of justice. The genuinely just person—the person who cultivates the sense of justice as a regulative sentiment—does not do so on the basis of a calculation that his life will go better by so doing. Rather, he commits to a specific understanding of what 'going better' means.

How does this affect the claim that the demand for congruence is plausible, and indeed attainable? I have suggested that the demand should be seen as one which ranges over the settled disposition to affirm justice, where the disposition to affirm justice itself influences what counts as my interest, or my good. Thus, and *pace* Hume, the just man is not vindicated if his decision to be just turns out to have long-term benefits, any more than the 'loving' husband is vindicated if his wife turns out to be wealthy, or well-connected, or able to promote his career. Loving another and being genuinely just preclude that kind of calculation, and they do so precisely because they require that one assess oneself *as a just person* or *as a loving spouse*. To be just is to adopt an attitude which itself dictates that my interests are not best served by acting unjustly. This, however, is not because there is any guarantee that justice will promote success, nor even is it because justice is a good bet all things considered. Rather, it is because, insofar as I am genuinely just, I will be reluctant to see the benefits that are purchased by injustice as genuine benefits at all.

But if this is right, then it has consequences for the denial that congruence is plausible. We can now see why we not only *need not*, but *must not* think that congruence requires that each and every just act bring benefit to the agent, for such an assumption takes decisions within a life as analogous to decisions within a game, where what counts as winning or losing is antecedently specified. However, not all decisions within a life have that form. The model is therefore defective, and the conclusion untenable. (In saying this, I do not of course mean to imply that there are no decisions of the 'game plan' type, nor even that it is always wrong to think of decisions on that model. My only concern is to indicate that when we consider the shape of our lives, and thus when we consider the good of the sense of justice, we are not characteristically engaged in strategic decisions of that sort. Nor should we be.)

Additionally, the discussion indicates how we might endorse the doctrine of congruence without thereby committing ourselves to a comprehensive conception of the good. In giving the example of the young person who is unsure whether to marry, I emphasized that the decision is not one which is taken on the basis of an antecedent and objectively determined idea of what his (or her) interests are. On the contrary, the example is intended to draw our attention to the fact that decisions within a life can themselves inform our understanding of what our interests are, or what our good consists in. It shows that what constitutes my good is malleable and indeed is moulded by my decisions themselves. So, far from implying comprehensiveness, the argument for congruence rests upon a denial of comprehensiveness. It succeeds (if at all) by emphasizing the ways in which people's conceptions of the good may change, and by resisting the thought that there is such a thing as a 'true' self which is best realized through the cultivation of a specific conception of the good. The argument does, however, assert the possibility of congruence because it implies that, where someone does endorse justice as a regulative sentiment, acting justly will be congruent with his good: to have a sense of justice is to see acting justly as congruent with my good, but that is not because there is something which is my good, and which can be stated as such in advance of the development of the sense of justice. It is because, in endorsing the sense of justice, I *become* the sort of person who is unwilling to consider a benefit purchased through injustice as a benefit at all. Here, then, we have a way of demonstrating the possibility of congruence while avoiding both absurdity and comprehensiveness. However, the demonstration does not succeed without remainder. I shall now note some residual questions before moving, finally, to a discussion of the political implications of the impartialist theory I have been advocating, and in particular to its ability to reconcile the permanence of pluralism with the priority of justice.

Moral Obligation and Personal Ideal

In arguing that the analogy between love and justice is able to secure congruence without comprehensiveness, I noted some differences between Rawls's view of love and Kant's view. Specifically, I traced the source of Kant's 'misamorism' to his insistence on the separateness of persons and the distinctness of individuals' ends, and I argued that it is this insistence which forces Kant to conclude that love is always, in reality, 'perilous' and 'risky'. Against this, I suggested that when we love another person, we will characteristically see our own interests as intimately bound up with theirs such that when they are harmed, we too are harmed; when they suffer, we too suffer, and I also noted that loving another person may involve the development of new interests which go beyond the pursuit of the other's self-interest in place of my own. As Fried puts it, those who love one another develop 'a new pattern or system of interests which both share and both value, in part at least just because it is shared' (Fried 1970: 70). In both these cases, the specification of my own interest will involve essential reference to the interests of the person I love and will thus undermine insistence on separateness.

These considerations were introduced in order to defend the doctrine of congruence against allegations of absurdity, but they also have implications for the account of impartialism which I have offered in the earlier chapters of this book. In giving that account I emphasized the significance of partial concerns to a defence of impartialism. In particular, I argued that any acceptable impartialist theory must take seriously the partial concerns we have *for others* and that, unless it does that, it will be unable to secure normative priority or even adequate motivational force. Connectedly, my account took issue with responses to the normative problem which elide the distinction between our partial concerns for others and our concern for our own integrity. Indeed, my reason for rejecting Korsgaard's response to the normative problem was exactly that it blurred the distinction between concern for others and concern for oneself, and I insisted that a concern for oneself and one's own integrity would be entirely the wrong reason (both morally and phenomenologically) for ignoring the requirements of impartiality. The troubling cases are troubling, I claimed, because they require the agent to abandon concern for those she loves, not because they require her to sacrifice her own integrity or sense of self.

However, this emphasis on the distinction between concern for oneself and concern for others, which was central to the argument in Chapter 2, is exactly what has been questioned in the earlier sections of the present chapter, where I have suggested that congruence can be demonstrated precisely because and insofar as our ends are not separate and distinct from the ends of those we care about. So while impartialism's ability to respond to the normative problem rests upon retaining the distinction between self and others, its ability to respond to the problem of congruence rests upon blurring that distinction. How, then, are these different claims to be reconciled? My contention is that they can be reconciled if we distinguish between impartiality as a theory of moral obligation and impartiality as a matter of personal ideal. I shall therefore explain that distinction and show how it contributes to the form of impartialism which I have been concerned to defend in this book.

In drawing the analogy between love and justice Rawls claims that to be genuinely just is to refuse to 'view the sense of justice as but one desire to be weighed against others. For this sentiment reveals what the person is, and to compromise it is not to achieve for the self free reign but to give in to the contingencies and accidents of the world' (Rawls 1971: 575). As we have seen, he has subsequently distanced himself from this claim, believing that it implies a comprehensive (because Kantian) conception of the good. I have denied that comprehensiveness need follow, but have concurred with the claim that justice is (or can be) congruent with the good of the agent himself, and the passage just quoted expresses that commitment to congruence. More specifically, it expresses the thought that being genuinely just involves seeing justice itself as amongst the things which contribute to my good because it is amongst the things I care about and deem to be important.

However, it is exactly this possibility (the possibility of caring about justice, or about impartial morality) which the opponents of impartialism often deny. In his article, 'Persons, Character and Morality', Bernard Williams writes:

The point is that somewhere one reaches the necessity that such things as deep attachments to other persons will express themselves in the world in ways which cannot at the same time embody the impartial view, and that they also run the risk of offending against it. They run that risk if they exist at all; yet unless such things exist, there will not be enough substance or conviction in a man's life to compel his allegiance to life itself. Life has to have substance if anything is to make sense, including adherence to the impartial system; but if it has substance, then it cannot grant supreme importance to the impartial system, and that system's hold on it will be, at the limit, insecure. (Williams 1981: 18)

Williams's analysis of the problem implicitly denies that impartial morality itself could be one of the things that gives life substance, and indeed he takes the fact of conflict between impartial and partial considerations to be evidence that impartial considerations do not give life substance. Similarly, in his discussion of utilitarianism Williams concludes (against the utilitarian) that: 'it is absurd to demand of a man, when the sums come in from the utility network which the projects of others have in part determined, that he should just step aside from his own project and decision and acknowledge the decision which utilitarian calculation requires. It is to alienate him in a real sense from his actions and the source of his actions in his own convictions' (Williams 1973: 116). Both quotations draw a distinction between the demands of impartialism and the things which give life its 'substance'. And both, by implication, doubt that impartial morality can be one of the things that gives life substance—one of the things we can care about.

Nor is Williams alone in drawing this conclusion. Frankfurt, too, doubts that morality is amongst the things we can care about and, as we have seen, he draws a very clear distinction between ethics, on the one hand, and the things we care about on the other. 'Ethics', he says, 'focuses on the problem of ordering our relations with *other people*. It is concerned especially with the contrast between *right* and *wrong*, and with the grounds and limits of *moral obligation*.' By contrast, what we care about is a matter of deciding 'what to do with *ourselves*, and we therefore need to understand what is *important* or, rather, what is *important to* us' (Frankfurt 1988: 80–1, emphasis original). And he goes on to deny that something's being important to me need be a matter of its moral value. Indeed, he is of the opinion that it is very unusual for people to consider morality to be amongst the things that are most important to them (Frankfurt 1988: 81, 82). For both Frankfurt and Williams, then, there is a clear distinction between morality (impartially understood) and the things we care about or deem to be significant in our lives. A large part of the argument of this book has been devoted to showing how this distinction might be softened by grounding impartial morality in the things we care about, and specifically in the partial concerns we have for particular people.

However, the defence of congruence raises a rather different possibility, which is that impartialist morality might itself be amongst the things we care about. Indeed, I take it that this possibility is exactly what is proposed by Rawls when he draws the analogy between love and justice. And this possibility is exactly what I have adverted to in defending the possibility of congruence. Congruence, I have argued, is plausible once we allow that the interests of the just man are, in part, determined by the very fact that he is just: to be just is not to gauge one's success against antecedent interests; it is to pursue justice for its own sake. However, it is exactly this possibility—the possibility of caring about justice itself—which Frankfurt and Williams rule out. How, then, might we defend the claim that morality can be one of the things we can care about, and how would that help to resolve the question of whether we ought to insist on the separateness of persons and the distinctness of ends?

In my discussion of Frankfurt in the previous chapter I denied that the distinction between ethics and what we care about could be retained in quite the stark form he suggests. I argued that our partial concerns are not simply statements of what we find important, but that they also imply evaluative, indeed moral, judgements. In that connection, I also noted Frankfurt's insistence that caring about things makes us vulnerable to loss, and I argued that that fact is in tension with his desire to distinguish sharply between morality and what we care about. Put starkly, my claim was that cases in which we become vulnerable through loving, or caring about, another are cases in which we risk a distinctively moral loss. Thus, we can fully understand the plight of Isabel Archer only by seeing her as someone who has invested herself in what is, objectively, unworthy of care. What she cares about is certainly, and as Frankfurt insists, a statement of who she is, but it is also a statement of what she deems to be morally valuable or worthwhile. Without this evaluative dimension her case cannot be distinguished from the case of someone who is disappointed because she fails to get what she wants. Isabel, however, is not simply disappointed, but morally undone, and to explain this we need to see the connections, as well as the distinctions, between morality and what we care about. So while morality and what we care about are distinct, they are not completely unrelated, since the things we care about serve both as statements of who we are and as statements of what we deem to be morally worthwhile.

The distinction between morality and what we care about was blurred yet further by the recognition that caring for another may involve seeing that person's ends as partly constitutive of my own. In explaining the source of Kant's 'misamorism' I noted that his perception of love as 'risky' stemmed from his neglect of this possibility and his consequent inability to acknowledge that the kind of vulnerability which is involved in loving another does not arise solely from the possibility that one's own projects and purposes will be thwarted. The risks which are involved in loving another are, by their very nature, risks that follow from an unwillingness (or inability) to see the ends of that person as sharply distinguishable from one's own.

The nature of our partial concerns themselves is therefore such as to cast doubt both on a stark contrast between morality and what we care about, and on the separateness of persons. Partial concerns give evidence not only of what is important to me, but also, and thereby, of what I deem to be morally valuable. This was the argument of the previous chapter. Additionally, partial concerns indicate how I may be damaged but not defeated when love fails. Since partial concerns can express who I am, and since who I am may involve essential reference to others whom I love, the damage which is consequent upon the failure of love is not a damage that consists simply in the thwarting of my own ends. On the contrary, it is a damage that is possible only on the assumption that I do not think exclusively in terms of my own ends, and of their contrast with the ends of others.

In 'The Importance of What We Care About' Frankfurt provides an example which is intended to highlight the distinction between morality and what we care about, but which can also cast light on the connections between the two, and on the possibility of caring about morality itself. He writes:

If a mother who is tempted to abandon her child finds that she simply cannot do that, it is probably not because she knows (or even because she cares about) her duty. It is more likely because of how she cares about the child, and about herself as its mother, than because of any recognition on her part that abandoning the child would be morally wrong... Especially with respect to those we love and with respect to our ideals, we are liable to be bound by necessities which have less to do with our adherence to the principles of morality than with integrity or consistency of a more personal kind... In a sense which a strictly ethical analysis cannot make clear, what they [the necessities] keep us from violating are not our duties or our obligations, but ourselves. (Frankfurt 1988: 90)

Of course, to abandon one's child would be to fail in a moral duty, but the point here is that the mother herself is unlikely to think of her action in that way, and equally unlikely to resist the temptation because she recognized that as her duty. Indeed, we might even be tempted to say that a mother who did resist because she recognized that it was her duty would be defective as a mother (just as the person who married in order to further his own life plan would be defective as a husband). And herein lies an important truth, which is (somewhat ironically) supportive of my claim that impartial morality, when grounded in our partial concerns, can be congruent with the good of the agent.

I take it that Frankfurt's main aim in this example is to distinguish between acting from moral obligation and acting from a personal ideal. And he explicates this distinction through the idea of betraying oneself. Thus, on his account, to be guided by an ideal is to conceive of oneself in a certain way, and it is for that reason that violating the ideal is felt as a betrayal of oneself. Its being felt in that way is, moreover, prior to and independent of any thought about one's ability or otherwise to justify oneself to others. So the mother's inability to justify to others her decision to abandon her child is largely irrelevant to her assessment of her own action and this, Frankfurt argues, is what shows us that we are here dealing with personal ideal, not (or not primarily) with moral obligation. Again, 'in a sense which a strictly ethical analysis cannot make clear, what they [the necessities] keep us from violating are not our obligations, but ourselves'.

However, exactly the same point may be made about the genuinely just person. Rawls tells us that the desire to act justly is 'a desire to conduct oneself in a certain way above all else, a striving that contains within itself its own priority... for this sentiment [the sentiment of justice] reveals what the person is, and to compromise it is not to achieve for the self free reign but to give way to the contingencies and accidents of the world'. And in saying this he implies that when the just person acts unjustly he, too, may see his act as a betrayal of himself, not (or not primarily) as a failure of moral obligation or a failure to justify to others. It is of course true that the person who acts unjustly fails in a moral duty, just as the mother who abandons her child fails in a moral duty. But in both cases the agent will be likely to perceive the failure as a failure to live up to his (or her) own ideals. The mother who abandons her child will, says Frankfurt, feel that she has 'violated herself', but the person who acts unjustly will also feel that he has violated himself, let himself down, or fallen short of the standards of behaviour which he sets for himself.

In short, what is implicit in both Frankfurt and Rawls is an insistence on the priority of being a certain sort of person. Frankfurt identifies the distinction between moral obligation and personal ideal as a distinction between justifying to others and justifying to oneself but, as his own example indicates, there can be cases in which what is (uncontroversially) a moral obligation is perceived by the agent as an ideal of personal integrity. In drawing the analogy between love and justice Rawls appears to be urging the possibility of just this perspective on moral duty. He appears to be suggesting that, when held as a fully regulative sentiment, justice is something which can itself mould and shape our other desires, just as love can mould and shape our desires. Like love, justice can have a transformative quality; like love, it can be understood as a reflection of the agent's desire to be a certain way, and when it is so understood its neglect can be characterized not simply as a failure of moral obligation, but as a betrayal of oneself and what one stands for.

If we take this thought seriously, then it delivers the conclusion that being genuinely just or genuinely moral need not stand in stark opposition to caring about things. This is partly because our partial concerns provide impartial morality with its motivational foundation, and partly because morality itself is (or can be) amongst the things we care about. Indeed, the two claims are connected: it is *because* impartial morality takes our partial concerns as central that it can itself come to command respect, and there need therefore be no sharp distinction between what we care about and what we are morally required to do. Indeed, my discussion in Chapter 2 was designed to show not only that this is possible, but that it is the most plausible way of responding to the normative problem. The mother who is tempted to pull strings for her child will, I argued, nonetheless feel the force of impartial demands when (and only when) she can see those demands as themselves flowing from a recognition of the significance of partial concerns. Without that assurance, impartial morality will appear alien to her, and her disposition to acknowledge it may be dismissed as dysfunctional.

I began this section with a puzzle: how can the defence of congruence be made compatible with the resolution of the normative problem? The defence of congruence required a recognition that our own ends are not clearly separable from the ends of others whom we care about or love. By contrast, the resolution of the normative problem required a clear distinction between acting from a concern for others and acting from a concern for oneself. These two requirements appeared to be in conflict. On inspection, however, they can be seen to be complementary aspects of impartialist morality: the insistence on separateness draws attention to the status of impartiality as a theory of moral obligation, while the denial that separateness is total draws attention to the possibility that morality itself may gain the status of personal ideal. When impartialism gains its motivational force from the centrality it accords to partial concerns, then it can itself become something we invest with import-ance. It can become something we are able to see as deserving of respect in itself, and as making our own life more worthwhile. But, to repeat, it does not have that status because its dictates conform to an antecedent understanding of what is worthwhile. It has that status because it is capable of transforming and enriching our sense of what it is for something to be worthwhile.

Conclusion

The aim of this chapter has been to argue that having a sense of justice (holding justice as a regulative sentiment) can be congruent with the good of the agent, and that such congruence need not imply commitment to a comprehensive conception of the good. The claim that congruence implies comprehensiveness appears most plausible on the assumption that life is like a path which forks, and that decisions within a life are strategic decisions taken in furtherance of an antecedently existent aim. However, this assump-tion is implausible: our lives do not characteristically have that form and, as a result, there may be no antecedently specifiable account of what is for the good of the agent. But it does not follow from this that 'anything goes' and that there are no constraints on the agent's good. Such constraints may be found by considering the things people care about, where caring itself has an evaluative dimension. Additionally, they may be found by noting that mor-ality itself, when suitably grounded, can become an object of concern or of love. It, too, can be amongst the things we care about and amongst the things which give life its substance. My conclusions therefore are that an impartial morality which is grounded in what we care about can provide an acceptable response to the normative problem (this was the purpose of Chapter 2); it can be commended to people who do not antecedently feel its force (this was the purpose of Chapter 3); and it can be congruent with the good of the agent (this is the purpose of the present chapter).

How, though, does all this reflect back on to the problem which prompted the entire discussion in the first place—the problem which is central to political philosophy in conditions of modernity? Recall that I began by concurring with Rawls's claim that 'the aims of political philosophy depend on the society it addresses' and that modern democratic societies are characterized by the fact of reasonable pluralism. They are societies in which people with different and conflicting comprehensive conceptions of the good must nonetheless agree upon a conception of justice and must, moreover, see justice as having some claim to priority in cases of conflict. In short, what is needed is that, somehow, people with different and conflicting comprehensive conceptions of the good shall agree upon a distinctively impartialist conception of justice and shall agree on the priority to be accorded to that conception in cases where it conflicts with their own comprehensive view. However, while their agreement must be more than a *modus vivendi*, it must not imply or demand commitment to a specific, and contested, comprehensive conception of the good, since such a demand would undermine the permanence of pluralism. In short, the problem of political philosophy is the problem of showing the priority of impartial justice to be compatible with the permanence of pluralism.

I have argued (Chapter 1) that epistemological arguments cannot pull off this trick: Barry's appeal to scepticism undermines the permanence of pluralism because it succeeds only by destabilizing the agent's own commitment to conceptions of the good. Similarly, Raz's argument from truth is at odds with the permanence of pluralism (although, of course, he himself will be untroubled by this implication), and while Rawls's own appeal to epistemological abstinence does indeed accommodate pluralism as a permanent fact, it struggles to demonstrate the priority of justice.

These considerations prompted a discussion of the *moral* foundations of impartiality. Since both Rawls and (yet more conspicuously) Nagel emphasize that impartiality is a moral doctrine, and since epistemological arguments have failed, this move seems a natural one. However, it, too, is fraught with danger because it threatens to demonstrate the priority of impartiality only by demanding commitment to a specific, and controversial, comprehensive conception of the good. I have argued that, despite this danger, impartiality can be defended on broadly moral grounds: it can be defended as grounded in our partial concerns generally, and in what we care about in particular, where care is understood as having a moral dimension, but not one which is allied to any particular comprehensive conception of the good. If these arguments are successful, then they provide a way in which the central problem can be resolved. They show how the permanence of pluralism can be reconciled with the priority of justice. Pluralism is acknowledged because the defence of impartialism does not require commitment to a comprehensive conception of the good; priority is acknowledged because the defence of impartialism is nonetheless a moral defence.

However, and in conclusion, it may be worth returning briefly to the political problems which prompted the discussion in the first place, and saying a little more about the character of a society grounded in the form of impartialism I have been advocating. Here, it is important to begin by noting what I have *not* shown (and have not attempted to show), namely that impartialism, suitably developed, will be compelling to all rational beings. To take the permanence of (reasonable) pluralism seriously just is to concede that there will always be people with comprehensive conceptions of the good which are in tension with the demands of impartiality. My aim has been to show how and why impartialism might nonetheless be commended to such people as an attractive and potentially fulfilling moral theory. Nonetheless, and given my conviction that rationally compelling arguments are not available, the political question that now arises is 'what are we to say to those who are not persuaded?' Here, two issues are paramount: the first is whether, for such people, the political principles advanced by impartialism can constitute more than a *modus vivendi*. The second, and related, issue is whether coercion is legitimate in the case of those who find their own comprehensive conception of the good at odds with the principles of impartiality. Both draw attention to the *status* of the theory I have been advocating.

On the first, I have argued that political impartialism must have a moral foundation. Indeed, the whole point of Chapter 1 was to deny that epistemological arguments could demonstrate the priority of justice, and to argue for the necessity of moral argument. However, if the moral argument is not one which all rational beings will find compelling, then it seems that the resultant political order can have no more than *modus vivendi* status—at least for those who are not persuaded. *Ex hypothesi*, if such people comply with the principles of justice delivered by impartialism that will not be because they think the principles to be morally right, and therefore (presumably) their only motivation for compliance will be pragmatic necessity. However, part of the reason for rejecting equality as the basis of impartialism and arguing instead for the centrality of partial concerns was to render impartialism more inclusive: where impartialism takes seriously our concern for others, it will, I have argued, have a wider constituency and will attract greater allegiance. Nonetheless, we cannot assume that it will secure universal acceptance and this raises the second issue—the legitimacy of coercion.

In his article, 'John Rawls and the Search for Stability', Brian Barry draws the following contrast between *A Theory of Justice* and *Political Liberalism*:

In *A Theory of Justice*, the validity of the theory was unaffected by any lack of success it might have in forming a part of people's conception of their good. For we could say that all conceptions of the good incompatible with the principles of justice were necessarily unreasonable. But in *Political Liberalism* Rawls denies that a regime can be legitimate if there exist people with 'reasonable comprehensive views' who reject its foundational principles. (Barry 1995a: 890)

In Barry's view, this change is a grave error, and it follows directly from Rawls's more recent insistence on yoking together legitimacy and stability. Whereas the legitimacy of the theory advanced in *A Theory of Justice* survives the fact that it might not command universal allegiance, the legitimacy of the theory advanced in *Political Liberalism* is destroyed by its inability to command allegiance. This is the cost of making legitimacy dependent on stability. However, my own account also yokes legitimacy to stability (or justification to motivation, as I have called them), so I too need to respond to Barry's challenge by saying what exactly the relationship between legitimacy and stability is, and whether, on my account, legitimacy is destroyed by failure to secure allegiance at the motivational level.

To be clear, the problem identified by Barry is this: if we follow the Rawls of *A Theory of Justice* and insist that all reasonable comprehensive conceptions of the good will be consonant with the principles of impartialism, then we are entitled to coerce those who would disregard impartialist principles. However, if we follow the Rawls of *Political Liberalism* and insist that impartialism is *legitimized* by its ability to accommodate all reasonable comprehensive conceptions of the good, then failure to secure allegiance does not licence coercion. Rather, it sounds the death knell for the theory, which staked its claim to legitimacy on its very ability to secure allegiance. The crucial question therefore is: 'what relationship holds between legitimacy and stability in the theory I have been advocating?' I have (I hope) made it clear that the theory cannot accommodate all reasonable comprehensive conceptions of the good. Indeed, I have urged that it should not aspire to do so, since such an aspiration would be at odds with liberal commitment to the permanence of pluralism. Legitimacy is not, therefore, dependent on the ability to secure stability. Nonetheless, the ability to secure stability is, as Rawls puts it, 'desirable': 'other things equal, the persons in the original position will adopt the more stable scheme of principles. However attractive a conception of justice might be on other grounds, it is seriously defective if the principles of moral psychology are such that it fails to engender in human beings the requisite desire to act upon it' (Rawls 1971: 455). My aim has been to show that a theory of impartialism grounded in what we care about can at least satisfy this, rather minimal, stability requirement. It can be commended as not dysfunctional and indeed those who embrace it will find it to be congruent with their own good, as then conceived. So while stability is not the determinant of legitimacy, stability is nonetheless a reasonable aspiration.

What, now, of those who have reasonable comprehensive conceptions, but ones which are at odds with the principles of impartialist political philosophy? Here, it seems clear that, if the principles are enforced politically, they can have no more than *modus vivendi* status for such people. Yet even here, the conclusion may be less dispiriting than at first appears, for the very ability of impartialism to command widespread, if not universal, respect, may itself secure converts to impartialism and may even serve to transform a *modus vivendi* agreement into something deeper. It is, presumably, something of this sort that Rawls has in mind when he suggests that:

initial acquiescence in a liberal conception of justice as a mere modus vivendi could change over time first into a constitutional consensus and then into an overlapping consensus... I have supposed that the comprehensive doctrines of most people are not fully comprehensive, and this allows scope for the development of an independent allegiance to the political conception that helps to bring about a consensus. This independent allegiance in turn leads people to act with evident intention in accordance with constitutional arrangements, since they have reasonable assurance (based on past experience) that others will also comply. (Rawls 1993: 168)

Thus, agreements initially entered into for pragmatic reasons might, if they prove stable and successful, generate a deeper allegiance precisely because they have shown themselves to be pragmatically effective. There is no reason in principle why an agreement which was initially made for reasons of expediency should not, in time, come to be accepted as morally right. And indeed the recognition that an arrangement 'works' may itself be an appropriate ground for coming to think of it as morally legitimate. Of course, it may not, but the point here is simply that although '*modus vivendi*' may be an accurate description of our motivation for entering into an agreement in the first place, it does not follow that it will accurately describe the manner in which we understand that agreement subsequently.

This last point, however, recalls the theory of stability advanced in *A Theory of Justice*, where (I have argued) Rawls is anxious to urge upon us the possibility that justice may itself be, or become, one of the things we care about, and that where we do come to care about it, we will find that to be congruent with our own good. Those who do not care about impartial justice in this way may be forced to agree to its principles as a pragmatic necessity, but what the preceding considerations suggest is that they, too, may come to value it in a deeper way when they see its benefits.

Politically, then, the form of impartialism which I have been advocating is one which does not make legitimacy dependent on stability. It does, however, acknowledge the importance of stability and it gives reason to believe that stability will be achievable when impartialism is rooted, not in the contested value of equality, but in those partial concerns for others which provide life's substance for (almost) all of us. These concerns may themselves lead us to an acknowledgement of the legitimacy of impartialism, but even where they do not, and impartial principles are initially accepted as a *modus vivendi,* there is still good reason to believe that they may ultimately come to be accepted as something more than that. Political impartialism, then, is not legitimised by its ability to secure stability, but stability is (or can be) a significant feature in the *moral* defence of impartialism.

Finally, and most importantly, although that defence takes the form of an appeal to partial concerns, it need not involve commitment to a specific comprehensive conception of the good, and can therefore acknowledge pluralism about the good as permanent. The things that people care about are many and various, and not all will be consonant with the principles of impartialist political philosophy. Nonetheless, impartialist philosophy, on my understanding, is a way of taking seriously the partial concerns we have for others, conceding that those concerns may be many and various, and yet emerging with a reason to be moral. The permanence of pluralism and the priority of justice can, I believe, be reconciled in a form of impartialism which has partial concerns at its foundations.

Bibliography

Baier, A. (1982). 'Caring About Caring: A Reply to Frankfurt', *Synthese*, 53/2: 93–108.

——(1994). *Moral Prejudices: Essays on Ethics* (Cambridge, Mass.: Harvard University Press).

Baron, M. (1991). 'Impartiality and Friendship', *Ethics*, 101/4: 836–57.

Barry, B. (1995). *Justice as Impartiality* (Oxford: Oxford University Press).

——(1995a). 'John Rawls and the Search for Stability', *Ethics*, 105/4: 874–915.

Becker, L. (1991). 'Impartiality and Ethical Theory', *Ethics*, 101/4: 698–700.

Blum, L. (1980). *Friendship, Altruism and Morality* (London: Routledge and Kegan Paul).

Cameron, J. (1974). *An Indian Summer: A Personal Experience of India* (Harmondsworth: Penguin).

Cocking, D., and Kennett, J. (2000). 'Friendship and Moral Danger', *Journal of Philosophy*, 97/2: 278–96.

Deigh, J. (1991). 'Impartiality: A Closing Note', *Ethics*, 101/4: 858–64.

Frankfurt, H. (1988). *The Importance of What We Care About* (Cambridge: Cambridge University Press).

——(1999). *Necessity, Volition and Love* (Cambridge: Cambridge University Press).

Fried, C. (1970). *An Anatomy of Values: Problems of Personal and Social Choice* (Cambridge, Mass.: Harvard University Press).

Gauthier, D. (1986). *Morals by Agreement* (Oxford: Oxford University Press).

Godwin, W. (1976). *Enquiry Concerning Political Justice* (Harmondsworth: Penguin).

Graham, G., and LaFollette, H. (1989). *Person to Person* (Philadelphia: Temple University Press).

Hampton, J. (1993). 'The Moral Commitments of Liberalism', in D. Copp *et al.* (eds.), *The Idea of Democracy* (Cambridge: Cambridge University Press): 292–313.

Hare, R. M. (1982). 'Ethical Theory and Utilitarianism', in A. Sen and B. Williams (eds.), *Utilitarianism and Beyond* (Cambridge: Cambridge University Press): 23–38.

Herman, B. (1991). 'Agency, Attachment and Difference', *Ethics*, 101/ 4: 775–97.

Hollis, M. (1996). *Reason in Action: Essays in the Philosophy of Social Science* (Cambridge: Cambridge University Press).

Hume, D. (1888). *A Treatise of Human Nature*, ed. L. A. Selby-Bigge (Oxford: Clarendon Press).

Ibsen, H. (1965). *Plays* (Harmondsworth: Penguin).

James, H. (1991). *The Portrait of a Lady* (London: Everyman).

Kant, I. (1964). *The Doctrine of Virtue: Part II of the Metaphysic of Morals*, ed. M. Gregor (Philadelphia: University of Pennsylvania).

——(1970). *Lectures on Ethics*, trans. L. Infield (London: Methuen).

Kelly, P. (1991). 'John Locke: Authority, Conscience and Religious Toleration', in J. Horton and S. Mendus (eds.), *John Locke: A Letter Concerning Toleration in Focus* (London: Routledge): 125–46.

Kelly, P. (1998). *Impartiality, Neutrality and Justice* (Edinburgh: Edinburgh University Press).

Korsgaard, C. (1996). *The Sources of Normativity* (Cambridge: Cambridge University Press).

Locke, D. (1980). *A Fantasy of Reason: The Life and Thought of William Godwin* (London: Routledge and Kegan Paul).

Locke, J. (1975). *An Essay Concerning Human Understanding*, ed. P. Nidditch (Oxford: Oxford University Press).

—— (1991). 'A Letter Concerning Toleration', in J. Horton and S. Mendus (eds.), *John Locke's Letter Concerning Toleration in Focus* (London: Routledge): 12–56.

Nagel, T. (1987). 'Moral Conflict and Political Legitimacy', *Philosophy and Public Affairs*, 16: 215–40.

Pippin, R. (2000). *Henry James and Modern Moral Life* (Cambridge: Cambridge University Press).

Putnam, H. (1992). *Renewing Philosophy* (Cambridge, Mass.: Harvard University Press).

Rawls, J. (1971). *A Theory of Justice* (Oxford: Oxford University Press).

—— (1993). *Political Liberalism* (Columbia: Columbia University Press).

—— (1999). *Collected Papers*, ed. S. Freeman (Cambridge, Mass.: Harvard University Press).

Raz, J. (1981). 'The Purity of Pure Theory', *Revue Internationale de Philosophie*, 35: 441–59.

—— (1994). *Ethics in the Public Domain: Essays in the Morality of Law and Politics* (Oxford: Oxford University Press).

Sandel, M. (1982). *Liberalism and the Limits of Justice* (Cambridge: Cambridge University Press).

Scanlon, T. M. (1998). *What We Owe to Each Other* (Cambridge, Mass.: Harvard University Press).

Stocker, M. (1976). 'The Schizophrenia of Modern Ethical Theories', *Journal of Philosophy*, 73: 453–66.

—— (1990). 'Friendship and Duty', in O. Flanagan and A. Rorty (eds.), *Identity, Character and Morality: Essays in Moral Psychology* (Cambridge, Mass.: MIT Press): 219–33.

Taylor, C. (1985). *Philosophical Papers I: Human Agency and Language* (Cambridge: Cambridge University Press).

—— (1989). *Sources of the Self: The Making of the Modern Identity* (Cambridge: Cambridge University Press).

Twain, M. (1950). *The Adventures of Huckleberry Finn* (London: Dent).

Waldron, J. (1991). 'Locke, Toleration and the Rationality of Persecution', in J. Horton and S. Mendus (eds.), *John Locke: A Letter Concerning Toleration in Focus* (London: Routledge): 98–124.

Williams, B. (1972). *Morality: An Introduction to Ethics* (Harmondsworth: Penguin).

—— (1973). 'A Critique of Utilitarianism', in J. J. C. Smart and B. Williams, *Utilitarianism: For and Against* (Cambridge: Cambridge University Press): 75–150.

—— (1981). *Moral Luck* (Cambridge: Cambridge University Press).

INDEX